I PROMISE
TO BE GOOD

THE LETTERS OF
ARTHUR RIMBAUD

I PROMISE
TO BE GOOD

RIMBAUD COMPLETE
VOLUME II

TRANSLATED, EDITED, AND
WITH AN INTRODUCTION BY
WYATT MASON

THE MODERN LIBRARY
NEW YORK

An earlier version of the Introduction appeared in *Harper's* magazine.
A version of "On the Subject of Flowers: Remarks, Addressed to the
Poet" appeared in *Circumference*.

LIBRARY OF CONGRESS CATALOGING-IN-PUBLICATION DATA
Rimbaud, Arthur, 1854–1891.
[Correspondence. English]
I promise to be good : the letters of Arthur Rimbaud / translated,
edited, and with an introduction by Wyatt Mason.
p. cm.
ISBN 0-679-64301-X (hc : alk. paper)
1. Rimbaud, Arthur, 1854–1891—Correspondence.   2. Poets,
French—19th century—Correspondence.   3. Rimbaud, Arthur,
1854–1891—Translations into English.   I. Mason, Wyatt
Alexander, 1969–   II. Title.

PQ2387.R5Z48 2003
841'.8—dc21
[B]   2003051036

*frontispiece: Les hôtes d'Hassan Ali, 1880, detail, from the collection of Pierre
Leroy.*

To the memory of
LEONARD MICHAELS
1933–2003

Come back, come back, dear friend, only friend, come back. I promise to be good.
—Rimbaud to Verlaine
July 4, 1873

CONTENTS

I Promise to Be Good

I. RESTLESS IN EUROPE (1870–1875)

II. FIRST TRANSIT (1876–1878)

III. CYPRUS (1879–1880)

VI. ADEN REDUX (1882–1883)

VII. HARAR REDUX (1883–1884)

VIII. ADEN AGAIN (1884–1885)

XIII. FINAL TRANSIT (1891)

XIV. AT REST (1891)

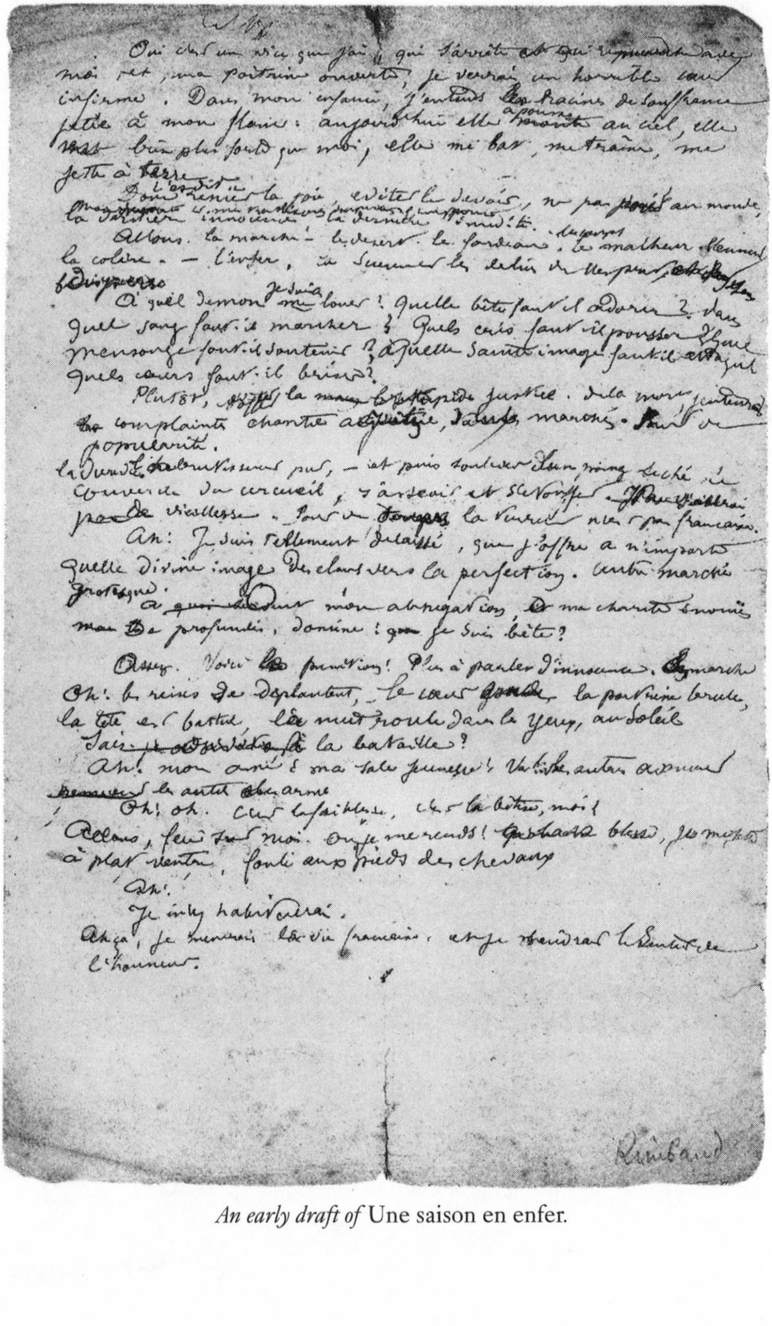
Oui c'est un vice que j'ai, qui s'arrête et qui reprend avec moi et, ma poitrine ouverte, je verrais un horrible cœur infirme. Dans mon enfance, j'entends ses racines de souffrance jetée à mon flanc : aujourd'hui elle a poussé au ciel, elle est bien plus forte que moi, elle me bat, me traîne, me jette à terre.

Donc renier la joie, éviter le devoir, ne pas porter au monde la dernière innocence, la dernière timidité.

Allons. La marche ! le désert, le fardeau, les coups, le malheur, l'ennui, la colère. — l'enfer, la science et les délices de l'esprit et des sens dispersés.

À quel démon je suis à louer ? Quelle bête faut-il adorer ? dans quel sang faut-il marcher ? Quels cris faut-il pousser ? Quel mensonge faut-il soutenir ? À quelle sainte image faut-il attaquer ? Quels cœurs faut-il briser ?

Plutôt, éviter la main brutale de la mort, j'entendrais les complaintes chantées aux marchés. Point de popularité.

La dure vie, l'abrutissement pur, — et puis soulever d'un poing séché le couvercle du cercueil, s'asseoir et s'étouffer. Je ne vieillirai pas de vieillesse. Point de dangers, la terreur n'est pas française.

Ah ! Je suis tellement délaissé, que j'offre à n'importe quelle divine image des élans vers la perfection. Autre marché grotesque.

Ô mon abnégation, ô ma charité inouïe, mais de profundis, domine ! que je suis bête ?

Assez. Voici la punition ! Plus à parler d'innocence. En marche ! Oh ! les reins se déplantent, le cœur gronde, la poitrine brûle, la tête est battue, la nuit roule dans les yeux, au soleil. Sais-je où je vais ? à la bataille ?

Ah ! mon ami ! ma sale jeunesse ! Va... les autres avancent les outils, les armes.

Oh ! oh. C'est la faiblesse, c'est la bêtise, moi !

Allons, feu sur moi. Ou je me rends ! Qu'on me blesse, je me jette à plat ventre, foulé aux pieds des chevaux.

Ah !

Je m'y habituerai.

Ah ça, je mènerais la vie française, et je suivrais le sentier de l'honneur.

Rimbaud

An early draft of Une saison en enfer.

INTRODUCTION

I

In the autumn of 1873, Arthur Rimbaud, aged nineteen, arrived at his family home in northeastern France bearing a large bundle. It contained nearly five hundred copies of his longest completed work, a seven-thousand-word prose poem entitled *Une saison en enfer*. The bundle originated in the Typographical Alliance of M.-J. Poot and Company, Brussels, where Rimbaud had gone to the trouble of having the poem printed in book form. Soon after his return to France, however, he threw the books into the family hearth, incinerating all but a handful of one of the most articulate documents of existential ambivalence in all literature.

This story, confirmed by Rimbaud's youngest sister, Isabelle, who witnessed the event, neatly symbolizes one of the most compelling aspects of Rimbaud's fame: after revolutionizing French poetry in his teens, he abandoned its pursuit, electing to live the rest of his life in the African desert. A novelist would be hard-pressed to come up with a truer image of artistic ambivalence, or an action that better revealed Rimbaud's conflicted character, than that of the poet incinerating the work upon which his posterity now rests. Alas, the one problem with this quintessential moment of truth is that it never happened.

We know that it never happened because of a man named Leon Losseau. Losseau was a lawyer who, on a certain day in 1901, visited the establishment of M.-J. Poot and Company. He was looking not for anything relating to Rimbaud but for a rare judicial publication he suspected might have originated there. The manager, a Monsieur Deghlislage, took Losseau to the attic of the shop. Together they dug through decades of accumulated crates. Losseau, who was also an avid, knowledgeable bibliophile, later explained what happened in a journal for book collectors:

You will understand the emotion a bibliophile felt the instant he saw the contents of a filthy, stained, dusty bundle which, one among many, he had just uncovered. Hundreds of copies of Rimbaud's *Season in Hell*!

Losseau hoarded his discovery for nearly a decade, quietly allowing it to increase in value. When word of the find finally got out, one man was particularly upset by the news: Paterne Berrichon, the writer most responsible for disseminating the tale of *A Season in Hell*'s destruction.

Berrichon was the posthumous brother-in-law of Arthur Rimbaud, having married Isabelle in 1897, the same year he published his first biography of the poet (he published a second in 1912). In his official capacity as literary executor, Berrichon contacted Losseau to confirm the discovery. The biographer then made a shocking request: He asked Losseau to "destroy the rediscovered edition to give the appearance of truth to his invention of the destruction."

The temptation is to think of Berrichon as simply a scoundrel, bent on nothing less than the destruction of the truth for the sake of a memorable scene. But within his fictional auto-da-fé, the ashes of a truth were buried. Once, in a letter, Rimbaud had asked a friend to "burn all the poems I was dumb enough to send you." Berrichon had been the first to publish the letter, in a 1912 issue of *La Nouvelle Revue française*. Perhaps he elected, in complicity with his wife, to fill a narrative gap in Rimbaud's life—the fate of all those missing copies of *A Season in Hell*—with a scene in keeping with Rimbaud's prior behavior. Whatever his ultimate reason, in the service of trying to tell the poet's story, of trying to have it make sense, Berrichon made an assumption. And, if we are feeling charitable, a not altogether unreasonable one.

II

The history of Rimbaud biography is one of not altogether unreasonable assumptions. In the hundred years since Berrichon's first biography appeared, dozens of authors have tried to tell Rimbaud's story. Between 1997 and 2001, four biographical studies—of varying length and ambition but all aimed at the general public—were published in English. Two were already in print. A seventh and eighth have just appeared in France, arguably making Rimbaud the most written-about literary figure of the past decade. This bounty is suspicious, for although new dribbles of information appear from time to time, the facts we have about Rimbaud's life have remained largely unchanged since Berrichon's time. What continues to change is our idea of Rimbaud, and these ideas have often been forged out of so much nothing.

There are countless scenes in the Rimbaud myth that, like the burning of *A Season in Hell,* seem to offer too telling a detail. Of a poet famous for proclaiming himself a seer, biographers have claimed that he was actually born with his eyes wide open; of a poet famous for fleeing Europe, some claim he was born literally crawling for the door. Because in his teens Rimbaud indisputably had at least one homosexual relationship, he has been portrayed as indisputably gay, despite the absence of any evidence of homosexual liaisons during his adulthood and the clear suggestion of a relationship with a woman. And because a letter dating from his years in Africa mentions his needing "two boy slaves," he has been called a slave trader (despite any shred of corroborating fact). Yet how infrequently a bibliophile appears out of the French countryside to set the record straight.

Myths deform. They obscure. At their best, biographies are a lifting of the veils. At their worst, they borrow novelistic means, dramatizing the unseen, suggesting the unknown, bridging gaps with guesses. Often the authors of such biographies fail to mention these departures from fact to their readers. As Virginia Woolf wrote in 1927:

> [T]he biographer's imagination is always being stimulated to use the novelist's art of arrangement, suggestion, dramatic effect. Yet if he carries the use of fiction too far, so that he disregards the truth ... he loses both worlds; he has neither the freedom of fiction nor the substance of fact.

Historical figures, rather than being revealed, become blurry; or else, made all too clear, they become fictional characters. And no figure in French literature has been more a victim of these unnecessary fictions than Arthur Rimbaud, who, when we think of him at all, continues to appear to us clothed not in the works he left behind but in the myths that won't leave him alone.

III

Perhaps the most curious aspect of the enduring Rimbaud myth is the degree to which modern biographers both acknowledge the need for its dismantling and unwittingly contribute to its maintenance. Yes, their introductions all address Berrichon in one way or another, either with amusement or scorn, though always ultimately to assure us that their own books will not fall prey to the temptations to which their predecessor and his followers succumbed. Some go so far as to state that, thanks to Berrichon, all subsequent biographies of Rimbaud have been "devotions wherein each author provides a demonstration of *his* Rimbaud... [erecting] an idol to their own measure," while others write that "the hagiography by... Paterne Berrichon, which he almost called *The Charming Life of Arthur Rimbaud,* is often derided but remains surprisingly influential." In their various ways, every Rimbaud biographer makes it very clear that he will set himself apart by writing neither a devotion nor a hagiography, and resisting the whisperings that go beyond interpretation.

And yet they still succumb. How? The answer differs little from the means by which the fish we caught last summer grows in size with each subsequent telling. Take, for example, a story of Rimbaud in Paris that appears in a recent, widely praised biography. An artist named Ernest Cabaner had been hosting Rimbaud in his home in Paris. Our biographer reports offhandedly: "On another occasion, when Cabaner was out, Rimbaud found [Cabaner's] daily glass of milk and neatly ejaculated into it." The footnoted source for this vivid incident is a memoir written by Rimbaud's closest school friend, Ernest Delahaye, considered by scholarly consensus a very dependable storyteller. Delahaye frequently provides transcripts of his conversations with Rimbaud, and the Cabaner story appears in one, after a fashion. Here is what one finds if one bothers to track it down. The voice below is Rimbaud's (as reported by Delahaye):

It's so annoying. I have a terrible reputation in Paris now. Reasons: friends' pranks, and also my own, moreover. I thought it would be fun—it was stupid—to pass myself off as an ignoble pig. They would take me at my word. One day, I tell them that I went into Cabaner's room while he was out and found a glass of milk that had been poured for him; that I jerked off into it, that I ejaculated into it. They laughed about it, and they went around repeating it as though it were true.

Clearly, Rimbaud is saying that he did not ejaculate into anyone's milk, "neatly" or otherwise. To my mind, the story of Rimbaud pretending to be a wild child is more nuanced and telling than the biographer's fictional version.

As with Berrichon's insistence on book burning, who can say what is responsible for this bald departure from a primary source? What is sure is that it happens over and over again in Rimbaud biographies, no matter how well intentioned. Gossip and conjecture are passed off brazenly as fact when not distorted altogether.

Another biographical means to mythic ends has been to read Rimbaud's poetry as a series of swashbuckling autobiographical snapshots. When relating a story that does have a factual basis (Rimbaud walking the roads of France, say), one biographer inserts details from poems as if they were items on a menu selling the facts of Rimbaud's life. Take "At the Cabaret-Vert, Five P.M.," a first-person account by a weary traveler:

> Eight days of shredding my boots
> On bad roads. Then, Charleroi.
> —And into the Cabaret-Vert. I ordered:
> Bread and butter with lukewarm ham.

Our biographer explicates it thus:

The next day [Rimbaud] crosses the border.... [H]e passes before an establishment with the surprising sign "Au Cabaret-Vert." Starving, he orders a solid meal: bread and butter, some ham....

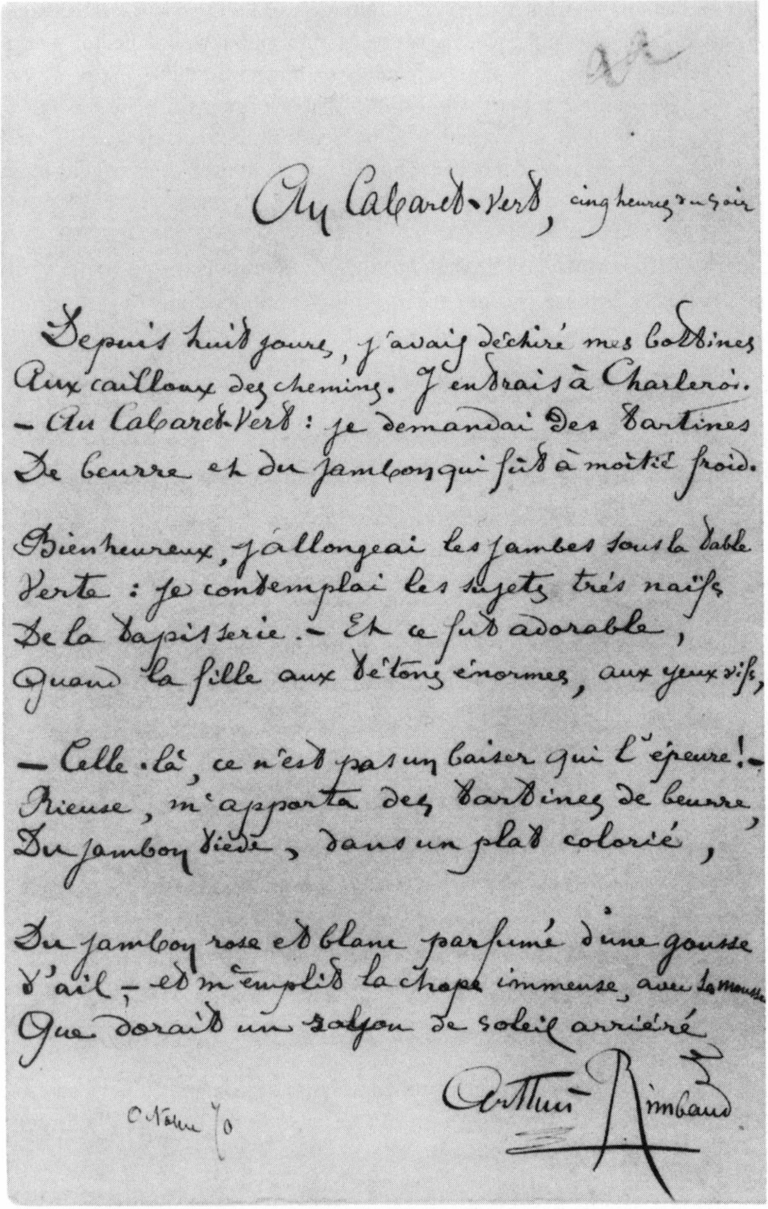
Au Cabaret-Vert, cinq heures du soir

Depuis huit jours, j'avais déchiré mes bottines
Aux cailloux des chemins. J'entrais à Charleroi.
– Au Cabaret-Vert : je demandai des tartines
De beurre et du jambon qui fût à moitié froid.

Bienheureux, j'allongeai les jambes sous la table
Verte : je contemplai les sujets très naïfs
De la tapisserie. – Et ce fut adorable,
Quand la fille aux tétons énormes, aux yeux vifs,

– Celle-là, ce n'est pas un baiser qui l'épeure ! –
Rieuse, m'apporta des tartines de beurre,
Du jambon tiède, dans un plat colorié,

Du jambon rose et blanc parfumé d'une gousse
D'ail, – et m'emplit la chope immense, avec sa mousse
Que dorait un rayon de soleil arriéré.

Arthur Rimbaud

Octobre 70

The manuscript of Rimbaud's "At the Cabaret-Vert, Five P.M."

And when not caulking narrative holes with poetic details, many biographers choose to read Rimbaud's poems as psychological broadsheets upon which the poet's innermost feelings and desires are written in large capital letters. As such, *A Season in Hell* becomes an "autobiographical project." These fashionably narcissistic readings are, inevitably, introduced by the biographer's halfhearted calling-into-question of such styles of interpretation:

> Of course, as a precaution, *A Season in Hell* can be attributed purely and simply to Rimbaud's imagination. [But] it is not difficult to... consider Verlaine as the "Foolish Virgin" and Rimbaud himself as the "Infernal Bridegroom." What personal diary could better describe the state of their daily relationship?

But such a "precaution" is only a formality: our biographer's giddiness at peeking into Rimbaud's presumptive "diary" is transparent enough. It may be "not difficult" to read the poem as something written under the covers by flashlight, but it is horribly limiting. It binds Rimbaud's poetry in a corset, allowing the poem to be read in only one way: as *A Season in Hell: The Love Story.* This ignores more pedestrian, but probably more accurate, alternatives, such as the one suggested by Rimbaud in a letter to his friend Delahaye:

> My fate rests with [*A Season in Hell*], and I've got to make up another half dozen horrible stories for it. And how can I invent such horrors here!... Soon I'll send you money so you can buy and send me Goethe's Faust.... Let me know if there aren't any translations of Shakespeare available.

Rimbaud may be bluffing, of course, but it wouldn't be bad to point out the language here: "stories" that he will "invent" and "make up." One biographer who does cite the letter passes over this aspect of it, instead doggedly focusing on a possible psychological reason why Rimbaud would want the books he is requesting: "When he asks Delahaye to send him Shakespeare or Goethe... he has in mind not so much transposing them as finding an answer to his fundamental anguish."

Is that the way an artist works? What about a craftsmanlike curiosity

From Rimbaud's school notebook, age 11.

about how others have done what he would do? But, of course, biographers frequently claim to know what Rimbaud "has in mind," just as they know that the poet would have read in order to answer "his fundamental anguish." Again and again, Rimbaud's biographers find it difficult to resist popping into the heads of their helpless victims, sprinkling unsubstantiated psychoanalytic verities like fairy dust: "Madame Rimbaud became even more authoritarian, a comforting role for her.... The failure of her marriage destroyed her most beautiful illusions." "Verlaine was...still dreaming of a reconciliation with [his wife]—too obvious an example of an unresolved Edipus [*sic*] complex." "Rimbaud and Verlaine made use of their hearts as if they were soulless objects. They didn't realize that they were thereby destroying in themselves the very substance of love."

With such interpretive hooey filling out so many biographies, it is no wonder that their authors end up differing on what one might think are the most basic details: some say Rimbaud was left-handed, others right-handed.

IV

Naturally, much of this misreading revolves around details more salacious than hands. Descriptions of body parts and bodily functions prove no less popular in literary biography than they were in high-school conversation. Naturally, we are mature enough to take this at face value, appreciating it as a function of human curiosity and nothing more. The trouble, of course, is the degree to which this sort of abundance creates its own lack, skewing whatever possible hope we might have of coming to a more balanced understanding of this life long past. However much we may be like Rimbaud, his life was most remarkable for the ways it was altogether unlike our own.

As such, it is not generally appreciated how methodical a student of poetry Rimbaud was. It is more pleasant, in the romantic sense, to suppose Rimbaud tossed off verses the way we like to think he tossed down drinks. But the evidence is clear that the wild metrical and musical departures of his middle and late poems were built on the back of the most

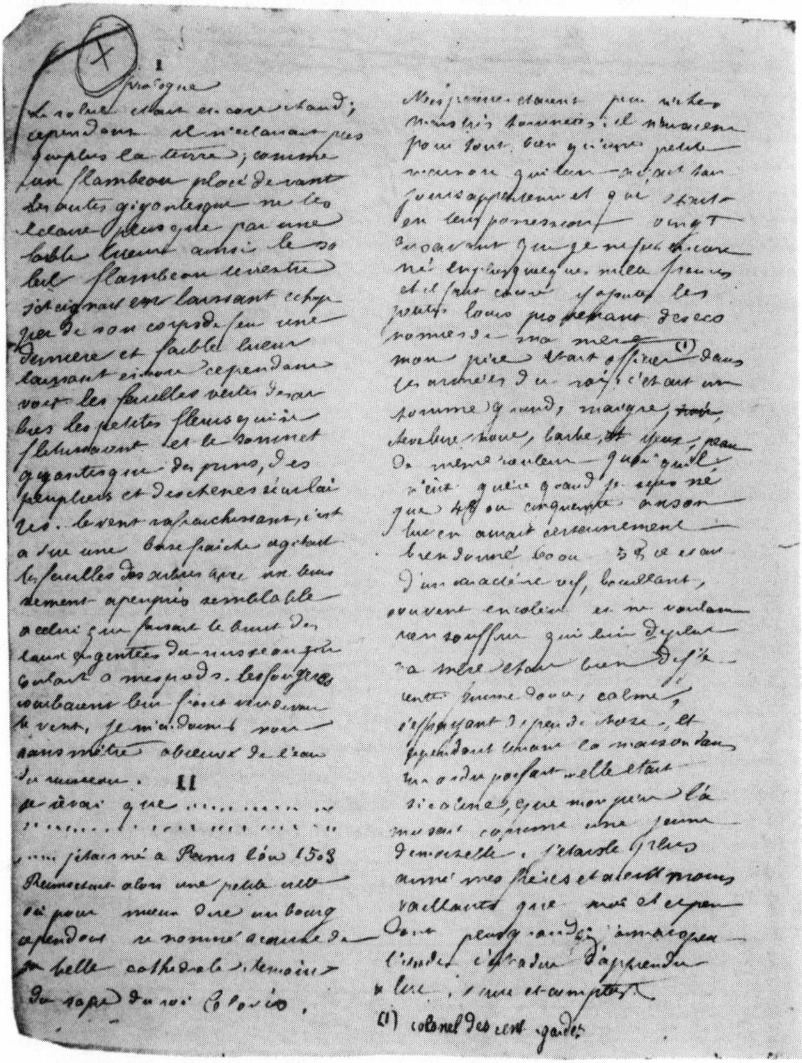

From Rimbaud's school notebook, age 11.

conventional beginnings, a succession of conventions he adopted and shredded over and over again. The cult surrounding Rimbaud's assertion that "the Poet makes himself into a seer by a long, involved, and logical derangement of all the senses" has obscured the inconvenient fact that Rimbaud made himself a poet by a long, involved, and sober study of the history of poetry.

The rigor of Rimbaud's evolving method is apparent in the earliest examples from his pen. Around his eleventh year, while exhibiting a normal schoolboy's zest for doodling, he also compiled, on the backs of the pages he filled with pictures, a sort of commonplace book in which he transcribed passages from his reading: animal fables out of Phaedrus, swaths from the Vulgate Bible, bits of Herodotus.

But these columned entries aren't rendered verbatim: Rimbaud expands and contracts his sources, plays with lines, exhibits a very early, very organic sort of literary criticism. This early workbook, then, lays the foundation for much that follows, most immediately a group of eight pieces he wrote in school in his early teens. In them, we see Rimbaud follow a Johnsonian apprenticeship of rigorous imitation: a prose piece in the style of Villon, an elaboration of a story from Horace's *Odes*, translations of various authors. Thus was crystallized a method of appropriation and play that Rimbaud would use throughout his writing life, until, at its end, Rimbaud the borrower finally became every bit the independent artist.

And it seems to me that the singular, indisputable hallmark of Rimbaud's life, both creative and lived, was the desire for independence. This imperative may reasonably be intuited from the thumbnail of his chronology without resorting to Berrichonism. For no one disputes that at a very early age Rimbaud ran away, repeatedly, as many children do. Precisely why need not concern us. The answer is the same for all such children: unhappiness, of some kind. The act of leaving the known in favor of the unknown is suggestive enough. And Rimbaud's actions remained suggestive, especially his endless running throughout his life, through France and England in his teens, across Europe in his twenties, and into and across Arabia and Africa, where he met the beginning of his early end and perhaps some kind of happiness, but who can say.

Some biographers, though, prefer to see these departures as a disorder with a clear source. They read them as the manifestation of an absence: Rimbaud's father—an officer in the army stationed in north Africa—left the family for good when Rimbaud was still a small child. Rimbaud's peregrinations, as apparently rudderless as his famous drunken boat, may then be read as a melancholy search for the father. Very like a myth. And seductively so.

But the problem is where this seduction leads. For the search for the father, in these biographical assemblages, soon undermines the seriousness of Rimbaud's artistic ambitions. The latest mythic turn to gain currency in the school of psychobiography is the idea that Rimbaud wrote poetry principally to please men he sought out as father replacements: his teacher, Georges Izambard, and the poets and musicians of Paris, not least of whom was Paul Verlaine. Rimbaud's wild productivity becomes, diagnostically, part of a larger pathology; his complete works, many thousands of lines of verse and prose that changed poetry in French and English for good, written over a mere five years, the final five years of his teens, were, the argument goes, wrought to win the admiration and love of his teachers and mentors.

While the other myths—of drugs, of debauch, and so on—are trivial and transparent enough to us now that they recede into the blurry background of the expected, the idea that Rimbaud was not diligent in his pursuit of his goals is the most in need of correction, for Rimbaud was, without question, wildly, soberly ambitious, in poetry, in everything.

As his letters teach us.

V

Rimbaud was a French poet, and, naturally, much of the source material that biographers draw upon for their accounts has not made it into English. Therefore, without a deep knowledge of French and unimpeded access to an excellent research library, those sources are out of reach for an interested English-language reader. The sources include memoirs by various friends, such as Delahaye and Izambard, but most important of them all is Rimbaud's own correspondence, only a fraction of which has been translated into English.

And once you have read these letters, this absence will seem, initially, troubling. But only initially, because to read them makes abundantly clear why they haven't appeared in English: they problematize many of our ideas of Rimbaud. They muddle the sexy myth by clarifying the sober man.

In their own way, the two hundred fifty Rimbaud letters are as important a body of information about Rimbaud as van Gogh's more voluminous correspondence is about him. The fundamental difference between these two groups of letters—both written largely during the 1880s by willful men, wanderers, who would die painfully a year apart, each at thirty-seven years of age—is their subject matter.

Van Gogh's letters are a testimonial to an idea of the artist; in many ways they are the modern foundation for that idea: a being who lives in poverty and obscurity, frequently in squalor, with few friends and even less encouragement, but who nevertheless works himself to death while obeying an inner imperative *to make*. Rimbaud's correspondence is an evolving document of a certain kind of endurance, a will no less manifest than van Gogh's own, but directed toward very different ends: to make himself rich. These differences alone, however, do not explain why van Gogh's letters have been available in English for fifty years, while Rimbaud's have not been available until now.

The easy and, I believe, utterly incorrect reason goes to the question of the letters' quality. Perhaps, one might suppose, the letters aren't very interesting. If one approaches them with the expectation of salaciousness, with a thirst for literary gossip, with the hope of discovering hidden troves of unpublished verses, with a deep interest in Rimbaud's sexuality, with a hunger for the confessional—yes, one would be guaranteed disappointment. There is little of that register in Rimbaud's correspondence. Rather, a sober impatience running from first letter to last. And it is the uniqueness of this tone—a relentless striving—that so informs our understanding of Rimbaud, both as poet and trader.

Only thirty of Rimbaud's letters were written during the period when he was writing poetry. The remainder document the last sixteen years of his life, as he first traveled Europe seeking work and then settled into Arabia and East Africa, where he would live the remainder of his years as a buyer and seller of various goods. While van Gogh literally wrote volumes on the subject of his art, Rimbaud wrote only a handful of lines on his. Due to their paucity, these thirty letters have been pored over and over-thought, are treated as Talmudic texts. And it is not that those letters—the *seer letters*, as they have come to be called by scholars and readers alike—are not interesting. Rather, they can only be viewed as a very small fraction of Rimbaud's thoughts on poetry, for his poetry exhibits so many more faces than simply that of the mystic. It is all too clear that in the absence of information, what little we have has swelled in significance for being the only thing in sight.

Take, in contrast to that scarcity, the sizable remainder of Rimbaud's African correspondence and its unifying theme: his frustration with his fate. Rimbaud complains, whines, roils, and fulminates through a dozen years in Africa and Arabia. I suspect that some have seen this strain as a kind of monotony, and have therefore judged a comprehensive presentation of the letters to be unnecessary. This is an error, I think, for if we read carefully, there is not a monolithic theme, but rather many variations. And those variations begin in the language in which their writer sets them.

For despite the vessel of a less vaunted form, the letters are nonetheless written by one of the most important poets in history. Rimbaud cannot write without frequent great beauty, and therefore we might read to find beauty alone: "Vernal ovens beckon; skins stream, stomachs sour, heads cloud, business is horrible, news is bad." Or to find evidence of Rimbaud's dry wit: "Think of me as a new Jeremiah, with my endless lamentation; there's nothing fun about my situation." Or we might read to find those occasions when Rimbaud looks up from the lap upon which his sorrows lie heaped and sees a vision of life that we have been taught not to expect of him:

> To what end these comings and goings, this exhaustion, these adventures among strange races, and these languages that fill my memory, and these nameless pains if I cannot, one day, after a few years, manage to rest in a lo-

cale that I more or less like and make a family, at least have one son whom I can spend the rest of my life raising as I see fit, adorning and arming with the most complete education one can currently imagine, and whom I will watch become a renowned engineer, a man made rich and powerful by his knowledge of science? But who can say how long my days amid these mountains will last?

We might read for all these reasons. But we can be forgiven if we find ourselves reading for story. An inadvertent narrative arises out of the episodic succession that its writer never could have presumed would be available to the world. Nonetheless, as a story it may be read, despite gaps of days, leaps of years. In the reader's mind, these voids are effortlessly filled, not with rubbery biographical inventions or facile psychological putty, but by Rimbaud's unmissable spirit, visible on every page.

That spirit is apparent in the very first letter—no more than a note, really. Written by the fifteen-year-old Rimbaud to his teacher Izambard, the boy writes to borrow some books. He says he needs one book "above all," and another "above all," too. That repeated "above all" is telling, typifying the inflexible, demanding person increasingly apparent as the letters move forward, in which an "above all" simmers beneath so much of what he says.

But while still in boyhood, this imperiousness takes baby steps as the boy moves from requesting books to, a few months later, forming adult opinions of them:

> I have Paul Verlaine's *Fêtes galantes,* in a pocket edition. Really strange, very funny; but, really, adorable. And sometimes he takes serious license.

And then, of course, on to writing work of his own, which he includes in letters he sends to poets of the day, not, I would argue, because he wants a daddy, but because he wants to get out of the small town he was born to. Later, Rimbaud would have guns and cloth and hides to sell in Africa, to keep him independent and far from home. But here, in a letter to the then-famous poet Théodore de Banville, Rimbaud at sixteen is pushing the only product he has:

Were these poems to find a place in *le Parnasse*, wouldn't they sing the poet's creed? I am unknown: so what? Poets are brothers. These verses believe; they love; they hope: that's enough. Help me, *Maître:* help me find my footing: I am young: give me your hand.

And, yes, we see Rimbaud fall in love, visit its states of rapture ("Listen to your heart.... My life is yours.... I promise to be good") and quarrel ("if you don't want to come back or me to rejoin you, you are committing a crime, and *you will repent its commission for MANY YEARS*"). And, in time, we see him depart for a new life as a desert merchant, where, like a boy reborn, he once again asks for books, requests that now are demands made of his family, as if he were ordering a trained bear to bring him honey:

—It's been two months since I wrote and I still haven't received the Arabic books I requested. Everything must be sent via the Messageries Maritimes. Be aware.

And not just Arabic books: *Topography, Geodesy, Trigonometry, Mineralogy, Hydrography, Meteorology, Industrial Chemistry, Traveler's Manual, Instruction for Travelers' Assistants, Cartwright's Manual, Tanner's Manual, The Compleat Locksmith, Operating Mines, Glassmaker's Manual, Brickmaker's Manual, Earthenware Manual, Metalforging Manual, Candlemaking Manual, Guide to Gunmaking*—in short, a library on how to build an entire civilization, piece by piece.

Time and again we meet proof of a clear, deliberate personality, whether it manifests in the maneuverings of a businessman—

Anyway, barely having said "hello" this sycophant leaving Azzaze for Farré with his mules just as I was leaving with my camels begins to insinuate that the Frangui, in whose name I had come, had a huge debt he owed him, and he demanded my entire caravan as a security against it. I calmed him down, briefly, by offering him a pair of my glasses and some laxatives....

—or in the frustration of a man for a woman he lived with for a year, perhaps two, and about whom we know almost nothing, only this:

Forgive me, but I have sent home that woman for good. I will give her a few thalers and she can leave for Obock by the dhow at Rasali where she can go where she wishes. I have seen quite enough of this masquerade. I would not have been so stupid as to bring her to Choa, I will not be so stupid as to feel responsible for returning her there.

Or in the self-pity he stores in inexhaustible supply:

I must therefore spend my remaining days wandering, in exhaustion and hardship, with nothing to look forward to but death and suffering.

Or even in the tenderness he reserves, occasionally, for his family:

I haven't forgotten you at all, how could I? And if my letters are too short, it's that, as I'm now always going on expeditions, I'm always in a rush at those moments when the mail is about to leave. But I think of you, and think of little but you.

Or, at last, in the resolve of the amputee confronting his end:

Where are the paths between mountains, the cavalcades and promenades, the deserts, rivers, and seas? And now living a *legless existence*! Because I am beginning to understand that crutches, wooden legs, and mechanical legs are all jokes that do no better than to allow you to drag yourself around without managing to accomplish a thing. All this just when I had decided to return to France and marry this summer! Goodbye marriage, goodbye family, goodbye future! My life is over, I'm nothing more than an immobile lump. [...]
    Were someone to ask my advice, I would tell him: you've come this far; now don't let them amputate. Get hacked up, ripped apart, torn to pieces, but don't tolerate amputation. If death comes, it's a far better thing than life with too few limbs. Many have said as much; and if I had it to do over again, I would do it differently. Better to live a year in hell than to be amputated.

These letters are proofs in all their variety—of impudence and precocity, of tenderness and rage—for the existence of Arthur Rimbaud.

And yes, letters are an odd sort of proof. They are necessarily performances, monologues written to the expectations of a particular audience.

The majority of these letters are to his family, the family he fled from, whom Rimbaud addresses as "My dear friends." That formal distance might put us on guard, as the rhetorical equivalent of a man who went bodily far from his mother and siblings but who never severed the ties completely, who ended his letters not with the stiff posture of the salutation but the droopily tender "Yours alone."

And certainly these letters do not tell the whole story. They do not begin to give us the depth of understanding of Rimbaud that the five thousand pages of Gustave Flaubert's correspondence give us of him. Nor do they offer the pure reading pleasure of Vladimir Nabokov's letters, or even the salacious entertainments of Philip Larkin's. The story Rimbaud's letters tell is frequently disagreeable and wildly incomplete, but honestly so, incomplete in the way life is, any life that is not ours to know from the inside.

These letters, then, cannot give us the man whole. And yet they give us significant pieces of him. They give us the opportunity, as readers, to form our own opinions. Of Rimbaud, not "Rimbaud."

And that is not nothing.

—Wyatt Mason
May 2003

1854 Born 20 October in Charleville, son of Frédéric Rimbaud, an infantry captain, and Vitalie Cuif, daughter of landowners.

1860 Frédéric leaves Vitalie and their four children, never to return.

1861–1869 Rimbaud enrolled in school, first Institut Rossat, then the collège de Charleville. Skips a grade, exhibiting academic gifts. Wins numerous regional and national competitions for schoolwork. Acquires reputation for excellence.

1870 Begins principal period of poetic production, which, by all signs, runs its course by 1874.

January: Georges Izambard hired by the collège to teach rhetoric. Develops a mentorial relationship with Rimbaud. Rimbaud's first poem is published, "Les Etrennes des orphelins," in *La Revue pour tous.*

May: Rimbaud writes letter and sends poems to Théodore de Banville, noted Parisian poet. Asks for encouragement; no response from Banville is known. In July, eruption of Franco-Prussian war.

August–November: Rimbaud runs away to Paris, where he is jailed. Upon release, retreats to Douai, home of Izambard's aunts. Remains several weeks. Fetched by Izambard at Rimbaud's mother's insistence. Rimbaud returns reluctantly, remains briefly, flees again, mostly on foot, around the region. Returns to Charleville in November. Schools remain closed due to war.

1871   Flees to Paris in February, returning in March. War comes to a close with the declaration of the Commune in Paris, to which Rimbaud may or may not have been a witness. In May, writes the so-called "seer letters." Summer: writes "The Drunken Boat." Letters to Banville and to Paul Verlaine, another noted poet. Verlaine responds enthusiastically: "Come, dear great soul, we call to you, we wait for you." Sends money and arranges for Rimbaud to come to Paris.

September: Rimbaud leaves for Paris. Put up by Verlaine, then by Banville and by Charles Cros. Becomes acquainted with Paris literary life. Acquires reputation for brilliance and brattiness. Develops relationship with Verlaine, to the consternation of Mathilde, Verlaine's wife. Volatility.

1872   Verlaine leaves wife, flees with Rimbaud. Reconciles with wife, leaves wife again, moves to London with Rimbaud. Melodrama.

1873   Winter: Rimbaud and Verlaine in London. Summer: upheaval, ending in July in Brussels, where Verlaine shoots Rimbaud in the wrist. Police interrogate. Verlaine given a penile/rectal exam, from which it is inferred he is a participant in "unnatural practices." Sentenced to prison: two years. Rimbaud returns to family home. October: at M.-J. Poot, Brussels, Rimbaud has his *Une saison en enfer* printed; takes a handful of copies, leaving over five hundred at the shop, to which he never returns.

1874–1879 Sees Verlaine for the last time in February 1875 upon his release from prison; gives him the manuscript of the poems known today as *Illuminations.* December 1875: death of sister Vitalie, of synovitis. Travels: to London, Stuttgart, Milan, Marseille, Paris, Vienna, Holland, Bremen, Stockholm, Alexandria, Cyprus, in search of work as a tutor, teacher, soldier of fortune, and foreman.

1880   Leaves Europe, to which he will not return for eleven years. March: employed as construction foreman in Cyprus. Leaves suddenly in June, in uncertain circumstances. Later a colleague, Ottorino Rosa, will claim in a memoir that Rimbaud told him he threw a stone that inadvertently struck a worker in the head and killed him.

August: in Aden, Arabia, hired as a clerk in the trading firm of Mazeran, Viannay, and Bardey. November: sent to work for the firm in Harar, Choa, in Africa.

1881   In Harar. Expedition into the interior in search of ivory. Finds the climate in the region unpleasant.

1882   Returns to Aden in service of the firm. Ponders a change of employment. Promoted instead.

1883   Returns to Harar, now as director of the agency. Various expeditions into the interior.

1884   Firm in bankruptcy. Harar and Aden branches closed. Firm reestablished in July by Alfred Bardey. Rimbaud's services retained. Returns to Aden.

1885   Continues to work for Bardey. Sells coffee and various goods. October: ends partnership with Bardey. Allies with another trader, Pierre Labatut, to form a caravan of arms and munitions for sale to the king of Choa, Ménélik. Prepares caravan: delays.

1886   Labatut falls ill: cancer. A new partner, Soleillet, dies. September: caravan at last departs.

1887   March: finds the king in Entotto, and liquidates caravan at what Rimbaud deems disastrous disadvantage. July: back in Aden. August: Massawa, to cash the king's checks. On to Cairo for a month, where he deposits money at a branch of a French bank, Crédit Lyonnais. In Aden by the end of the year. First complaints of knee pain.

1888   Various arms caravans. Partnership with César Tian, an Aden merchant, to begin a firm in Harar.

1891   February: debilitating knee pain. March: seeks local medical attention. April: unable to walk. Borne on a litter to the coast, a twelve-day trip in terrible weather. May: Arrives Marseille, hospitalized. Mother arrives soon thereafter. May 27, right leg amputated above the knee.

July: released from the hospital, returns to the family home in Roche. August: condition worsens, returns to Marseille. Hospitalized again, for good. Weeks pass, disease spreads, limbs fail, delusions come.

November 9: dictates final letter, sister Isabelle at his side.

November 10: dies, at ten in the morning.

RIMBAUD'S YOUTHFUL TERRAIN

BELGIUM

Givet

Vireux

Meuse

Fumay

Paliseul

Gespunsart

Bouillon

Charleville
Mézières

FRANCE

Sedan

Meuse

Tourteron

Aisne

Amagne

Rethel

Charbogne

Mont-de-Jeux

Rilly

Attigny

Roche

Voncq

Chuffilly

Ste-Vaubourg

Coulommes

Méry

Vouziers

Area of
Detail

FRANCE

0   10   20 miles

RIMBAUD'S ADULT TERRAIN

CYPRUS

Alexandria

Port Saïd
Suez

Cairo

EGYPT

Nile

Red Sea

SUDAN

Persian Gulf

Jeddah

Suakin

ARABIA

Hodeidah

Massawa

TIGRE

Adoua

Assab

Mokha

Aden

Tadjoura

Obock

Gulf of Aden

Djibouti

Zeila

Berbera

CHOA

Ankober

Entotto

Addis-Ababa

GALLA

Harar

Bubassa

OGADEN

Area of
Detail

INDIAN OCEAN

-------- Rimbaud's caravan trails

A NOTE ON THE TEXT

Thirty-three of Rimbaud's letters have not been included in this edition. Thirty-two were sent to one man, Alfred Ilg, a trading colleague of Rimbaud's during the late 1880s. These letters are of interest almost exclusively and certainly exhaustively for their enumeration of goods bought and sold. They are, for the most part, lists or descriptions of merchandise either sent or requested, which, in the editor's opinion, is an aspect of Rimbaud's commercial existence already more than adequately documented in the following selection. The dates of these letters are listed in an appendix at the back.

I PROMISE
TO BE GOOD

How lucky you are to be out of Charleville! In all the world, no more moronic, provincial little town exists than my own.

AUGUST 25, 1870

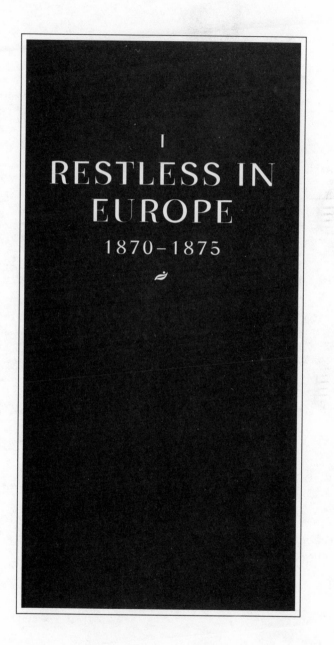

I
RESTLESS IN
EUROPE
1870–1875

The earliest known letter of Rimbaud's to have survived, written when he was fifteen to his teacher Georges Izambard, late winter 1870.

NOTE LEFT IN THE MAILBOX OF GEORGES IZAMBARD
[Charleville; undated, most likely late winter 1870]

	If you have, and if you can lend me:
(above all)	1: Historical Curiosities, volume one by (I think) Ludovic Lalanne;
	2: Bibliographical Curiosities, volume one by same;
	3: French Historical Curiosities, by P. Jacob, first series, including the Feast of Fools, the King of the Ribauds, the Francs-Taupins, and Jesters of France,
(And above all)	... and the second series of same.

I'll come by for them tomorrow, around ten or ten-fifteen. —I'll be in your debt. They will be most useful.

Arthur Rimbaud

Georges Izambard: Rimbaud's rhetoric teacher of the period. He quickly became mentor, confidant and, eventually, ex-friend.

TO THÉODORE DE BANVILLE
Charleville (Ardennes), May 24, 1870

Cher Maître,

These are the months of love; I'm seventeen, the time of hope and chimeras, as they say, and so, a child blessed by the hand of the Muse (how trivial that must seem), I've set out to express my good thoughts, my hopes, my feelings, the provinces of poets—I call all of this spring.

For if I have decided to send you a few poems—via the hands of Alp. Lemerre, that excellent editor—it is because I love all poets, all the good Parnassians—since the poet is inherently Parnassian—taken with ideal beauty; that is what draws me to you, however naïvely, your relation to Ronsard, a brother of the masters of 1830, a true romantic, a true poet. That is why. Silly, isn't it? But there it is.

In two years, perhaps one, I will have made my way to Paris. —*Anch'io,* gentlemen of the press, I will be a Parnassian! Something within me...wants to break free...I swear, Master, to eternally adore the two goddesses, Muse and Liberty.

Try to keep a straight face while reading my poems: You would make me ridiculously happy and hopeful were you, Maître, to see if a little room were found for "Credo in Unam" among the Parnassians...I could appear in the final issue of *le Parnasse:* it would be a Credo for poets! Ambition! Such madness!

Arthur Rimbaud

Théodore de Banville: a well-established poet of the era whose posterity today rests on the collection *Odes funambulesques.* Rimbaud's letter was sent care of Banville's publisher, Alphonse Lemerre. The assistance for which "seventeen"-year-old Rimbaud (who, at writing, was actually fifteen and a half) asked would not come until autumn of 1871, when Banville became one of several poets who gave Rimbaud a room in Paris. *Anch'io:* an allusion to the remark by Correggio, who as he stood before Raphael's canvas of Saint Cecilia said, "Anch'io son pittore" ("I too will be a painter"). *"Credo in Unam":* an earlier version of Rimbaud's "Sun and Flesh."

Through blue summer nights I will pass along paths,
Pricked by wheat, trampling short grass:
Dreaming, I will feel coolness underfoot,
Will let breezes bathe my bare head.

Not a word, not a thought:
Boundless love will surge through my soul,
And I will wander far away, a vagabond
In Nature—as happily as with a woman.

April 20, 1870
A.R.

OPHELIA

I

On calm black waters filled with sleeping stars
White Ophelia floats like a lily,
Floating so slowly, bedded in long veils...
—Hunting horns rise from the distant forest.

A thousand years without sad Ophelia,
A white ghost on the long black river;
A thousand years of her sweet madness
Murmuring its ballad in the evening breeze.

Through blue summer nights...: Rimbaud would later title the poem "Sensation."

The wind kisses her breasts, arranges her veils
In a wreath softly cradled by waters;
Shivering willows weep at her shoulder,
Reeds bend over her broad dreaming brow.

Rumpled water lilies sigh around her;
And up in a sleeping alder she sometimes stirs,
A nest from which a tiny shiver of wings escapes:
—A mysterious song falls from golden stars.

II

O pale Ophelia. Beautiful as snow.
You died, child, borne away upon waters.
Winds from high Norwegian mountains
Whispered warnings of liberty's sting;

Because a breath carried strange sounds
To your restless soul, twisting your long hair,
Your heart listened to Nature's song
In grumbling trees and nocturnal sighs,

Because deafening voices of wild seas
Broke your infant breast, too human and too soft;
Because one April morning, a pale, handsome knight,
A poor fool, sat silent at your feet.

Sky. Love. Liberty. What dreams, poor Ophelia.
You melted upon him like snow in flame:
Visions strangled your words
—Fear of the Infinite flared in your eyes.

III

—And the poet says you visit after dark
In starlight, seeking the flowers you gathered,
And that on the water, sleeping in long veils
He saw white Ophelia floating like a lily.

15 May 1870
Arthur Rimbaud

CREDO IN UNAM...

....

The sun, hearth of tenderness and life,
Spills molten love onto a grateful earth,
And, when you're asleep in a valley, you can feel
The earth beneath you, nubile and ripe with blood;
Her huge breast, rising with the soul within,
Is, like god, made of love; like woman, made of flesh;
Heavy with sap and sunlight,
And embryonic swarms.

How it all grows, how it all rises.
—O Venus, O Goddess.
I long for the lost days of youth,
For wanton satyrs and beastly fauns,
Gods who, for love, bit the bark of branches
And kissed blonde Nymphs in water-lily pools.
I long for lost days: when the rosy blood
Of green trees, the water in rivers,
When the world's sap flowed,

Pouring a universe into Pan's veins.
When the green ground breathed beneath his goat's feet;
When his lips, softly kissing his syrinx,
Sent a song of love into the sky;
When, standing on the plain, he heard
Nature respond to his call;
When the silent trees cradled the songbird,
When the earth cradled man, the blue seas
And the beloved beasts—beloved in God.

I long for lost days when great Cybele
In all her boundless beauty was said
To cut across magnificent cities
In a great bronze chariot, both of her breasts
Spilling the pure stream of eternal life
Unto the breach. Mankind suckled
Her blessed breast like a delighted little child.
—Because he was strong, Man was gentle and chaste.

. . . .

Misery! For now he says: I know everything,
And therefore wanders, eyes closed, ears shut. —And yet,
No more gods! No more gods! Man is King.
Man is God! But Love remains our Faith.
O Cybele! O grandmother of gods and men,
If only man could linger at your breast,
If only he hadn't forsaken immortal Astarte
Who, flower of flesh, odor of oceans,
Once rose from the vast brightness of the blue waves,
Baring a rosy belly snowing foam, goddess
With great black conquering eyes
Who made the nightingale sing in forests
And love in human hearts.

. . . .

I believe in You! I believe in You! Divine Mother,
Aphrodite of the sea! Oh the way is bitter
Now that another God has yoked us to his cross;
Flesh, Marble, Flower, Venus: I believe in you!
—Man is sad and ugly, sad beneath an enormous sky,
He is clothed for he is no longer chaste,
He has sullied his godly head,
And his Olympian body is stooped
In dirty servitude, an idol in the fire.
Yes, even in death, even as a pale skeleton
He would live on, an insult to his original beauty.
—And the Idol upon whom you lavished your virginity,
In whom you made mere clay divine, Woman,
So that Man might illuminate his poor soul
And slowly climb, in limitless love,
From the earthy prison to the beauty of light—
Woman has forgotten her virtue.
—Such a farce! And now the world snickers
At the sacred name of mother Venus.

. . . .

If only lost time would return.
—Man is done for, has played his part.
In the light, weary of smashing his idols
He revives, free from his Gods,
And, as if he were from heaven, searches the skies.
The idea of an invincible, eternal Ideal,
The god who endures within clayey flesh,
Will rise and rise until he burns his brow.
And when you see him sound the horizon,
Shrugging off old yokes, free from fear,
You will offer him divine Redemption.

—Splendid, radiant in the bosom of endless oceans
You will rise, releasing infinite love across
An expanding universe with an infinite smile.
The World will quiver like an enormous lyre
In the tremblings of an enormous kiss.
—The World thirsts for love: you slake it.

. . . .

Free and proud, Man lifted his head.
And the first glimmer of original beauty
Shakes the god in the altar of flesh.
Happy with the present good, sad for sufferings past,
Man would sound the depths—would know.
Thought, a mare long stabled though broken,
Leaps from his brow. She must learn *Why*...
Let her leap, let Man find Faith!
—Why this azure silence, this unsoundable space?
Why these gold stars streaming like sand?
Were one to climb the skies
Forever, what would one find?
Does some shepherd guide this great flock
Of worlds, wandering through the horror of space?
And these worlds that the great ether embraces,
Do they tremble at the sound of an eternal voice?
—And Man, can he see? Can he say: I believe?
Is the voice of thought more than a dream?
If man is so recently born, and life is so short,
Where does he spring from? Does he sink
Into the deep seas of Germs, Fetuses, Embryos,
To the bottom of a vast Crucible where
Mother Nature revives him—living thing—
To love amidst roses and to grow with the wheat...?

We cannot know. —Our shoulders bear
A cloak of ignorance and confining chimeras.
Men are monkeys fallen from their mothers' wombs,
Our pale reason hides any answers.
We try to look: —Doubt punishes us.
Doubt, doleful bird, beats us with its wings...
—And the horizon flees in perpetual flight...

. . . .

The heavens are wide open! All mysteries are dead
In Man's eye, who stands, crossing his strong arms
Within the endless splendor of nature's bounty.
He sings... and the woods with him, and the rivers
Murmur a jubilant song that rises into the light....
—It is Redemption. It is love. It is love!

The splendor of flesh! The splendor of the *Ideal!*
The renewal of love, a triumphant dawn
When, Gods and Heroes kneeling at their feet,
White Callipyge and little Eros
Blanketed in a snow of roses,
Will lightly touch women and flowers
Blossoming beneath their beautiful feet.
O great Ariadne whose tears water
The shoreline at the sight of Theseus' sail,
White in sun and wind. O sweet virgin
By a single night undone, be silent.
Lysios in his golden chariot embroidered
With black grapes, strolling in the Phrygian fields
Among wanton tigers and russet panthers,
Reddens the moss along blue rivers.
Zeus, the Bull, cradles the naked, childlike body of Europa

Around his neck as she throws a white arm
Around the God's sinewy shoulders, trembling in a wave,
He slowly turns his bottomless stare upon her;
Her pale cheek brushes his brow like a blossom;
Her eyes close; she dies
In a divine kiss; and the murmuring wave's
Golden spume blossoms through her hair.
—Through oleander and lotus
Lovingly glides the great dreaming Swan
Enfolding Leda in the whiteness of his wing;
—And while Cypris, so strangely lovely, passes,
And, arching her richly rounded hips,
Proudly bares her large golden breasts
And her snow white belly embroidered with dark moss,
Hercules—Tamer of Beasts, who as if with a nimbus
Girds his powerful form with a lion skin, his face
Both terrible and kind—heads for the horizon.
In the muted light of the summer moon,
Standing naked and dreaming in the gilded pallor
Staining the heavy wave of her long blue hair,
In the dark clearing where the moss is stung with stars,
The Dryad stares at the silent sky...
—White Selene floats her veil
Timidly across the feet of fair Endymion,
And sends him a kiss in a pale beam of light...
—The distant Spring weeps in endless ecstasy...
Our Nymph, elbow on her urn, dreams
Of the fair white lad her wave had touched.
—A breeze of love passed in the night,
And in the sacred woods, surrounded
By terrible trees, majestic marble forms,
Gods whose brows the Bullfinch makes his nest,
—Gods watch over Man and the unending Earth.

. . . .

April 29, 1870

Were these poems to find a place in *le Parnasse,* wouldn't they sing the poet's creed?

I am unknown: so what? Poets are brothers. These verses believe; they love; they hope: that's enough.

Help me, *Maître:* help me find my footing: I am young: give me your hand...

TO GEORGES IZAMBARD
Charleville, August 25, 1870

Monsieur,

How lucky you are to be out of Charleville! In all the world, no more moronic, provincial little town exists than my own. I have no illusions about this any more. Because it is next to Mézières—which no one has heard of—because two or three hundred infantrymen wander its streets, my sanctimonious fellow residents gesticulate like Prudhommesque swordsmen, not at all like those under siege in Metz and Strasbourg! How dreadful, retired grocers donning their uniforms! How marvelous, as though that's all it takes, notaries, glaziers, tax inspectors, woodworkers, and all the well-fed bellies, which, rifles held to their hearts, make their shivering show of patriotism at the gates of Mézières; my countrymen unite! I prefer them seated; keep it in your pants, I say.

I'm disoriented, sick, angry, dumb, shocked; I was looking forward to sunbaths, endless walks, rest, travel, adventure, bohemianism, but: I was most looking forward to newspapers, books... —Nothing! Nothing! The mail brings nothing new to bookstores; Paris is having a fine time at our expense: not one new book! It's like death! I've been reduced to reading the estimable *Courrier des Ardennes,* owned, run, directed, edited-in-chief and edited-at-all by A. Pouillard! This newspaper sums up the hopes, dreams, and opinions of the local population; see for yourself! —I've been exiled inside my own country!!!!

Happily, I have your room: —You do recall that you gave me your permission. —I've borrowed half your books! I took *Le Diable à Paris.* And is there anything more ridiculous than Grandville's drawings? I took *Costal l'indien,* and *La Robe de Nessus,* two interesting novels. What else? I read all your books, all; three days ago, I sank as low as *Les Epreuves,* and then to *Les Glaneuses*—yes, I went so far as to reread it—but that was it. Nothing more; I've exhausted my lifeline, your library. I found *Don Quixote;* yesterday, I spent two hours looking at Doré's woodcuts; now I have nothing! I'm sending you some poetry; read it one morning. In the sun, as I wrote it: I hope you aren't a teacher anymore!

It seemed to me that you had wanted to know more of Louisa Siefert when I lent you her most recent poems; I just managed to find some pieces from her first book, *Les Rayons perdus,* 4th edition. In it I found a very moving and beautiful poem, "Marguerite":

Off to one side, bouncing on my thighs
Was my little cousin with big sweet eyes.
Marguerite is a ravishing girl,
Blonde hair, little lips like pearls
And transparent skin...

Marguerite is too young. Were she mine...
Had I a child so sweet, blonde and fine...
A delicate creature in whom I could be reborn
Pink and guileless with a stare so forlorn
That tears rise to the rims of my eyes
When I think of her bouncing on my thighs.
Never to be mine—an absence I mourn
Because fate, heaping me with scorn,
Delights to see love devoured by flies.

No one will say of me: ah, such a good mother!
No child will look at me and say: *mommy!*
A chapter unwritten in this heavenly homily
To which every girl hopes to contribute another.

Eighteen, and my life is over.

—I think that's as beautiful as Antigone's laments in Sophocles.
—I have Paul Verlaine's *Fêtes galantes,* in a pocket edition. Really strange, very funny; but, really, adorable. And sometimes he takes serious license, like:

And the ter
rible tigress

...is a line in the book. You should buy a little book of his called *La Bonne Chanson:* it just came out with Lemerre; I haven't read it; nothing comes here; but more than one newspaper has had good things to say about it;

—So good-bye, send me a 25-page letter—general delivery—and right away!

A. Rimbaud

P.S. —Soon, revelations about the life I'll lead...after vacation...

Envelope to the letter of September 5, 1870.

TO GEORGES IZAMBARD
Paris, September 5, 1870

Cher Monsieur,

What you told me I shouldn't do, I did: I went to Paris, abandoning my maternal home! I left August 29. Stopping when getting off the train because I was penniless and owed the railroad thirteen francs, I was taken to the prefecture, and today I am awaiting my verdict in Mazas! Oh! —I depend on you as though on my mother; you have never been less than a brother to me: so I ask for the immediate help you've offered before. I wrote my mother, the imperial prosecutor, the Charleville chief of police; if you don't hear anything from me on Wednesday, before the train for Paris leaves from Douai *take that train, come here and claim me by letter or go to the prosecutor yourself,* beg, *vouch for me, pay my debt! Do everything you can,* and, when you get this letter, write, you too, *I order you,* yes, *write to my poor mother* (quai de la Madeleine, 5, Charlev.) *to console her, write me* too, do it all! I love you like a brother, I will love you like a father.

Taking your hand, your poor Arthur Rimbaud
From Mazas.

And if you are able to set me free, take me to Douai with [you].

Rimbaud had run away to Paris, fleeing there by train without a ticket. Upon arrival, he was arrested and thrown in jail, wherefrom this letter. *Mazas:* the Paris prison on boulevard Diderot.

PROTEST LETTER
September 18, 1870

We the undersigned, members of the legion of the sedentary national guard of Douai are protesting against the letter of Monsieur Maurice, mayor of Douai, brought to order on September 18, 1870. In response to the numerous complaints by unarmed members of the national guard, Monsieur the Mayor refers us to the orders given by the Minister of War; in a letter ripe with insinuation, he seems to accuse the Ministers of War and the Interior of ill-will or lack of foresight. Without going so far as to establish ourselves as defenders of a battle already won, we do feel it is our right to assert that the lack of arms at present is attributable only to the lack of foresight and ill-will of the deposed government, to which consequences we are still being subjected. We all should understand the grounds by which the government presiding over the national defense reserves its remaining arms for its soldiers on active duty as well as those on patrol: naturally they all should be armed by the government well before us. Is this the same as saying that three quarters of the national guard cannot be armed, even though they are resolved to defend themselves if attacked? Not at all: they do not wish to remain useless: they must be armed at all costs. It is up to the town council—officials whom we elected—to procure them. The mayor, in such cases, must take the initiative, and, as has already been done in many French communities, he must put in play all means necessary and available to purchase and distribute arms in his community.

Elections for the town council are next Sunday, and we wish to lend our support only to those who, in their words and deeds, will show themselves devoted to our best interests. Now, in our opinion, the Mayor of Douai's letter, read publicly last Sunday after the review, strove, voluntarily or not, to cast discredit on the government of the national defense, to sow discouragement in our ranks, as if there were nothing remaining of the municipal will: which is why we have felt it necessary to protest against the apparent intentions with this letter.

F. Petit

Protest Letter: penned pseudonymously by Rimbaud in an effort to secure rifles for the national guard that had formed as a result of France's invasion by Prussia.

TO PAUL DEMENY
Douai, September 26, 1870

I came to say good-bye to you. But you aren't here.

I don't know if I will be able to come back; I am leaving tomorrow morning for Charleville—I have a safe-conduct pass. —I am infinitely sorry not to have been able to say good-bye to you.

A handshake in thought, with all my force. With every hope—I will write you—you will write me? Right?

Arthur Rimbaud

Paul Demeny: 1844–1918, friend of Rimbaud's via Georges Izambard. Demeny was a very minor poet, author of *Les Glaneuses* (The Lazy Women), which Rimbaud had read. Also part owner of a Paris publishing firm. Rimbaud sent him many poems.

TO LÉON BILLUART

Charleroi, October 8, 1870

... I suppered on odors rising from cellar windows from which wafted aromas of roasted meats and birds in the good bourgeois kitchens of Charleroi, then went off to nibble a bar of Fumay chocolate under the moonlight...

Léon Billuart: A school friend from Rimbaud's time at the collège de Charleville. The letter is a fragment.

TO GEORGES IZAMBARD
Charleville, November 2, 1870

Monsieur
—For your eyes only.—

I got back to Charleville the day after leaving you. My mother was here to meet me, and I—am here... utterly idle. My mother will be sending me to boarding school, but not until January of '71.

But! I kept my promise.

I'm dying, decomposing under the weight of platitude, of crap, of gray, of the daily grind. What else would you expect, I stubbornly continue to love free freedom, and... so many things that are "so very unfortunate," am I right? —I should just leave again today; I could do it: I was wearing new clothes, I could have sold my watch, and so hooray for freedom! —But I stayed put! I stayed put! And I will want to leave again and again. And off I'll want to go, hat, greatcoat, fist in my pockets and away...! But I will stay, I will stay. I didn't promise that. But I will do it to prove myself worthy of your affection: you said as much. And I will be worthy.

I have such gratitude for you that I wouldn't be able to express it any more today than I was the other day. I will just have to prove it to you. I will by doing something for you that will kill me—I will give you my word. —I still have so much to say...

Your "heartless"
A. Rimbaud

War: Mézières has been besieged. When? No one knows. —I gave your message to M. Deverrière, and, if there is anything else, I will do it. —Sniper fire here and there. The popular mind here is like one stupid, ceaseless itch. The things people say. Depressing.

TO PAUL DEMENY
Charleville, April 17, 1871

Your letter arrived yesterday, the 16th. Thanks. —As for what I asked of you: I must have been out of my mind. Knowing nothing of what I should know, and resolved to doing nothing of what I should do, I am condemned, forever and ever. Live for today, live for tomorrow! Since the 12th, I've been opening the mail for the *Progrès des Ardennes:* today, sure enough, the newspaper ceased operations. But at least I briefly appeased the mouth of darkness.

Yes, you are happy, you. I'll say this—whether woman or idea, miserables never find their *Sister of Charity.*

But today I would suggest you ponder these verses from Ecclesiastes: "And he would have seven flights of madness in his soul, who, having hung his clothes beneath the sun, would groan at the hour of rain," but I heap scorn upon wisdom and 1830: let's talk about Paris.

There are a few new things at Lemerre: two poems by Leconte de Lisle, *Le Sacre de Paris, le Soir d'une bataille.* —By F. Coppée: Lettre d'un Mobile breton. —Mendès: *Colère d'un Franc-tireur.* —A. Theuriet: *L'Invasion.* A. Lacaussade: *Væ victoribus.* —Poems by Félix Franck, by Émile Bergerat. —A *Siège de Paris,* really good, by Claretie.

While I was there I read *Le Fer rouge, Nouveaux châtiments,* by Glatigny, dedicated to Vaquerie; available through Lacroix, probably in both Paris and Brussels.

At La Librairie artistique—from Vermersch's address—they asked me what was new with you. I said you were still in Abbeville.

Every bookstore had its *Siège,* its *Journal de Siège;* Sarcey's is in its 14th printing; I saw endless streams of photographs and drawings about the *Siège;* you wouldn't have believed it. The most interesting were of A. Marie, *Les Vengeurs, Les Faucheurs de la Mort;* above all Dräner and Faustin's comic drawings. —As far as theaters went, it was abomination

---

the mouth of darkness: Rimbaud's nickname for his mother, borrowed from Victor Hugo. *"And he would have seven ... the hour of rain":* Actually, from the gospel according to Rimbaud: no such verse exists in Ecclesiastes.

and desolation. —The dailies were represented by *Le Mot d'ordre* and *Le Cri du Peuple*, with Vallès's and Vermersch's admirable imaginations.

So that was literature from February 25 to March 10. —But I may not have told you anything you didn't already know.

If so, turn your face towards the lances of rain, the soul towards ancient wisdom.

And may Belgian literature take us under its wing.

Au revoir,

A. Rimbaud

TO ERNEST DELAHAYE
Charleville, May 1871

...Physically, he was strikingly Psukhé's double...His brother had the
soul of a magistrate; his mother the soul of a Catholic...
...his suspicious looks...nervous as thirty-six million poodle pup-
pies...

Ernest Delahaye: 1853–1930, Rimbaud's oldest friend. Wrote several important books about his
years with Rimbaud, and is our only source for a great deal of what we know of Rimbaud. This
fragmentary letter exists because Delahaye quoted from it, from memory, in a note he wrote fifty
years after the fact.

TO GEORGES IZAMBARD
Charleville, May 1871

And so you're a professor again. You've said before that we owe something to Society; you're a member of the brotherhood of teachers; you're on track. —I'm all for your principles: I cynically keep myself alive; I dig up old dolts from school: I throw anything stupid, dirty, or plain wrong at them I can come up with: beer and wine are my reward. *Stat mater dolorosa, dum pendet filius.* I owe society something, doubtless—and I'm right. You are too, for now. Fundamentally, you see your principles as an argument for subjective poetry: your will to return to the university trough—sorry!—proves it! But you will end up an accomplished complacent who accomplishes nothing of any worth. That's without even beginning to discuss your dry-as-dust subjective poetry. One day, I hope—as do countless others—I'll see the possibility for objective poetry in your principles, said with more sincerity than you can imagine! I will be a worker: it's this idea that keeps me alive, when my mad fury would have me leap into the midst of Paris's battles—where how many other workers die as I write these words? To work now? Never, never: I'm on strike. Right now, I'm encrapulating myself as much as possible. Why? I want to be a poet, and I'm working to turn myself into a *seer:* you won't understand at all, and it's unlikely that I'll be able to explain it to you. It has to do with making your way toward the unknown by a derangement of *all the senses.* The suffering is tremendous, but one must bear up against it, to be born a poet, and I know that's what I am. It's not at all my fault. It's wrong to say *I think:* one should say *I am thought.* Forgive the pun.

I is someone else. Tough luck to the wood that becomes a violin, and to hell with the unaware who *quibble* over what they're completely missing anyway!

You aren't my *teacher.* I'll give you this much: is it satire, as you'd say? Is it poetry? It's fantasy, always. —But, I beg you, don't underline any of this, either with pencil, or—at least not too much—with thought.

TORTURED HEART

My sad heart drools on deck,
A heart splattered with chaw:
A target for bowls of soup,
My sad heart drools on deck:
Soldiers jeer and guffaw.
My sad heart drools on deck,
A heart splattered with chaw!

Ithyphallic and soldierly,
Their jeers have soiled me!
Painted on the tiller
Ithyphallic and soldierly.
Abracadabric seas,
Cleanse my heart of this disease.
Ithyphallic and soldierly,
Their jeers have soiled me!

When they've shot their wads,
How will my stolen heart react?
Bacchic fits and bacchic starts
When they've shot their wads:
I'll retch to see my heart
Trampled by these clods.
What will my stolen heart do
When they've shot their wads?

Which isn't to say it means nothing. —WRITE BACK.

With affection,
Ar. Rimbaud

LETTER TO PAUL DEMENY
Charleville, May 15, 1871

I resolved to provide you with an hour of new literature; I'll jump right in with a psalm on current events:

THE BATTLE SONG OF PARIS

Spring is here, plain as day,
Thiers and Picard steal away
From what they stole: green Estates
With vernal splendors on display.

May: a jubilee of nudity, asses on parade.
Sèvres, Meudon, Bagneux, Asnières—
New arrivals make their way,
Sowing springtime everywhere.

They've got shakos, sabers, and tom-toms,
Not those useless old smoldering stakes,
And skiffs that "*That nev-nev-never did cut...*"
Through the reddening waters of lakes.

Now more than ever we'll band together
When golden gems blow out our knees.
Watch as they burst on our crumbling heaps:
You've never seen dawns like these.

Thiers and Picard think they're artists
Painting Corots with gasoline.
They pick flowers from public gardens,
Their tropes traipsing from seam to seam...

They're intimates of the Big Man, and Favre,
From the flowerbeds where he's sleeping,
Undams an aqueductal flow of tears: a pinch
Of pepper prompts adequate weeping...

The stones of the city are hot,
Despite all of your gasoline showers.
Doubtless an appropriate moment
To roust your kind from power...

And the Nouveau Riche lolling peacefully
Beneath the shade of ancient trees,
Will hear boughs break overhead:
Red rustlings that won't be leaves!

Now, prose on the future of poetry.

All ancient poetry culminated with Greek poetry—Harmonious Life.

From Greece to the romantic movement—the Middle Ages—there are
writers and versifiers. From Ennius to Theroldus, from Theroldus to
Casimir Delavigne, it's all rhymed prose, a game, the sloppiness and glory
of innumerable ridiculous generations: Racine is the standout, pure, strong,
great. Had his rhymes been ruined and his hemistiches muddled, the Divine Dunderhead would be as forgotten today as the next author of the *Origins.* —After Racine, the game got old. It kept going for two thousand years!

Neither joke nor paradox. Reason fills me with more certainty about
all this than a Young France would have been with fury. So the *neophytes*
are free to curse their forebears: it's their party and the night is young.
Romanticism has never been fairly appraised; who would have? Critics!!
The romantics, who so clearly prove that the song is infrequently the
work of a singer, which is to say rarely is its thought both sung and *understood* by its singer.

For I is someone else. If the brass awakes as horn, it can't be to blame.
This much is clear: I'm around for the hatching of my thought: I watch it,
I listen to it: I release a stroke from the bow: the symphony makes its rum-
blings in the depths, or leaps fully formed onto the stage. If old fools

Voici de la prose sur l'avenir de la poésie —
Toute poésie antique aboutit à la poésie grecque,
Vie harmonieuse. — De la Grèce au mouvement
romantique, — moyen-âge, — il y a des lettres,
des versificateurs. D'Ennius à Théroldus, de
Théroldus à Casimir Delavigne, tout est
prose rimée, un jeu, avachissement et gloire
d'innombrables générations idiotes : Racine est
le pur, le fort, le grand. — On eût soufflé
sur ses rimes, brouillé ses hémistiches, que le
Divin Sot serait aujourd'hui aussi ignoré que
le premier venu auteur d'Origines. — Après
Racine, le jeu moisit. Il a duré deux mille ans!

Ni plaisanterie, ni paradoxe. La raison
m'inspire plus de certitudes sur le sujet
que n'aurait jamais eu de colères un Jeune-France.
Du reste, libre aux nouveaux! d'exécrer
les ancêtres : on est chez soi et l'on a le temps.

On n'a jamais bien jugé le romantisme
qui l'aurait jugé? Les critiques!! Les romantiques
qui prouvent si bien que la chanson est si
peu souvent l'œuvre, c'est-à-dire la pensée chantée
du chanteur? et comprise

Car Je est un autre. Si le cuivre
s'éveille clairon, il n'y a rien de sa faute. Cela
m'est évident : j'assiste à l'éclosion de ma
pensée : je la regarde, je l'écoute : je lance un
coup d'archet : la symphonie fait son

From the "seer letter" of May 15, 1871.

hadn't completely misunderstood the nature of the Ego, we wouldn't be constantly sweeping up these millions of skeletons which, since time immemorial, have hoarded products of their monocular intellects, a blindness of which they claim authorship!

In Greece, as I mentioned, poems and lyres turned *Action into Rhythm.* Later, music and rhyme became games, mere pastimes. The study of this past proves precious to the curious: many get a kick out of reworking these antiquities: let them. The universal intelligence has, of course, always shed ideas; man harvests a portion of these mental fruits: they measured themselves against them, wrote books about them: so things progressed, man not working to develop himself, not yet awake, or not yet enveloped in the fullness of the dream. Functionaries, writers: author, creator, poet—such a man never existed.

The first task of any man who would be a poet is to know himself completely; he seeks his soul, inspects it, tests it, learns it. And he must develop it as soon as he's come to know it; this seems straightforward: a natural evolution of the mind; so many *egoists* call themselves authors; still others believe their intellectual growth is entirely self-induced! But all this is really about making one's soul into a monster: like some *comprachico!* Like some man sewing his face with a crop of warts.

I mean that you have to be a *seer,* mold oneself into a *seer.*

The Poet makes himself into a *seer* by a long, involved, and logical *derangement of all the senses.* Every kind of love, of suffering, of madness; he searches himself; he exhausts every possible poison so that only essence remains. He undergoes unspeakable tortures that require complete faith and superhuman strength, rendering him the ultimate Invalid among men, the master criminal, the first among the damned—and the supreme Savant! For he arrives at the *unknown!* For, unlike everyone else, he has developed an already rich soul! He arrives at the unknown, and when, bewildered, he ends up losing his understanding of his visions, he has, at least, seen them! It doesn't matter if these leaps into the unknown kill him: other awful workers will follow him; they'll start at the horizons where the other has fallen!

—more in six minutes—

At this point I'll insert another psalm from *off book:* lend a forgiving ear—and everyone will be delighted. —Bow in hand, I begin:

MY LITTLE LOVES

A teary tincture slops
  Over cabbage-green skies:
Beneath saplings' dewy drops,
  Your white raincoats rise

With strange moons
  And bony spheres,
Knock your knees together
  My disgusting dears.

How we loved each other then
  My blue, disgusting dear:
We ate eggs and chickenweed...
  Now you're no longer here.

One night you named me *poet,*
  My blonde, disgusting dear:
Over my knees I spanked you...
  Now you're no longer here.

Your brilliantine made me sick,
  My dark, disgusting dear:
Your brow could break a guitar...
  Now you're no longer here.

My dry jets of sputum,
  O red, disgusting dear,
Fester between your breasts...
  Though they're no longer here.

O my little loves, I come
  To hate you all the more.
I hope your disgusting tits
  Grow ripe with painful sores.

You trampled my stores of caring
   Now dance for me once again,
No break is ever past repairing
   But Love—broken, ne'er we mend.

My loves' shoulders dislocate:
   An ever-increasing trend.
Stars brand your hobbled hips,
   I won't fall for your tricks again.

And yet, for these sides of beef
   I rhymed the lines above:
Their hips I should have broken
   Than fill with acts of love.

Guileless clumps of fallen stars
   Accumulate in flurries;
You'll die alone, with God,
   Saddled by your worries.

Beneath strange moons
   And bony spheres,
Knock your knees together
   My disgusting dears!
A.R.

There it is. And please be aware that were it not for fear of making you spend 60 centimes on postage—I who, frozen in fear, have been broke for seven months—would be sending you, Monsieur, my one hundred hexameter "Lovers of Paris," and my two hundred hexameter "Death of Paris"!—

But I digress:

The poet is really a thief of fire.

Humanity, and even the *animals,* are his burden; he must make sure his inventions live and breathe; if what he finds *down below* has a form, he offers form: if it is formless, he offers formlessness. Find the words.

—What's more, given every word is an idea, the day of a single universal language will dawn! Only an academic deader than a fossil could compile a dictionary no matter what the language. Just thinking about the first letter of the alphabet would drive the weak to the brink!

This language will be of the soul, for the soul, encompassing everything, scents, sounds, colors, one thought mounting another. The poet will define the unknown quantity awaking in his era's universal soul: he would offer more than merely formalized thought or evidence *of his march on* Progress! He will become *a propagator of progress* who renders enormity a norm to be absorbed by everyone!

This will be a materialistic future, you'll see. These poems will be built to last, brimming with *Number* and *Harmony*. At its root, there will be something of Greek Poetry to them. Eternal art would have its place; poets are citizens too, after all. Poetry will no longer beat *within* action; it *will be before* it. Poets like this will arrive! When woman will be freed from unending servitude, when she too will live for and by her *self,* man—so abominable up until now—having given her freedom, will see her become a poet as well! Women will discover the unknown! Will her world of ideas differ from ours? She will find strange, unfathomable, repugnant, delicious things; we will take them in, we will understand.

In the interim, we require new ideas and forms of our *poets.* All the hacks will soon think they've managed this. —Don't bet on it!

The first romantics were *seers* without even really realizing it: their soul's education began by accident: abandoned trains still smoking, occasionally taking to the tracks. Lamartine was a seer now and again, but strangling on old forms. Hugo, too pigheaded, certainly *saw* in his most recent works: *Les Misérables* is really a *poem.* I've got *Les Chatiments* with me; *Stella* gives some sense of Hugo's vision. Too much Belmontet and Lamennais with their Jehovahs and colonnades, massive crumbling edifices.

For us, a sorrowful generation consumed by visions and insulted by his angelic sloth, Musset is fourteen times worse! O the tedious tales and proverbs! O his *Nuits*! His *Rolla, Namouna, La Coupe.* It's all so French, which is to say unbearable to the *n*th degree; French, but not Parisian. Another work by that odious genius who inspired Rabelais, Voltaire, and

Jean La Fontaine, with notes by M. Taine! How vernal, Musset's mind! And how delightful, his love! Like paint on enamel, his dense poetry! We will savor *French* poetry endlessly, in France. Every grocer's son can reel off something Rollaesque, every seminarian has five hundred rhymes hidden in his notebook. At fifteen, these passionate impulses give boys boners; at sixteen, they've already resolved to recite their lines *with feeling;* at eighteen, even seventeen, every schoolboy who can write a *Rolla* does— and they all do! Some may even still die from it. Musset couldn't do anything: they were mere visions behind the gauze curtains: he closed his eyes. French, half-dead, dragged from tavern to school desk, the beautiful corpse has died, and, ever since, we needn't waste our time trying to rouse him with our abominations!

The second romantics are true *seers;* Th. Gautier, Lec. de Lisle, Th. de Banville. But to explore the invisible and to hear the unheard are very different from reviving the dead: Baudelaire is therefore first among seers, the king of poets, *a true God.* And yet even he lived in too aestheticized a world; and the forms for which he is praised are really quite trite: the inventions of the unknown demand new forms.

In the rut of old forms, among innocents, A. Renaud did a *Rolla;* L. Grandet did his; the Gauls and Mussets; G. Lafenestre, Coran, Cl. Popelin, Soulary, L. Salles; schoolboys Marc, Aicard, Theuriet; the dead and the dumb, Autran, Barbier, L. Pichat, Lemoyne, the Deschamps, the Desessarts; the journalists, L. Cladel, Robert Luzarches, X. de Ricard; the fantasists, C. Mendes; the bohemians; the women; the prodigies, Leon Dierx, Sully Prudhomme, Coppée; the new so-called Parnassian school has two seers, Albert Mérat and Paul Verlaine, a true poet. —There it is. So I work to turn myself into a *seer.* And conclude with a pious song.

SQUATTING

Later, when he feels his stomach grumble,
Brother Milotus—an eye on the skylight
Where bright as a scoured pot the sun

Shoots him a migraine and briefly blinds him—
Shifts his priestly belly beneath the sheets.

He thrashes about beneath the covers
And sits up, knees against his trembling belly,
Upset like an old man who's swallowed his snuff,
Because he still must hike his nightshirt up
Over his hips, clutching the handle of his chamberpot.

Now, squatted, shaking, his toes
Curled, shivering in the bright sunlight that plasters
Brioche-yellow patches on the paper windowpanes;
And the fellow's shiny nose ignites
With light, like a fleshy polyp.

. . . .

The fellow simmers by the fire, his arms in a knot, his lip
Hanging to his belly: he feels his thighs slipping towards the fire,
And his chausses glow red hot, and his pipe goes cold;
Something like a bird barely stirs
In his belly, serene as a pile of tripe.

Around him, a jumble of beaten furniture sleeps
Amidst filthy rags and dirty bellies;
Stools like strange toads sit hunched
In dark corners: sideboards with mouths like cantors
Gaping with carnivorous sleep.

Sickening heat crams into the narrow room;
The fellow's head is stuffed with rags.
He listens to the hairs growing on his moist skin,
And, at times, ridiculous hiccups
Escape, shaking his wobbly stool . . .

And at night, in the light of the moon
That drools its beams onto the curves of his ass,
A shadow squats, etched onto a backdrop
Of rosy snow, like a hollyhock...
Remarkable: a nose hunts for Venus in the deep dark sky.

You'd be a son-of-a-bitch not to respond: quickly: in a week I'll be in Paris,
maybe.

Au revoir, A. Rimbaud

TO PAUL DEMENY
Charleville, June 10, 1871

POETS, AGE SEVEN

And the Mother, closing the workbook,
Departed satisfied and proud, without noticing,
In blue eyes beneath a pimply forehead,
The loathing freighting her child's soul.

All day he sweated obedience; clearly
Intelligent; and yet, black rumblings, hints
Of bitter hypocrisies, hidden, underneath.
In shadowy corridors hung with moldy drapes
He'd stick out his tongue, thrust his fists
In his pockets, shut his eyes till he saw spots.
A door opened onto the night: by lamplight
You could see him, up there, moaning from the banister,
Beneath a bay of light under the roof. Above all,
In summer, beaten and dumb, he was bent
On locking himself in cool latrines:
He could think there, peacefully, filling his lungs.
In winter, when the garden behind the house
Was bathed in the day's fragrances, illunating,
Lying down at the foot of a wall, interred in clay
He pushed on his eyes until they swam with visions,
Listening to the rustling of mangy espaliers.
What a shame! His only friends were bareheaded runts
Whose eyes leaked onto their cheeks, who hid
Skinny fingers mottled yellow-black with mud
Beneath ragged clothes that stunk of the shits,

And who spoke as blandly as idiots.
And when his Mother found him wallowing among them
She was shocked; but seeing such tenderness
In her child muted her surprise. For an instant:
Her blue eyes lied.

At seven years old, he wrote novels
About life in the desert, where Freedom reigns,
Forests, suns, riverbanks, plains. —Inspiration
Came in the form of illustrated papers where he
Blushingly saw laughing girls, from Italy and Spain.
When the daughter of the laborers next door
Came by, eight years old, wild brown eyes,
In a calico dress, he backed her into a corner
And the little brute pounced onto his back,
Pulling his hair, and so, while under her,
He bit her ass, since she never wore panties;
—And bruised by her fists and heels,
He carried the taste of her skin back to his room.

He hated dreary December Sundays,
His hair greased flat, sitting on a high mahogany table,
Reading from a Bible with cabbage-green edges;
Dreams overwhelmed him each night in his little room.
He didn't love God; instead, the men returning to the suburbs
After dark, in jackets, in the tawny dusk,
Where the town criers, after a trio of drumrolls,
Would stir up crowds with edicts and laughter.
He dreamt meadows of love, where luminous swells
Of nourishing scents and golden pubescence
All move about calmly and take wing!

And as he especially relished darkness,
When he was alone in his room, shutters shut,

High and blue, painfully pierced by damp,
He read his endlessly pondered novel,
Overflowing with heavy ochre skies and drowning forests,
Flowers of flesh scattered through the starry woods,
Vertigo, collapse, routs in battle and lasting pity.
—While the noise in the neighborhood continued
Below—alone, reclined on cream canvas,
He had a violent vision of setting sail.

A.R. 26 May 1871

THE POOR AT CHURCH

Parked on oak benches in church corners
Warmed by stale breath, eyes fixed
On the chancel's glittering gold, the choir's
Twenty mouths mumble pious hymns;

Inhaling in the scent of melting wax like the aroma
Of baking bread, the Happy Poor,
Humiliated like beaten dogs, make stubborn dumb prayers
To the good Lord, their patron and master.

After six dark days of suffering in God's name,
The women don't mind wearing the benchwood smooth.
In dark cloaks they cradle ugly children
Who cry as if on the brink of death.

Dirty dogs dangle from these soup eaters,
Prayer in their eyes but without a prayer
They watch as a group of girls parades by
Wearing ugly hats.

Outside: cold; hunger; carousing men.
But for now all's well. One more hour; then,
Unmentionable evils! —For now, wattled old women
Surround them groaning, whining, whispering:

Idiots abound, and epileptics
You'd avoid in the street; blind men
Led by dogs through the squares
Nose through crumbling missals.

And all of them, drooling a dumb beggars' faith,
Recite an endless litany to a yellow Jesus
Who dreams on high amidst stained glass,
Far from gaunt troublemakers and miserable gluttons,

Far from scents of flesh and moldy fabric,
This dark defeated farce of foul gestures;
—And prayer blossoms with choice expressions,
And mysticisms take on hurried tones,

Then, from the darkened naves where sunlight dies,
Women from better neighborhoods emerge,
All dim silk, green smiles, and bad livers—O Jesus!—
Dipping their long yellow fingers in the stoups.

June 1871

Look—don't be mad—at these notions for some funny doodles: an
antidote to those perennially sweet sketches of frolicking cupids, where
hearts ringed in flames take flight, green flowers, drenched birds, Leucadian
promontories, etc.... —These triolets are also as good as gone...
    Perennially sweet sketches
    And sweet verse.
    Look—don't be mad—

HEART OF STONE

My sad heart drools on deck,
A heart splattered with chaw:
A target for bowls of soup,
My sad heart drools on deck:
Soldiers jeer and guffaw.
My sad heart drools on deck,
A heart splattered with chaw!

Ithyphallic and soldierly,
Their jeers have soiled me!
Painted on the tiller
Ithyphallic and soldierly.
Abracadabric seas,
Cleanse my heart of this disease.
Ithyphallic and soldierly,
Their jeers have soiled me!

When they've shot their wads,
How will my stolen heart react?
Bacchic fits and bacchic starts
When they've shot their wads:
I'll retch to see my heart
Trampled by these clods.
What will my stolen heart do
When they've shot their wads?

So that's what I've been up to.
    I have three requests:
    Burn, *I'm not kidding,* and I hope you will respect my wishes as you
would a man on his deathbed, burn *all the poems I was dumb enough to send you*
when I was in Douai: be so kind as to send me, if you can and if you want
to, a copy of your *Glaneuses,* which I want to reread and is impossible for

me to buy since my mother hasn't given me a penny in six months—*oh too bad!* Finally, please respond, anything at all, to this and my previous letter. I wish you a good day, which is something.

Write to: M. Deverrière, 95 sous les Allés, for

A. Rimbaud.

TO GEORGES IZAMBARD
Charleville, July 12, 1871

Cher Monsieur,

[So you're going swimming in the ocean], you've been [sailing... Boyards: that seems very far away, so you've had enough of my jealousy, of hearing how I'm suffocating here!] Anyway, I'm driving myself to unspeakable distraction and can barely get anything down.

Nonetheless, I need to ask you something: an enormous debt—to a bookstore—has fallen upon me, and I don't have a dime to my name. I have to sell back my books. You must remember that in September of 1870, having come—for me—to try to soften my mother's hardened heart, you brought, upon my recommendation, [several books, five or six, that in August I had brought to you, for you.]

So: do you still have Banville's *Florise* and *Exiles?* Given I must sell back my books to the bookstore, it would help me to get these two back: I have some other books of his here; with yours, they would make up a small collection, and collections sell better than books by themselves.

Do you have *Les Couleuvres?* I would be able to sell this as new. —Did you hold onto *Nuits persanes?* An appealing title even second-hand. Do you still have the Pontmartin? There are still people around here who would buy his prose. —What about *Les Glaneuses?* Ardennais schoolchildren will spend three francs to fiddle in his blue skies. I would be able to convince my crocodile that the purchase of this collection would bring considerable benefits. I'd be able to put the best face on the least book. The audacity of all this second-hand shenanigans is wearying.

If you knew the extent to which my debt of 35 fr. 25 c. was driving my mother to her worst, you wouldn't hesitate to get those books to me. You would send the bundle care of M. Deverrière, 95 sous les Allées, which I would be waiting for. I will pay back your postage, and I would be over-overflowing with gratitude!

The brackets indicate sentences destroyed by glue, which Izambard reconstructed from memory.

Were there any other volumes that would be out of place in the library of a professor with which you felt like parting, feel free. But hurry, please, I'm under the gun.

Cordially, and with thanks in advance.

A. Rimbaud

P.S. —In a letter from you to M. Deverrière, I noticed that you were worried about your crates of books. He will get them to you as soon as you tell him where to send them.

A handshake in thought.

A.R.

TO THÉODORE DE BANVILLE
Charleville, Ardennes, August 15, 1871

ON THE SUBJECT OF FLOWERS:
REMARKS, ADDRESSED TO THE POET

To Monsieur Théodore de Banville

I

There, bordering blue black skies
Where wavecrests tremble gold,
Lilies stimulate evening ecstasies,
Enemas thrust between bardic folds.

After all, times have changed:
Plants now labor—aloe and rose.
Lilies arranged in bunches
Decorate your religious prose.

Kerdrel disappeared behind them
In the Sonnet of eighteen thirty.
Poets are buried beneath them,
In amaranth and carnation flurries.

Lilies, lilies. So often mentioned,
So seldom seen. In your verses, though
They blossom like good intentions
As sinners' resolutions come and go.

Why, even when you bathe, Dear Sir,
Your sallow-pitted gown must bloom

With morning breezes: sleeves confer
High above forget-me-nots in swoon.

Yes: our garden gates let lilacs pass.
But such candied clichés have a cost:
Pollinating spit on petals looks like glass
But is still spit. Our poor flowers? Lost.

II

And when you get your hands on roses,
Windwhipped roses red on laurel stems,
Their effect upon you one supposes
Irresistible: bad verses just never end.

BANVILLE's roses fall like snow,
Their whiteness flecked with blood.
A pricking feeling readers know:
Incomprehension chafes and rubs.

Through grassy banks and wooded ways
Feast your shutterbugging eyes.
What they seize on sure amazes:
A monotony of pretty lies.

Why this mania for floral wrangling?
Why does it prompt such turgid lines?
Low-slung hounds with bellies dangling
French poets are tickled by muddy vines.

As if the lines weren't bad enough,
Consider the pictures they adjoin...
A first communion? Either option's rough:
Sunflowers or Lotuses? Flip a coin.

Can French poets resist an Ashokan ode?
Can addicts resist a bag of blow?
As if butterflies take the high road,
To avoid shitting on daisies below.

All this greenery is becoming mulch.
Blossoms plucked to raise the stakes.
Salons bedecked like a flowery gulch
Better for beetles than rattlesnakes.

Grandville's sentimental sketchings
Fill margins with mawkish blooms,
Caricatures of flowery retchings
Evening stars the dark consumes.

Saliva drooling from your pipings
Is all we have for nectar: Pan now dozes.
His song has become mere guttersniping
About Lilies, Ashokas, Lilacs, Roses.

III

O White Hunters: your barefoot excursions
Trample the pastoral into derision;
Shouldn't your flowery poetic diversions
Exhibit a modicum of botanical precision?

You deploy Crickets and Flies indiscriminately
Conflating Phylum and Genus. Rio's gold
And Rhine's blue are switched inadvertently,
Poor Norway becomes "Florida, but cold."

In the past, Dear Master, Art may have settled
For the alexandrine's hexametrical constrictions;

But now, shouldn't the stink of fallen petals
Rotting, make a clean sweep of our ambitions?

Our botanically challenged bards forever bungle:
Mahogany is "a flower found in the country":
Who could imagine that in the Guyan jungle
The real trees support armies of monkeys?

If decadent decoration is the answer that looms
To prettify your pages, the larger question's clear:
Is this riotous, ceaseless, vomitation of blooms
Worth a seagull's turd or one candle's tear?

I think I've made my point: sitting there,
A poet in his far-flung bamboo hut,
Draped with Persian rugs in the Sahara,
You resolutely keep the shutters shut:

And then describe the sands as full
Of flowers, ignoring barren dunes:
This sort of thing—so disgraceful—is bull.
Keep it up, and drive poetry to its doom.

IV

Heard of the notion of "keeping it real"?
Your efforts until now have been rotten.
Enough of this milk-fed literary veal:
Try describing tobacco and cotton.

Why not render Pedro Velazquez' face
And the dollars his cash-crop brings;
Let sun brown skin, your pallor erase,
Describe the shit on swans' white wings:

Yes: the Sorrento sea is full of feathers,
But an ocean of crap floats there too;
Are your stanzas equipped for all weathers?
Are there hydras in the waters with you?

Thrust quatrains into the bloody woods
And report the news that we need.
Expostulate on sugar and durable goods
Whether pansements or rubbers that bleed.

Your job? Deliver truth on these matters,
Such as what covers our tropical peaks;
Is what crowns them like snow-scatters
Lichen, or eggs from insectoid beaks?

O White Hunters, we really must insist
You find us perfumed madders' hues;
Nature nurtures, we gather: fat fists
Dye trousers our infantrymen abuse.

Find flowers that look like muzzles,
At forest fringes dead with sleep;
Unpack oozing botanical puzzles,
Ochre ointments that they leak.

Find calyxes full of fiery eggs
Cooking in aestival juices
In meadows gone insane with legs:
Pubescent insects Spring seduces.

Find cottony thistledown in bunches
By which donkeys' vision is impaired.
Nature never pulls her punches,
Some flowers even look like chairs.

Yes: find in the heart of dark divides
Flowers that look like precious gems;
Pistils and stamens the darkness hides
But crystally encrusts with faceted hems.

For once—Sad Jester—just serve it up;
Lay our table with a purple platter.
Fill it with a lily stew's sweet syrup:
Fill our spoons with the heart of the matter.

V

And, of course, we now arrive at *love:*
Surely it should be the poet's thing.
Yet Renan below and Murr above
Avoid all Dionysian blossoming.

Put your perfumes to good use:
Scent our stink of torpid lust;
Redeem the wanting we produce,
Lift us heavenward on verbal gusts.

Let *practicality* be a poetic criterion,
As for any Soldier, Psychic, or Salesman.
Awake us from thiopentalic delirium
Like rubber trees, tear us open.

Let strange fruit fall from stanzas,
Prismatic light refract from verses;
Black wings, lepidoptric memorandas,
Flutterings full of electric purpose.

An Age of Hell is now upon us:
The earthly body pierced with spears.

Telegraphic poles limn each Gowanus
Helplessly broadcasting silent tears.

Spin, my poet, tales of earthly blight,
Exalt, somehow, in the potato's sorry life;
Rhyme all ruin to make wrong right
Feed your poems on terrestrial strife—

Whether in Babylon or Bayonne—
Let them ramble, let them range
Over paper like low moans:
Graze the poem: make it strange.

Alcide Bava
A.R.
July 14, 1871

Monsieur and Maître,

Perhaps you recall, in June of 1870, having received a hundred or a hundred fifty mythological hexameters for the provinces entitled *Credo in Unam?* You were so good to respond!

The same idiot is sending you more of his stuff, this time signed Alcide Bava—Sorry.

I'm eighteen. —I still admire Banville's poetry.

Last year I was only seventeen!

Am I progressing?

Alcide Bava
A.R.

My address:
Monsieur Charles Bretagne,
Avenue de Mézières, Charleville,
for
A. Rimbaud.

------

eighteen: seventeen, actually.

TO PAUL DEMENY
Charleville, August 28, 1871

You would suggest I say my prayers again: fine. This is my complaint in full. I'm trying to chose peaceful words: but that isn't my strong suit. But here we go.

The situation as it stands: a year ago, I abandoned ordinary life in favor of one you now know well. Trapped without end in this unspeakable Ardennais countryside, seeing no one, consumed by revolting, inane, dogged, mysterious work, answering questions with silence, answering rude, cruel remarks with silence, attempting to appear dignified in my extralegal circumstances, and ending up provoking appalling resolutions from a mother as set in her ways as seventy-three administrations in lead helmets.

She wanted to make me work—for good, in Charleville (Ardennes)! Either take a job on such-and-such a day, or hit the road. —I rejected that life, without giving my reasons: it would have been pathetic. And until now, I had been able to ignore her schedule. She has come to this: she longs for little more than my immediate departure, my flight! Poor, inexperienced, I would end up in a house of correction. And from that moment forward, not a word from me would be heard!

This is the rag of disgust that has been shoved in my mouth. Simple as that.

I am not asking for anything, only information. I want to be free when I work: but in the Paris I love. Here: I am a pedestrian, no more, no less; I come to the great city without the least material resource: but you have said in the past: Whosoever wishes to work for fifteen sous a day can go here, do that, live like so. I'll go, do, live. I begged you to advise me on what were the least demanding occupations, as though this takes up a great amount of time. Poetic absolution, this materialist see-saw has its charms. I am in Paris: I need some savings! You know I'm sincere, right? To me, this all seems so strange that I have to stress just how serious I am.

I had the idea above: it was the only reasonable alternative: I'll put it another way: I'm determined, I do my best, I speak as well as any other malcontent. Why scold a child who, not blessed with much zoological understanding, wishes for a five-winged bird? Why not have him believe in six-tailed birds with three beaks? Why not loan him a family Buffon: that would cure him of his delusions.

So, uncertain as to how you might respond, I'll put an end to my explanations and put my faith in your experienced hands, in your blessed kindness, in awaiting your letter, in awaiting what you think of my ideas—if you will think of them . . .

Would you tolerate seeing a few samples of my work?

A. Rimbaud

Buffon: Georges-Louis Buffon (1707–88), writer of a classic work of natural history.

TO PAUL VERLAINE
[Charleville, September 1871]

[...] I have been planning a long poem, but I can't work in Charleville any more. But I'm without resources, so I can't come to Paris. My mother is widowed and extremely religious. She gives me ten centimes a week, to pay for my church pew.

[...] dirty girl [...]

[...] less trouble than a Zanetto [...]

This letter and the next are fragmentary reconstructions of letters Rimbaud sent to Paul Verlaine (1844–1896). Verlaine was an influential poet of the day to whom Rimbaud wrote requesting help (as he did of Banville). Verlaine's poetic posterity rests on the collections *Fêtes galantes* and *Romances sans paroles,* but his fame has come for being remembered as the teenaged Rimbaud's lover. These letters have been cobbled together from separate published recollections by Verlaine and his wife, Mathilde, of letters that were destroyed. The "Zanetto" reference— a fey boy commedia dell'arte archetype that functioned as a seducer—has been fodder for generations of writers who claim this was Rimbaud's code to Verlaine that he would provide his potential patron with pleasurable recompense. Undependable.

TO PAUL VERLAINE
Charleville, April 1872

[...] Right now work is about as far from my thoughts as my finger-nails are from my eyes. Tough shit! Tough shit! Tough shit! Tough shit! Tough shit! Tough shit! Tough shit! Tough shit!

When you see me actually eat shit, then only you will no longer think that I am expensive to feed!...

TO ERNEST DELAHAYE
The Big Shitty, Juneteenth 1872

Yes, life in the Ardennais cosmorama is filled with surprises. I do not miss this province where we eat flour and mud, where we drink local wine and beer. You are perfectly justified in continuing to denounce it. But here: distillation, composition, narrow-mindedness; and the oppressive summers: the heat isn't without respite, but given that good weather is in everyone's interests, and that everyone is a pig, I hate how summer kills me when it appears even briefly. I'm so thirsty you would think I have gangrene: Belgian and Ardennais rivers, caves, these I miss.

There is one place to drink here I like. Long live the Academy of Abseenth, however surly the waiters! Such delicate, tremulous attire— drunkenness delivered by abseenth, that glacial sage! All so we may sleep in shit when we're through.

The whining never changes! What is for certain: fuck Perrin. And why not on the bar of the Café de l'Univers, whether it faces the square or not. —My greatest wish is that the region were occupied and squeezed tighter and tighter. But this is a commonplace.

The worst is that all of this will bother you as much as it will. It seems for the best that you read and walk as much as possible. Reason enough not to remain confined to offices and homes. Mindlessnesses must be given free reign, far from confinement. I am not about to be selling balm, but I imagine habit isn't much consolation on the worst days.

Now I'm crossing through night. Midnight to five A.M. The past month, my room, rue Monsieur-le-Prince, overlooking a garden in the Lycée Saint-Louis. There were enormous trees beneath my narrow window. At three A.M., the candle dimmed: all the birds in the trees called out together: the end. No more work. I had the trees to look at, the sky, held in this unspeakable hour, morning's first. I saw the lycée dormitories, utterly silent. And already there was the wonderful melodic staccato of the carts on the streets. —I smoked my hammer pipe, spitting on the tiles, my room high in the garret. At five A.M., I went down to buy bread: that's the time. Workers are everywhere. For me, it's the time of day to go get drunk at the wine merchants'. I came back home to eat, and then went to sleep at seven A.M., when the sun stirs the wood lice from under the tiles. The first summer morning, and the December nights, that's what always delighted me here.

But now I have a pretty room, on an endless courtyard, but three meters square. —La rue Victor Cousin and the Café Bas-Rhim form a corner on the Place de la Sorbonne, and face rue Soufflot on the other side. —There I drink water all night, I don't see the dawn, I don't sleep, I suffocate. So there it is.

Your complaints will be lodged, remedy granted! And don't forget to shit on *La Renaissance,* that arts and letters daily, should you come across it. Until now I've been able to avoid those shitty slickers from home. And fuck the seasons too.

Courage.

A.R.

TO ERNEST DELAHAYE
Laïtou (Roche), (Attigny canton), May 1873

Dear friend, my life right now is pretty much like what you see in this watercolor below:

O Nature! O my mother!

What a pain in the ass, and what monstrous innocents these peasants are. At night, if you want to drink you have to walk at least two leagues. *Mother* is responsible for putting me in this grim pit.

I have no idea how I'm going to get out of this: but I will. I miss unbearable Charleville, l'Univers, the Librar...etc.... I am working fairly regularly; I'm doing some little prose pieces under the general title *The Pagan Book* or *The Black Book*. It is stupid and innocent. O innocence! Innocence; innocence, innoc...scourge!

Verlaine must have saddled you with the unfortunate responsibility of debating Lord Devin, printer of the *Nord-Est*. I think this Devin could do Verlaine's book reasonably and perfectly well. (As long as he avoids the *Nord-Est*'s shitty font. I could just see the guy inserting an ad or a picture!)

I have nothing more to tell you, I'm up to my ass in introspection and Nature-watching. I am yours, O Nature, O my mother!

A handshake in thought, a hoping my efforts towards reunion bear fruit.

R.

I have reopened my letter. Verlaine must have suggested a rendezvous on Sunday the 18th in Bouilon. I can't make it. If you go, he'll probably give you a few prose fragments of mine to give back to me.

Mother Rimb. will return to Charleville sometime in June. This is certain, and I'll try my best to remain in this pretty town as long as I can.

The sun is strong and mornings are cold. The day before yesterday I went to see the Prussians in Vouziers, an underprefecture of some 10,000 souls, seven kilometers from here. This brightened my spirits.

I am unbelievably bothered. No books, no bar nearby, nothing going on in the streets. The French countryside is death. My fate rests with this book for which I still have a half-dozen horror-stories to make up. How does one make up atrocities here? I won't send you any of them yet, while I already have three: *it costs too much!* So there!

Au revoir, and you'll see it soon enough.

Rimb.

I'll soon send you stamps so you can buy and send me Goethe's *Faust*, in the Bibliotheque Populaire edition. Mailing it will cost a sou.

See if there is any Shakespeare coming out in that series.

And if you could send me their latest catalogue, do.

TO PAUL VERLAINE
London, Friday afternoon [July 4, 1873]

Come back, come back, dear friend, only friend, come back. I promise to be good. If I was short with you, I was either kidding or just being stubborn; I regret all this more than I can express. Come back and all is forgotten. It is unbearable to think you took my joke seriously. I have been crying for two days straight. Come back. Be brave, dear friend. All is not lost. You only need to come back. We will live here once again, bravely, patiently. I'm begging you. You know it is for your own good. Come back, all of your things are here. I hope you now know that our last conversation wasn't real. That awful moment. But you, when I waved to you to get off the boat, why didn't you come? To have lived together for two years and to have come to that! What will you do? If you don't want to come back here, would you want me to come to you?

Yes, I was wrong.

Tell me you haven't forgotten me.

You couldn't.

I always have you with me.

Listen, tell me: should we not live together anymore?

Be brave. Write immediately.

I can't stay here much longer.

Listen to your heart.

Now, tell me if I should come join you.

My life is yours.

Rimbaud

Write now: I can't stay here past Monday night. I don't have a penny to my name; I can't even mail this. I gave *Vermersch* your books and papers for safekeeping.

If you say you don't want to see me again, I'll join the army or the marines.

Come back, come back, I cry and cry. Tell me to come join you and I'll come. Tell me, wire me. —I have to leave Monday night. Where will you go? What will you do?

One of Rimbaud's lists of English vocabulary words.

TO PAUL VERLAINE
[London, July 5, 1873]

Dear friend,

I have your letter dated "at sea." You are wrong, this time, very wrong. First, there is nothing positive in your letter. Your wife isn't coming, or will come in three months, three years, who knows. As to your dropping dead, please. So while waiting for your wife and your demise, you're just going to flail around, wander aimlessly, piss people off. Right? Haven't you yet realized that each of our angers was as wrong as the other's? But you're going to end up being wrong all by yourself, because even after I called you home you refused to drop the act. Do you really believe that life can be better with someone other than me? *Think about it.* I thought so.

You can be free only with me, and, since I swear I'll be kinder from now on, since I can't stand the part I've played in all of this, since my conscience is now clear, since I adore you, if you don't want to come back or me to rejoin you, you are committing a crime, and *you will repent its commission for MANY YEARS in the form of freedom lost and boredom more unbearable* than any you've known. So think of what you were before we met.

As for me, I'm not going back to my mother's. I'm going to Paris. I'll try to be gone by Monday night. You're making me resort to selling your clothes, as I have no other choice. I haven't sold them yet: they won't come for them until Monday morning. If you want to write me in Paris, send letters to L. Forain, 289 rue Saint-Jacques (for A. Rimbaud), which will be my address there.

Of course, if your wife returns, I won't compromise your situation by writing you—I won't write again.

The only words with any meaning are these: come back. I want to be with you, I love you. If you hear this, you will prove yourself courageous and sincere.

Otherwise, I pity you.

But I love you, embrace you, and know we'll see each other again.

Rimbaud

8 Great Colle...etc....
Until Monday night, or Tuesday midday, if you call.

TO PAUL VERLAINE
Monday, Noon [London, July 7, 1873]

My dear friend,

I saw the letter you sent to Madame Smith.
Unfortunately it arrives too late.
You want to return to London. You have no idea how everyone will receive you. The look that Andrieu and the others will give us if they see
me with you. But I'll be brave. Tell me what you want. Are you coming
back to London for me? What day? Did my letter convince you? There's
nothing left in your room. —Everything's been sold except a jacket. I got
two pounds ten. But the wash is still with the woman, and I kept a few
things for myself: five vests, all the shirts, some boxers, collars, gloves, and
all the shoes. All your books and ms's are in good hands. So, the only thing
left to sell are your pants, black and gray, a jacket, and a vest, the bag and
the hatbox. But why don't you write me directly?
Yes, dear boy, I'm going to stay here another week. And you'll come,
right? Be honest. You're being brave. I hope you mean it. Trust me, I will
be on my best behavior.
I'm yours. I'm waiting.

Rimb.

\

Lundi midi.

Mon cher ami

J'ai vu la lettre que tu
envoyée à Mme Smith.
et malheureusement trop
tard. Tu veux revenir à Londres?
Tu ne sais pas comme tout le
monde t'y recevrait! Et la
mine que me feraient Andrieu
et autres s'ils me revoyaient avec
toi! Néanmoins, je serai très
courageux. Dis moi ton idée
bien sincère.. Veux tu retourner
à Londres pour moi? Et quel jour?
Est ce oma lettre qui te conseille?
Mais il n'y a plus rien dans les
chambres. — Tout est rendu, sauf
un paletot. J'ai eu deux lettres
d'ix. Mais le linge est encore chez
la blanchisseuse, et j'ai conservé
un tas de choses pour moi.

From the Monday, Noon letter opposite.

TO ERNEST DELAHAYE
Stuttgart, [March 5] 1875

Verlaine arrived here the other day, clutching a rosary... Three hours later he had renounced his god and reopened the 98 wounds of Our Savior. He stayed two and a half days, was altogether sensible, and upon my remonstration returned to Paris to go, straightaway, to study over there on the island.

I have only one week left of Wagner and I regret this hateful use of money, this time wasted. By the 15th I'll have *Ein freundliches Zimmer* somewhere, and

---

1875: On the letter, Rimbaud wrote "5 February," but its postmark read March 6. Rimbaud did not leave Charleville for Stuttgart until February 12, leading scholars to believe he meant March 5 instead.

Wagner: Wagnerstrasse, the street where Rimbaud was living.

Ein freundliches Zimmer: Gr. a pleasant room.

I'll tear through this language, such that I'll have it all settled in two months at the most.

Everything is pretty much inferior here, with one exception: Riessling, ein glasovich ei vould derink befronten der hillen ver itz growen! Idtz tsunnie unt den knot: inferniating!

(After the 15th, Stuttgart general delivery).
Yours,

Rimb.

TO HIS FAMILY
[Stuttgart] March 17, 1875

My dear friends,

I decided not to write until I had a new address. Today I acknowledge receipt of your last mailing, of 50 francs. Here's a model of how to make out envelopes meant for me:

"3 tr." means 3rd floor.

I have a big room here, very well furnished, in the middle of town, for ten florins, which is 21 francs 50 centimes, tax included; room and board would be 60 francs a month: but I don't need to do that: those deals always end up being a liability, either through dependence or deceit, whatever bargain they might at first seem. I'll try to go until April 15 with what I have on me (another 50 francs) since I'll still need an advance by then: because either I have to stay another month to get myself up to speed, or I have to place some ads for various positions the pursuit of which (traveling there, for example) requires money. I hope that you find this moderate and reasonable. I'm trying to assimilate all the local ways of doing things by every available means, gathering all the information I can, although their attitude is for the most part insufferable. Regards to the military, I hope that Vitalie and Isabelle are well, I hope you let me know if there is anything I can get you from here, and know I remain devoted to you.

A. Rimbaud

My dear friends: in French, "Mes chers amis," an unusual greeting from a son to his mother and sisters. *the military:* Rimbaud's brother, Frédéric, was doing his military service at the time.

TO HIS SISTER ISABELLE [FRAGMENT]
[undated]

[...] I am in a lovely valley that leads to Lac Majeur and old Italy. I slept in the heart of Tessin in a lonely barn where a bony cow was ruminating and willing to relinquish some of its straw. [...]

This is a fragment of a letter believed to be in the hands of a private collector.

TO ERNEST DELAHAYE
October 14, 1875

My dear friend,

Got the Postcard and V.'s letter a week ago. To keep things simple, I told the post office to send general delivery to me, so that you could write me here. I won't respond to any of the most recent Loyola-inspired rudenesses, and I have no energy to devote to that right now, as it seems that the 2nd "portion" of the "74th class's contingent" will be called up next November 3, or the one after that: the barracks at night: "Dream."

In the barracks, hunger finds you
      It's true...
Outpourings and explosions. The ingenuity
      Of the engineer: "That's me, Gruyère!"
Lefêvbre: "Keller!"
The ingenious engineer: "I'm Brie!"
Soldiers cut their bread: "C'est la vie!"
The ingenious engineer: "I'm Roquefort!"
                    —"We're done for...!"
                    —"That's me, Gruyère!"
                       And Brie...! etc.
                —Waltz—
Lefêvbre and I are one...   etc...

It's easy to become consumed by worries of this kind. Nonetheless, kindly send along whatever "Loyolas" should crop up.

One thing: would you be able to tell me exactly and briefly what the Baccalaureates in Sciences, Classics, and Math require. —The grade required on each part: math, physics, chemistry, etc, and the titles—immediately (and how to go about getting them)—of the books used in your

---

Loyola: a reference to Verlaine, who, upon his release from prison, revealed a new religiosity, thus the Ignatius quips by an unconvinced Rimbaud.

M__   14 8bre 75

Cher ami
Reçu le Postcard et la lettre de V. il y a
huit jours. Pour tout simplifier, j'ai dit
à la Poste d'envoyer ses restantes chez moi
de sorte que tu peux écrire ici, ni encore ici,
aux restantes. Je ne comprends pas les
dernières grossièretés de Loyola, et je
n'ai plus d'activité à me donner de ce côté là
à présent, comme il paraît que la 2ᵉ
"portion" du "contingent" de la "classe 74"
va-t-être appelée le trois novembre "suivᵗ"
ou prochain : la chambrée de nuit : "Rêve"

            On a faim dans la chambrée —
                C'est vrai….
Émanations, explosions. Un génie :
        " Je suis le Gruère ! —
    Lefèbvre :   " Keller !"
Le génie : " Je suis le Brie ! —
Les soldats coupent sur leur pain :
            " C'est la vie !
Le génie.   — " Je suis la Roquefort !
            — " Ça s'ra not' mort !….
            — J' suis le Gruère
                Et le Brie !…. etc.
            — Valse —
On nous a joints, Lefèvre et moi —
                    etc.
De telles préoccupations ne permettent que de

From the letter of October 14, 1875.

school; for example, for this Bac, those books that would be the same no matter where you were in school: If you could, ask some competent professors and students about this matter. The more specific the better, as the next step would be for me to buy the books. Between military service and studying for the Bac, you see, would provide me with two or three agreeable seasons. Anyway, to hell with "good works." Just be good enough to let me know as best you can the way to go about all this.

Here, nothing at all.

I like to think that the Gooniversity student and the slimeballs full of patriotic beans or not aren't driving you to distraction. At least it doesn't stink with snow there, as it does here.

To you "to the extent of my limited powers."

Write:

A. Rimbaud
31, rue St-Barthélémy,
Charleville (Ardennes), it goes without saying.

P.S. The wrangling with the mail has gotten to the point where Némery gave Loyola's newspapers to *a police officer* to bring me!

Cette idole, yeux noirs et crin jaune,
sans parents ni cour, plus noble que la
fable, mexicaine et flamande; son
domaine, azur et verdure insolents, court
sur des plages nommées, par des vagues
sans vaisseaux, de noms férocement
grecs, slaves, celtiques.

People unaccustomed to the sight of mountains quickly learn that a mountain may have peaks but that a peak is not a mountain.

NOVEMBER 17, 1878

II

FIRST
TRANSIT

1876–1878

The undersigned Arthur Rimbaud —
Born in Charleville (France) — Aged 23 —
5 ft 6. height — good healthy, — Late a
teacher of sciences and languages — Recently
deserted from the 47? Regiment of the
French armies, — Actually in Bremen without
any means, the French Consul refusing
any Relief, —

Would like to know on which conditions
he could conclude an immediate engagement
in the American navy.

Speaks and writes English, German, French,
Italian and Spanish.

Has been four months as a sailor in
a Scotch bark, from Java to Queenstown.
from August to December 76.

Would be very honoured and grateful
to receive an answer.

John Arthur Rimbaud

TO THE UNITED STATES CONSULATE IN BREMEN
May 14, 1877

The untersigned Arthur Rimbaud; Born in Charleville (France); Aged 23; 5 ft. 6 height; Good healthy; Late a teacher of sciences and languages; Recently deserted from the 47th Regiment of the French army; Actually in Bremen without any means, the French Consul refusing any Relief;
Would like to know on which conditions he could conclude an immediate engagement in the American navy.
Speaks and writes English, German, French, Italian and Spanish.
Has been four months as a sailor in a Scotch bark, from Java to Queenstown, from August to December 76.
Would be very honoured and grateful to receive an answer.

John Arthur Rimbaud

This letter was written in English. All errors are Rimbaud's.

TO HIS FAMILY
Gênes, Sunday, November 17, 1878

Dear friends,

This morning I arrived in Gênes and received your letters. You have to pay for passage to Egypt in gold, so there's no way to make it cost less. I leave Monday the 19th, at 9 P.M. We get in by the end of the month. As for how I got here, it was full of wrong turns and sporadic seasonal surprises. From Remiremont, I had to go through the Vosges in order to meet the German connection at Wesserling; first in a carriage, then on foot, for after a certain point no carriage could get through with an average of fifty centimeters of snow and a storm brewing. The Gothard crossing was supposed to be the route; you can't get through by carriage in this season, and so I couldn't get through either.

At Altdorf, on the south side of lake Quatre-Canton along the border of which we strolled through steam, the Gothard road begins. At Amsteg, fifteen kilometers from Altdorf, the road begins to climb and follow the contours of the Alps. Valleys are long gone by this point, and all the climbing that's left is the cliffs above the decametrical mile markers that line the road. Before arriving in Andermatt, you pass a place of real horror called the Devil's Bridge—less beautiful though than the Via Mala in Splügen, an engraving of which you have. At Göschenen, a village that has become a market town because of the affluence of its workers, you see the opening of the famous tunnel at the back of the gorge, the studios and canteens of businesses. Moreover, this seemingly rough-hewn countryside is hardworking and industrious. Even if you can't see the threshers going in the valley, you can hear the scythes and mattocks against the invisible heights. It goes without saying that most of the local industry manifests in wood. There are many mining operations. Innkeepers show you mineral samples of every variety, which Satan, they say, buys on the cheap and resells in the city.

The real ascent begins at the Hospital, I think: sidestreets lead to the road the carriages use. Because you can imagine you wouldn't want to go that way all the time with its zigzags and gentle terraces (which would take forever), particularly when you see the elevation of the adjoining countryside: each cliff rises only to 4,900 meters, or even less. And you don't go straight up: you take the well-marked routes, which is not to say they're easy going. People unaccustomed to the sight of mountains quickly learn that a mountain may have peaks but that a peak is not a mountain. The Gothard summit covers an area of several kilometers.

The road, which is never wider than six meters, is filled the whole way with nearly two meters of fallen snow, which, at any moment, might collapse, covering you with a meter-thick blanket you have to hack through during a hailstorm. And then: no more shadows above, below, or beside, despite being surrounded by these massive things; no more road, or precipices, or gorges or sky: just whiteness out of a dream, to touch, to see or not to see, since it's impossible to look away from the white annoyance in the middle of the road. Impossible to lift your head with the biting wind, eyelashes and mustaches becoming stalactites, ears torn, necks swollen. Without the shadow that is oneself, and without the telegraph poles to mark what one must assume remains of the road, you would be as flustered as a sparrow in an oven.

All this, just to get through snow a meter high, a kilometer long. You haven't seen your knees in some time. It's exhausting. Breathless—since in a half-hour the storm can bury you effortlessly—you offer each other shouts of encouragement (you never climb all alone, only in groups). Finally a road-mender appears: you buy a bowl of saltwater for 1.50. And then back at it. But the wind picks up, you see the road begin to fill. Here's a convoy of sleighs, a fallen horse half-buried. The road disappears. Are we on the road or next to it? (There are markers only on one side of the road.) You get off course, sink into the snow up to your ribs and then your armpits . . . A pale shadow behind a clear path: the Gothard hospice, a civil and medical facility, a hulking mass of pine and stone; a steeple. When you ring the bell, a seedy-looking young man comes to the door; you take the steps to a dirty, low-ceilinged room where you are given the legally determined minimum of bread and cheese, soup and drink. You see the great big yellow hounds everyone has heard of. Soon, half-dead latecomers come in off the mountain. At night, after soup, the thirty of us spread out on hard mattresses under inadequate covers. At night, we hear our hosts exhaling holy canticles in praise of another day of theft from the government that subsidizes their little hovel.

In the morning, after a morsel of bread and cheese, steadied by this free hospitality that will last as long as the storm dictates, you leave: this morning, in the sun, the mountain is a marvel: no more wind, all downhill, taking shortcuts, making leaps, tumbling for kilometers that leave you at Airolo, the other end of the tunnel, where the road reverts to alpine expectations, roundabout and full of obstructions, but descending. That's Tessin.

There's snow on the road for the thirty kilometers from Gothard. Only after thirty km, at Giornioco, the valley widens a little. A few vine-covered bowers and a few patches of meadow that we light carefully with leaves and other detritus from fir trees that must have served as bedding. Goats move down the roads, gray cows and bulls, black pigs. At Bellinzona, there is a major livestock market. At Lugano, twenty leagues from Gothard, you get the train and go from pleasant Lake Lugano to pleasant Lake Como. After that, the expected route.

Thinking of you all, thanking you, and in twenty days or so you will have a letter.

Your friend.

TO HIS FAMILY

Alexandria, [December] 1878

My dear friends,

I arrived here after a ten-day crossing, and, after having been here another fifteen, things are only now starting to improve! I'll soon be employed, and am already finding enough work to get by, if barely. Either I'll work for a large agricultural concern about ten leagues from here (I already went there, but there won't be any work for a few weeks); or I'll join the Anglo-Egyptian Customs office, at a good wage; —or, I think it more likely still I'll leave for Cyprus, the English island, as an interpreter for a group of laborers. In any case, I have been offered one thing that's certain; it is with a French engineer—a kind, talented man—with whom I'm dealing. But they want something from me: a letter from you, mother, notarized by city hall, and stating:

"I the undersigned, wife of Rimbaud, a property owner in Roche, declare that my son Arthur Rimbaud recently worked on my land, left Roche of his own free will, October 20, 1878, and has conducted himself honorably here and elsewhere, and that he is not presently liable to military law. Signed: Wife of R ..."

And the stamp from city hall is the most important part.

Without this letter I will not be given a regular position, although I think I could work part-time. Be careful not to say I was only in Roche briefly, because they would ask for an explanation, and that would go on and on; this will make the people from the agricultural concern here believe that I am able to get things done.

I pray that you send me this note as soon as you can: it's all very straightforward and will take care of things for here, at the very least giving me work through the winter.

I'll soon send you details and descriptions of Alexandria and Egyptian life. No time today. I'll say good-bye. Hello to F[rédéric] if he's home. It's hot here, like August in Roche.

Send news.

A. Rimbaud
French mail, Alexandria
Egypt

What's more, while the plains are very hot, at our elevation it is, and has been, disagreeably cold for over a month; it rains, hails, and the wind can knock you over.

MAY 23, 1880

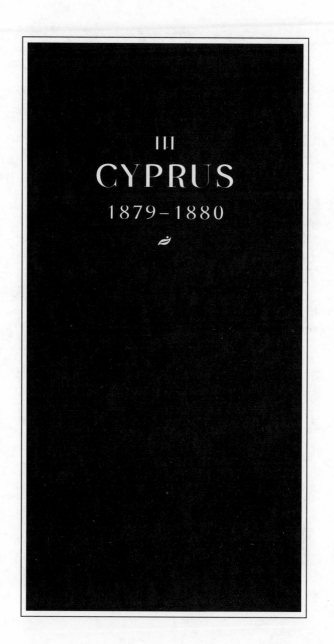

III

CYPRUS

1879–1880

TO HIS FAMILY
E. Jean et Thial Sons, Larnaca (Cyprus), Entrepreneurs
February 15, 1879, Larnaca (Cyprus)

Dear Friends,

I didn't write you sooner, not knowing precisely where I would be sent.
But you should have received a letter from Alexandria where I mentioned
a possible job in Cyprus. Tomorrow, February 16, I will have been employed here for exactly two months. My employers are in Larnaca,
Cyprus's main port. I'm the supervisor of a quarry in the desert by the
sea: a canal is also being dug. And stones have to be loaded onto the company's five boats and one steamer. There is also a lime kiln, a brickworks,
etc.... The nearest village is one hour away on foot. There is nothing here
but a jumble of rocks, a river, and the sea. There are no houses. No soil,
no gardens, no trees. In summer, the heat goes up to 80 degrees centigrade. Now it's usually around fifty. It's winter. It rains occasionally. We
eat small game, chickens, etc.... all the Europeans are sick but me. There
are no more than twenty of us here. The first of them arrived December
9. Three or four have died. The Cyprian workers come from the surrounding villages; we employ up to sixty a day. I'm in charge: I organize
the schedules, arrange for materials, report to the Company, am account-
able for the food and all expenses; and I do payroll; yesterday, I paid some
Greek workers five hundred francs.

I am paid by the month, five hundred francs, I think: all I've received so
far is twenty francs or so. But soon I'll be paid in full and then dismissed,
as I believe that a new company is coming to take the place of our own
and therefore clean house. Because of this uncertainty I put off writing
you. In any case, my food only costs me 2.25 per day, and as I owe nothing
to my boss there will be enough left over that I'll be able to make ends
meet until I find other work, and there will always be more work for me
in Cyprus. They are building railroads, forts, barracks, hospitals, ports,
canals, etc.... On March 1 they will be distributing deeds to the land,

OPPOSITE: *Maison Bardey, c. 1880.*

without any other cost beyond the administrative fees associated with the issuing of deeds.

What is going on back home? Would you prefer that I come back? How are things? Write me as soon as you can.

Arthur Rimbaud.
General Delivery, Larnaca
(Cyprus).

I am writing this in the desert and don't know when I will be leaving.

TO HIS FAMILY
Larnaca (Cyprus), April 24, 1879

Only today am I supposed to be able to secure my power of attorney from the Ministry of Justice; but I think that it won't make the boat and won't arrive until next Thursday.

I am still the head of the quarry construction site for the Company, and load, transport, and cut stone.

The heat is intense. We're harvesting grain. The flies are a horrible torture, night and day. The mosquitoes are worse. We have to sleep right by the edge of the sea, in the desert. I argued with some of the workers and had to send for guns.

I'm spending a lot. By the 16th of May I'll have been here five months.

I think I'll come back; but before that, I would like it if you were first to bring me up to date.

So write me.

I won't give you my address at the quarry because the mail never makes it out this far, only to the town six leagues away.

A. Rimbaud,
General delivery, Larnaca (Cyprus)

TO HIS FAMILY
[undated]

So it's been fifteen days since I was told that the tent and the dagger had been sent from Paris and still I've received nothing.

Annoying.

TO HIS FAMILY
Mont-Troodos (Cyprus), Sunday, May 23, 1880

Sorry I didn't write you sooner. Perhaps you needed to know where I was; but up until now I have been in a situation where it wasn't possible for me to have brought you up to date on all that's new.

I didn't find anything to do in Egypt and left again for Cyprus almost a month ago. Upon arrival, I found that my old employers were bankrupt. After a week, I nonetheless managed to find the job I have now. I am supervising a palace being built for the governor-general, at the top of Mount Troodos, the tallest mountain in Cyprus [2,100 meters].

Up until now it was just me and the engineer, in one of the wooden barracks that make up the camp. Fifty workers arrived yesterday and the work will now go forward. I am the supervisor, but I'm only making two hundred francs per month. I was paid two weeks ago, but I have many expenses: you have to go everywhere on horseback; shipping is extremely difficult, villages very far apart, food very expensive. What's more, while the plains are very hot, at our elevation it is—and has been—disagreeably cold for over a month; it rains, hails, and the wind can knock you over. I had to buy a mattress, covers, a jacket, boots, etc., etc.

At the summit, there is a camp at which a battalion of English troops will arrive in a few weeks, as soon as it's too cold on the plains and cooler on the mountain. That should at least guarantee that enough provisions will make it up here.

So for the time being I am serving at the behest of the British administration: I expect to get a raise soon enough if I remain with them until the end of construction here, around September. As such, I could earn a good letter of recommendation, which would help me get work elsewhere in the future, as well as save a few hundred francs.

I don't feel well; I'm bothered by heart palpitations. I feel better when I don't think about it. What else can I do? The air here, however, is very clean. On the mountain, there are only fir trees and ferns.

I'm writing this letter on Sunday; but the post office is ten leagues away, in a port called Libassol, and so I don't know when I'll be able to get there to mail it. Probably not for a week or so.

Now I have to ask a favor of you. For work, I really need two books: *The Illustrated Book of Agricultural and Forestry Sawmills*, in English, 3 francs, with 128 pictures.

(To find it, write to M. Arbey, mechanical engineer, cours de Vincennes, Paris).

And:

The Pocket Book of Carpentry, with 140 diagrams, by Merly, 6 francs. (Get it from Lacroix, editor, rue des Saints-Pères, Paris.)

I need you to request and obtain these two books as soon as possible, sending them to the following address:

Monsieur Arthur Rimbaud
General Delivery
Limassol (Cyprus)

Please pay for these yourselves. *The mail here won't accept money, so I can't send you any.* It would be better were I to buy you something here, which the post office would accept, and hide the money inside. But that's prohibited and I would prefer to avoid it. Soon, though, if there is anything else I have to send you, I will try to send you money this way.

You know how long it takes for things to make a round trip to and from Cyprus; and where I am, I'm not counting on getting these books for *six weeks*.

Until now I have only spoken of myself. Sorry. I was only thinking that you must all be feeling well and doing even better. I'm sure it's warmer there than it is here. Tell me anything that's new, even the least nothing. Father Michel? Cotaîche?

I will do my best to send you some of the famous wine that belongs to the military here.

Father Michel: an old farmhand on the family farm. *Cotaîche* is how a Frenchman from Luxembourg would pronounce "Countess," in this case the name of the horse that Michel used to lead around.

Don't forget about me.
Yours.

Arthur Rimbaud
General Delivery, Limassol (Cyprus).

Of the military, I forgot to mention the matter of the military service. I will alert that French consul here, and what happens happens.

Of the military . . . happens: Rimbaud's concerns over military service will come up for the rest of his life in the letters.

TO HIS FAMILY
Friday, June 4, 1880

Dear friends,

I haven't yet been able to find the time to make sure a letter gets to you. Tomorrow, however, I'll give this to someone going to Limassol. Be ever so kind as to respond and send me what I ask of you, I need all of it. I am still employed here. Weather is beautiful. In a few days I'll leave to check out a business that deals in very large stones and lime, where I hope to earn something.
Soon.

A. Rimbaud
General Delivery
Limassol
(Cyprus)

Envelope of a letter from Cyprus to Rimbaud's mother, 1879.

Aden is a hideous rock, without a blade of grass or a drop of decent water: we drink water distilled from the ocean.

AUGUST 25, 1880

IV

ADEN

1880

TO HIS FAMILY
Aden, August 17, 1880

Dear Friends,

   I left Cyprus with 400 francs, after nearly two months, after disagreements with the paymaster and my engineer. If I had remained, I would have gotten a good position a few months down the line. But I can always go back.

   I looked for work in all the ports along the Red Sea, at Djeddah, Souakim, Massaouah, Hodeidah, etc. I came here after trying to find something to do in Abyssinia. I was sick when I got here. I'm now working for a coffee-seller, and I've only earned seven francs so far. When I have a few hundred, I'll leave for Zanzibar, where, they say, there is work.

   Tell me all that's new.

Rimbaud
Aden-camp.

Postage is more than 25 centimes. Aden isn't a part of the postal Association.

   —By the way, did you send those books to Cyprus?

OPPOSITE: *Aden, c. 1880.*

TO HIS FAMILY
Aden, August 25, 1880

Dear friends,

I believe that the last letter I sent you told how I sadly had to leave Cyprus and how I had arrived here after crossing the Red Sea.

Here I'm working in the office of a coffee-seller. The administrator of the Company is a retired general. Things are going reasonably well, and will get even better. I'm not earning very much, no more than six francs a day; but if I stay here, and I must stay here, as it's too far from everything not to stay here for a few months and earn a few hundred francs to use in case the need to leave arises, and if I stay, I believe that they will give me more responsibility, perhaps in an agency in another city, and that way I could earn more faster.

Aden is a hideous rock, without a blade of grass or a drop of decent water: we drink water distilled from the ocean. The heat is excessive, worst of all in June and September, which are the two real scorching months, the dog days. The constant temperature, night and day, in an office that is very cool and well ventilated, is 35 degrees. Everything is very expensive and so on. But what can you do: I am something of a prisoner here and, absolutely, I have to stay here a minimum of three months before I'm on my feet enough to find better work.

And at home? The harvest is complete?

Tell me what's new.

Arthur Rimbaud

TO HIS FAMILY
Aden, September 22, 1880

Dear Friends,

I just got your letter of September 9, and as the mailman leaves again tomorrow I'm writing you now.

I'm doing as well here as one can. The company does a few hundred thousand francs worth of business each month. I am the only employee and everything passes through my hands, meaning I'm completely up on things as far as the coffee trade by now. I have the complete confidence of my employer. The only problem is how poorly I'm paid: I'm getting five francs a day, fed, housed, clothed, etc., etc., with a horse and carriage, which all would cost twelve francs a day. But as I'm the only semi-intelligent employee in all of Aden, after two months here, which is to say the 16th of October, if they won't give me 200 francs a month above all my expenses, I'm out of here. I'd rather leave than be taken advantage of. Right now I have about 200 francs to my name. I'll probably go to Zanzibar, where there's work. Here too, by the way, there's plenty of work. Many trading companies are setting up shop here on the Abyssinia coast. My company has caravans all over Africa; it's still possible that I might go there, where I could make some profit of my own and be less bored than in Aden, which is, everyone knows, the most annoying place on earth, second only to where you live, of course.

It's 40 degrees here, indoors: you sweat out liters of water every day. But it could be 60, as it was when I was in Massaouah!

So you're having a lovely summer. Good for you. It's in return for your famous winter.

The books never came, because (I'm certain) someone took them in my absence, as soon as I had left for Troodos. I still need them, as well as others, but I won't ask this of you, because I don't dare send any money until I'm sure I won't need it, if, say, I were to have to leave at the end of the month. I wish you every bit of good fortune and a summer fifty years long.

Reply to the same address still; if I leave, I'll have it forwarded.

Rimbaud.
Maison Viannay,
Bardey and Co.
Aden.

—Be careful when writing my address, because there's another Rimbaud here in the Messageries Maritimes. They made me pay an extra ten centimes in postage.

I don't think Frédéric should be encouraged to go to Roche to start his career, given how few opportunities there are there. He'd quickly grow bored, and you can't expect him to stay there. As far as the idea of getting married, when one has no money or plans or means to earn one or the other, it seems like a terrible idea. As far as I'm concerned, were I condemned to marriage in such a situation it would be better were I assassinated straightaway. But everyone has their opinion, what people think doesn't give me a second thought, doesn't bother me in the least, and I wish them every possible earthly joy, particularly those in the canton of Attigny (Ardennes).

Yours.

TO HIS FAMILY
Aden, November 2, 1880

Dear Friends,

I'm still here a little while longer, although I have been hired for another position I'll be taking soon. The company opened an agency in Harar, a land you'll find on a map in southeast Abyssinia. We export coffee from there, skins, rubber, etc., which we acquire in exchange for cotton and other merchandise. The country is very clean and cool because of its elevation. There are few roads and nearly no communications. From Aden to Harar: initially by boat, from Aden to Zeila, a port on the African coast; from there to Harar, twenty days by caravan.

M. Bardey, one of the heads of the organization, has already made a trip there, establishing the agency and bringing back lots of merchandise. He left a representative of his there, under whose direction I will be. I have been contracted, as of the first of November, at the rate of 150 rupees per month, which is 330 francs, or 11 francs a day, plus food, all travel expenses and 2% of the profits. Meanwhile, I won't leave for another month to six weeks, because I have to take a large sum of money there which isn't yet available. It goes without saying that one must go there armed, and one is at risk of falling into the clutches of the Galla—whatever danger they might present proving relatively minor in reality.

Now I must ask a favor of you which—given that you shouldn't be too busy these days—shouldn't present much trouble. I'd like to place an order for some books. I am asking that the company send you one hundred francs from the Lyon office. I won't send it myself because I'd be charged an 8% commission from here. The company will draw this sum upon my account. Nothing could be simpler.

M. Bardey: Alfred Bardey (1854–1934), with whom, in various situations, Rimbaud will be employed for much of his time abroad. *Galla:* an indigenous tribe that had only just recently encountered whites, a caravan of whom they tore apart. Also called the Oromo.

When you receive it, send the following note, which you should re-
copy and stamp, to the following address: "*Lacroix, éditeur,* rue des Saints-
Pères, Paris."

TO M. LACROIX

Roche, le ... etc.

Monsieur,

Kindly send me, as quickly as possible, the works listed below,
noted in your catalogue:

Treatise on Metallurgy	4 fr.
Urban and Agricultural Hydraulics	3 fr.
Piloting Steamboats	5 fr.
Naval Architecture	3 fr.
Powders and Saltpeters	5 fr.
Geology	10 fr.
Masonry by Demanet	6 fr.
Pocket Book of Carpentry	6 fr.

There is also a treatise on artesian wells, by F. Garnier. I would be
exceedingly grateful to you were you able to find it for me, even were
it to turn out that it isn't published by your firm, and in your reply were
you to also furnish the address of makers of tools for drilling, were it
possible.

Your catalogue features, if I remember correctly, a *Guide to the Building
of Sawmills.* I would be most appreciative were you to include it too.

I would prefer it were you to send me the total cost of these
volumes by return mail, indicating the method of payment you would
prefer.

I hope you can find the treatise on *Artesian Wells,* as I have been asked
for it. I have also been asked to inquire after the cost of a work called
Metalworking, which should also be in your catalogue, as well as a
comprehensive work on *Textiles,* which I ask you to send straightaway.

I await your information eagerly, as these books must be sent to
someone who is leaving France in four days.

If you would prefer to be paid upon my receipt, send the order directly.

Rimbaud

Roche, etc.

With that, you will send the requested sum, and forward me the package.

This letter will reach you around the 20th of November, around the same time as the postal order from the house of Viannay in Lyon in the sum indicated here. The first boat of the Messageries leaves from Marseille for Aden on November 26 and arrives here the 11th of December. In eight days, you would have sufficient time to do as I ask.

I would also ask that from *M. Arbey, Builder,* cours de Vincennes, Paris, you request the *Illustrated Book of Agricultural and Timber Sawmills,* which you must have sent to Cyprus but which I never received. That one costs three francs.

Also ask that *M. Pilter,* quai Jemmapes, send you his *Illustrated Catalogue of Agricultural Machines,* by FRANCO.

Also, at *Librairie Roret:*

> *Cartwright's Manual*
> *Tanner's Manual*
> *The Compleat Locksmith,* by Berthaut
> *Operating Mines,* by J. F. Blanc
> *Glassmaker's Manual*
> *Brickmaker's Manual*
> *Earthenware Manual*
> *Metalforging Manual*
> *Candlemaking Manual*
> *Guide to Gunmaking*

See how much these cost, and request them C.O.D., if available; and as soon as possible: above all I need the *Tanner.*

Request the *Complete Catalogue of the Bookstore of the École centrale,* Paris.

I have been asked for the address of the *Builders of Diving Equipment.*

You can ask Pilter for this address at the same time you request the machine catalogue.

I would be very upset if all of this weren't to arrive by December 11. As such, make sure everything gets to Marseille by the 26th of November. To the package, add a *Telegrapher's Manual, The Little Woodworker,* and *House Painter's Manual.*

—It's been two months since I wrote and I still haven't received the Arabic books I requested. Everything must be sent via the Messageries Maritimes. Be aware.

I am really too busy today to write much more. I only hope that you are all well and that winter isn't too harsh. Tell me all of your news in detail. Here, I'm just trying to save a little money.

When you send me the receipt for the 100 francs I am having sent to you, I will reimburse the firm immediately.

Rimbaud.

A photograph by Rimbaud of a local Harar artisan.

I would like to learn about the best instruments made in France (or abroad) used in the following disciplines: mathematics, optics, astronomy, electrical engineering, meteorology, pneumatics, mechanics, hydraulics, and mineralogy. I do not need surgical equipment. I would be very happy were someone able to gather all the catalogues devoted to these products, and thus rely on your benevolent expertise for the above. I also require catalogues devoted to novelties, pyrotechnics, magic, mechanical models and construction summaries, etc. If there are any factories in France of interest in this vein, or if you know better ones abroad, I would be more obliged to you than I can say to provide me with their addresses or catalogues.

—JANUARY 30, 1881

V

HARAR

1880–1881

A photograph by Rimbaud of a square in Harar.

TO HIS FAMILY
Harar, December 13, 1880

Dear friends,

   I arrived in this country after twenty days on horseback through the Somali desert. Harar is a city colonized by Egyptians and dependent on their government. The garrison is made up of many thousands of men. Our agency and our storehouses are here. The salable products of the country are coffee, ivory, skins, etc. The country is at an elevation, but the land is cultivable. The climate is cool and not unhealthy. European merchandise of every variety is available here by camel. Moreover, there is much work available. We don't have regular mail delivery. We must send our mail to Aden, but only do so occasionally. So this will take some time to reach you. I hope that you received the *100 francs* that I had sent to you via the firm in Lyon. And that you found a means of expediting the items I requested. It doesn't matter when they come, so long as they do.
   I am surrounded by the Gallas. I think I will have to go further forward next time. I ask that you send me news as often as you can. I hope that your work is going well and you are all feeling well. I will find a way to write to you soon. Send your letters or packages here:

M. Dubar, agent général à Aden.
For M. Rimbaud, Harar.

TO HIS FAMILY
Harar, January 15, 1881.

Dear Friends,

I wrote you twice in December of 1880 and haven't heard from you at all. I wrote in December that you were sent a second hundred francs, which perhaps already arrived and which you can use as I said. I have an urgent need of everything I requested, and I imagine that the first of them has already arrived in Aden, but it takes another month to go from Aden to here. Soon a great quantity of merchandise will arrive here from Europe and we will have our work cut out for us. Soon I will be making a long tour of the desert to buy camels. Of course, we have horses, guns, and everything else. The country isn't unpleasant: right now the weather is like May in France.

I received both of your November letters; but I lost them immediately. Nonetheless, having had the time to skim them, I recall that you acknowledged receipt of the first hundred francs I had sent to you. I am having another hundred sent just in case, to cover shipping. This will be the third such mailing, and for now I'll stop there; when the order comes through it will most likely be April. I have not yet told you that I am contracted here for three years; this will assure me a meritorious departure from a position of trust, even if they give me a hard time. I receive 300 francs per month above and beyond all expenses, and a percentage of the profits.

We will have, in this city, a Catholic bishop who will probably be the only Catholic in the country. We are in the heart of Galla.

We have ordered a camera, and I will send you images of the country and its people. We have also received equipment used by natural historians, and I will be able to send you birds and animals that no one has yet seen in Europe. I have already collected a few curiosities that I await the opportunity to send you.

I am happy to hear that you think of me and that business is going well there. I hope it goes as well as possible. On my end, I try to make my work interesting and profitable.

I have a few simple errands to ask you to run. Send the following letter to M. Lacroix, bookseller-publisher, Paris:

TO M. LACROIX

Monsieur,

There is a work by a German or Swiss author, published in Germany a few years ago and translated into French, bearing the title: *Traveler's Guide or Theoretical and Practical Manual of Exploration.* Something like that. This work, I am told, is an intelligent compendium of all the knowledge necessary for an explorer in topography, mineralogy, hydrography, natural history, etc., etc.

As I now find myself in a place where I cannot procure the name of the author, nor the address of its publisher-translators, I supposed that this book might be known to you and that you might give me more information. I would be equally happy were you kind enough to send it to me straightaway, choosing whichever means of payment you preferred.

With thanks,

Rimbaud
Roche, par Arrigny, Ardennes (France)

Send this next one to M. Bautin, maker of precision instruments, Paris, rue, du Quatre-September, 6:

TO M. BAUTIN
Aden, January 30, 1881

Monsieur,

As it is my desire to import a variety of precision instruments for sale in the Orient, I permit myself to contact you to ask you the following:

I would like to learn about the best technical instruments made in France (or abroad) used in the following disciplines: mathematics, optics, astronomy, electrical engineering, meteorology, pneumatics, mechanics, hydraulics, and mineralogy. I do not need surgical equipment.

I would be very happy were someone able to gather all the catalogues devoted to these products, and rely on your benevolent expertise for the above. I also require catalogues devoted to novelties, pyrotechnics, magic, mechanical models and construction summaries, etc. If there are any factories in France of interest in this vein, or if you know better ones abroad, I would be more obliged to you than I can say to provide me with their addresses or catalogues.

You may address your replies in this matter to: "Rimbaud, Roche, par Attigny, Ardennes. France." Naturally I will pay any shipping charges, and will have them forwarded the instant you should require them.

Also please send, should a serious, modern example exist, a *Complete Manual for the Manufacture of Precision Instruments.*

With cordial thanks,

Rimbaud
Aden, Arabia

Please preface the above with the following notes:

Monsieur,

We enclose the following memorandum on behalf of one of our relations presently in the Orient, and would be most delighted were you to give it your attention. We are at your service for whatever expenses should arise.

Rimbaud,
Roche, par Attigny, Ardennes.

And apprise yourself if there isn't in Paris a bookstore associated with the School of the Regulation of Weights and Measures; and if it should exist do please send its catalogue.

With all my heart.

Rimbaud,
Maison Viannay, Bardey,
Aden, Arabia.

TO HIS FAMILY
Harar, February 15, 1881

Dear friends,

I received your letter of December 8, and I think I have written you once before as well. I have, however, forgotten if that is so while in the countryside.

I remind you that I had 300 francs sent to you: first from Aden; second from Harar on or around December 10; third from Harar on or around January 10. I trust that by now you have received these three mailings of one hundred francs and sent off all that I asked. I thank you in advance for the mailing you alert me to, but which I most likely will not receive for two months, perhaps.

Please send me the *Metalworking* book, by Monge, 10 francs.

I don't expect to stay here long; I will soon know when I'll be leaving. I did not find it as I expected; my current mode of existence is extremely annoying and unprofitable. As soon as I manage to save 1,500 to 2,000 francs, I'll leave, and will be very pleased. I expect to find things better a bit farther on. Write me concerning the work going on in Panama: as soon as it opens, I'll go. From this moment forward, I will be very pleased to leave here; I caught an illness which on its own isn't very serious; but the climate here is treacherous on any disease. Wounds never heal. A cut a millimeter long to a finger suppurates for three months and becomes gangrenous easily. The other problem is that the Egyptian administration has very inadequate doctors and medicines. The climate is very humid in summer: it is unhealthy; I don't like it here at all, it's far too cold for me.

Regarding books: don't send any more of the *Roret* manuals.

It's been four months since I ordered a variety of things from Lyon and I don't expect to have received anything for another two.

Panama: as soon as it opens, I'll go: to the construction of the Panama Canal, where, like Zanzibar, he never went (that we know). *illness:* The verb in French is *pincé,* which in the slang of the era usually indicated a venereal disease.

You shouldn't believe that this country is completely wild. We have the Egyptian army, artillery and cavalry, and their administration. It's just as it is in Europe; the only difference is the abundance of dogs and thieves. The Gallas are poor farmers and shepherds: peaceful people when not attacked. The land is excellent, however cold and humid it may be; but agriculture is still very backwards. Trade doesn't amount to much more than skins and animals, animals traded during the duration of their lives and then skinned; and coffee, ivory, gold; perfumes, incense, musk, etc. The bad part is being 60 leagues from the sea and having transportation be so expensive.

I am glad to see that your little operation is going as well as possible. I hope you won't get a repeat of the winter of 1879–80, which I remember well enough to wish to avoid anything remotely like it again.

Should you find an odd volume of Bottin, *Paris and Abroad* (a used one), for *a few francs,* send it to me, right away: I have great need of it. Also stick a half pound of sugarized beetroot powder in the corner of your next package.

Request—if you have any of the money left—a *Dictionary of Engineering, Military and Civil,* from Lacroix, 15 francs. This isn't urgent.

You can be sure I'll be careful with my books.

Our photographic and natural history equipment has yet to arrive, and I think that I'll be gone before it gets here.

I have a great many things to ask of you; but you have to send the Bottin first.

On that subject, how is it that you haven't been able to find an Arabic dictionary? It should be in the house somewhere.

Tell Frédéric to look in all the Arabic papers for a folder called: *Jokes, word games, etc.,* in Arabic; and he should also find a collection of *dialogues* there, and *songs* and other things, useful to those learning a language. If there is a book in Arabic, send it; but all of this as wrapping: it alone isn't worth the postage.

I will soon send you twenty-odd kilos of mocha-coffee on my account, as long as the customs duty isn't unreasonable.

I'll tell you: I have every hope for better times and more interesting work soon! Because, were you to suppose that I'm living the life of a prince, I should assure you that I am living a really stupid, tiresome existence.

This letter leaves with a caravan, and won't reach you before the end of March. One of the true delights of this predicament. Perhaps the worst.

Yours,

Rimbaud.

TO HIS FAMILY
Harar, March 12, 1881

Dear friends,

Yesterday I received a letter from you without a date but postmarked, I think, February 6, 1881.

In your earlier letters, I already received news about your mailing; and the parcel should already have reached Aden. The only thing I don't recall is when it will be put on a train for Harar. This company's dealings are somewhat mixed up.

But you say you received my letter of December 13, 1880. Well, at the same time you should have received the sum of one hundred francs which I requested the firm advance you on December 13, 1880; and, given your letter left around February 10 or thereabouts, you should also have received a 3rd sum of one hundred francs that I ordered the firm advance you on January 10, 1881, by letter, and heard of via my letter on this same date of January 10.

I wrote to find out how all of this worked out. It is possible that you still hadn't received my letter of January 10 by the date you wrote your letter, which is to say February 16, but I wonder what happened to the money order which accompanied my letter of December 14, 1880, a letter which you say you received. In any case, there is nothing lost if nothing was sent. I will find out the definitive answer myself. Think about how I ordered two pieces of woolen clothing from Lyon in November 1880 and it will still probably be some time before I get them. In the interim, I am cold here, in cotton clothing from Aden.

In a month, I will know if I must remain here or clear out, and I will be back in Aden by the time you receive this. I experienced some ridiculous annoyances in Harar, and there is nothing that can be done about them, for the moment, it seems. If I leave the region, I will probably go down to Zanzibar, and I will perhaps find work around the Great Lakes. —I would like it better were they to open up some interesting work somewhere, and here news doesn't come often enough.

I hope that distance isn't a reason not to share your news with me.

Continue to send your letters to Aden, where they'll make their way to me.

More news soon.

Good health and happiness to all.

Rimbaud.

TO HIS FAMILY
Harar, Sunday, April 16, 1881

Dear friends,

I received your letter, the date of which I can no longer recall: I recently lost it. You acknowledge the receipt of the sum of one hundred francs; you say this was the second such sum. That's right. The other, I think, which is to say the third, must not have reached you: my request must have gotten misplaced. Hang on to the hundred francs for now.

Things are still unresolved here. Business hasn't been great. Who knows how long I'll stay? Maybe next I'll make a trip into the country. A group of French missionaries arrived; and I just may follow them into parts of the country that up until now have been inaccessible to whites from this part of the country.

Your mailing still hasn't arrived; it must be in Aden, and I hold on to the hope of receiving it in the next few months. Can you believe that I ordered some clothes from Lyon six months ago that, at this point, remain little more than a dream.

Nothing very interesting to report for now.

Wishing you stomachs less besieged than my own right now, and work less annoying than mine too.

Rimbaud.

TO HIS FAMILY
Harar, May 4, 1881

It's summer there now, and it's winter here, which is to say it is pretty hot, but it rains often. This will last a few months.

The coffee harvest is six months away.

As for me, I'm about to leave this city to fiddle with the unknown. There is a big lake a few days away, and it's in ivory territory: I will try to get there. But it is most likely hostile territory.

I will buy a horse and go. In the event this ends badly, and I don't come back, know that I have a sum totaling 7 times 150 rupees belonging to me in the Aden office, and which you could claim, if you thought it was worth it.

Send me any newspaper you can get your hands on devoted to civil engineering, so I can know what's going on. Is work under way in Panama?

Write to *MM. Wurster et Cie, Publishers,* in Zurich, Switzerland, and ask them to send you their *Traveler's Manual,* by M. Kaltbrünner, either C.O.D. or however they prefer. Have them also send *Building at Sea,* by Bonniceau, from Lacroix.

Send them to the Aden office.

Be well. Adieu.

A. Rimbaud

TO HIS FAMILY
Harar, May 25, 1881

Dear friends,

Dear Maman, I received your letter dated May 5. I am happy to know that your health has returned and that you are resting better. At your age, it would be unfortunate to have to work. Alas! I am not very fond of life; and if I live, I am used to living with exhaustion; but if I am forced to continue to exhaust myself like this, and to feed on sorrows as unremitting as they are ridiculous in these horrible climates, I suspect it will lead to an abridgement of my existence.

I am still here in the same conditions, and in three months I can send you 5,000 francs I've saved; but I think that I'll hang on to it to start a little business of my own in these neighborhoods, because it is not my intention to spend the rest of my existence in slavery.

Finally, might we enjoy a few years of real rest in this life; and happily this life is the only life, and that is evident, as one could not possibly imagine another life more boring than this one.

All for you,

Rimbaud.

TO HIS FAMILY
Harar, June 10, 1881

I have returned from a campaign outside the city, and I am leaving again tomorrow for a new ivory campaign.

My address is still the same, and I will be happy to have news from you.

Rimbaud.

—I've heard nothing from you in a very long while.

TO HIS FAMILY
Harar, July 2, 1881

Dear friends,

I have just returned from the interior, where I bought a large supply of leather.

I have a slight fever right now. I will depart once again in a few days for territory as yet completely unexplored by Europeans; and if I really succeed, the trip will take six weeks, difficult and dangerous, but likely very profitable. —I am in charge of this little expedition. I hope it will all be for the best. In any case, don't worry about me.

You must be very busy right now; and I wish you the best in your various endeavors.

Yours,

Rimbaud.

P.S.—Am I in violation of military law? I still have no idea where I stand on this matter.

TO HIS FAMILY
Harar, Friday, July 22, 1881

Dear friends,

The last letter I received from you was from May or June. You seem surprised by the delays with the mail, but it isn't entirely a matter of delays: the mail arrives very regularly however long the interim since its mailing; and as for packages, boxes, and books you had sent, they all arrived at once, over four months ago, of which I sent you an acknowledgment of their receipt.

The distance is great, that's all; the desert has to be crossed twice, a distance twice that which the post office has to cover.

I haven't forgotten you at all, how could I? And if my letters are too short, it's that, as I'm now always going on expeditions, I'm always in a rush at those moments when the mail is about to leave. But I think of you, and think of little but you. And what should I tell you about my work, which disgusts me already to no end, and the country, which I can't stand, and on and on. Should I tell you the various efforts I have made and their price, yielding me little more in return than a fever, a fever I've been running for two weeks like the one I had two years ago in Roche? What would you like to hear? I can withstand anything at this point, I fear nothing.

I'm about to make an arrangement with my firm whereby my salary will be paid directly to you each trimester. At first, the payments will balance out what I already owe you, and then we'll take it from there. What use is money here in Africa?

With the money I send you, straightaway you should get the title to some property or stocks and register them in my name with a notary: or make whatever arrangements you feel appropriate, or entrust them to a reliable notary or banker. The only two things that matter to me are that the money be secure and in my name; and that it yield some sort of regular income.

And it is essential that I know that I am not in violation of military law, so that no one can intervene in my affairs no matter what.

You are of course welcome to whatever share of the profits you feel are appropriate in return for your careful attention in all of this.

The first payment you should expect in three months may be as much as 3,000 francs.

All of this is absolutely normal. I have no need of money for the time being, and can do nothing to make it grow here.

I wish you the best in your doings. Don't work too hard, there's no reason to! Health and life are more precious than all the other crap in the world.

Live peacefully.

Rimbaud.

TO HIS FAMILY
Harar, August 5, 1881

Dear friends,

I just made the request that my firm in France pay you, in French currency, the sum of eleven hundred sixty-five rupees and fourteen anas, which would make, with the rupee worth about 2 francs 12 centimes, two thousand four hundred seventy-eight francs. However, the exchange rate fluctuates. As soon as you have received this little sum, do with it as you see best, and alert me promptly.

From now on, I'll try to make sure that my salary is paid directly to you in France, every three months.

All this, alas, isn't very interesting. I'm beginning to feel somewhat better in the wake of my illness. I count on your being well and that your doings are going as you would hope. As for me, I got the wind knocked out of my sails here, but I am hoping that a tour of the coast or of Aden will get me back in shape.

And what devil knows the road where we'll find our fortunes?
Yours,

Rimbaud.

TO HIS FAMILY
Harar, September 2, 1881

Dear friends,

I believe I wrote you once before your letter of July 12.
I'm still really not enjoying this part of Africa. The weather is miserable and humid; the work I'm doing is ridiculous and stultifying, and the general quality of life is for the most part ridiculous as well. I've had a few unpleasant wrangles with the directors and others, and I've nearly decided to get a change of scenery in the near term. I'll try to set aside something in my account here; and if that doesn't work out (which will quickly become apparent), I'll leave straightaway, I hope, for more intelligent work beneath more favorable skies. Anyway, it remains possible that I'll remain affiliated with the firm—elsewhere.

You tell me that you sent me things, crates, effects, which I have yet to receive. I just received a shipment of shirts and books according to your list. Anyway, my requests and letters have always circulated nonsensically around this place.

Think how I've ordered two wool uniforms from Lyon in November of last year, and they still haven't come!

I needed medication six months ago; I ordered it from Aden, and I still haven't gotten it!

—All of this stuff is en route, to hell.

All I ask for in this life is a pleasant climate and agreeable work, something interesting: and I'll find it, one day or another! I also hope only to have good news of you and your health. My greatest pleasure comes from hearing from you, dear friends; and I wish you better luck and happiness than myself.

Au revoir.

Rimbaud.

—I had my request made to the firm in Lyon to send you in Roche, by mail, the total of my salary in cash, from December 1, 1880, to July 31,

1881, as much as 1,165 rupees (at about 2 francs 12 right now). Do let me know when you will have received it, and do with the sum as you see best.

—Regarding military service, I continue to believe that I'm not in violation; and would be very upset to learn that I were. Let me know about this. I will soon need to get a passport in Aden, and I'll need to know what to say on this count.

Hello to F[rédéric].

TO HIS FAMILY
Harar, September 22, 1881

Dear friends,

News from you is late, it seems: I haven't gotten anything here for a long while. They don't make a big deal about letters in this branch!

Winter is about to start where you are. Here, rainy season is about to end, and summer begin.

I'm in charge now, for the time being, of the branch, while the director is away. I resigned three weeks ago, and await a replacement. Nonetheless, I may stay in this country,

They should have written to the Lyon branch to have the sum of 1,165 rupees sent along, covering my salary from December 1 through 31 July. Have you gotten them?

—If yes, do with them as you see fit. —For the time being, I'll get money from my account, so I can do as I need to.

Why haven't you sent me, as I requested, the following books:

1st *Traveler's Manual,* by Kaltbrünner (available at *Reinwald and Company,* 15 rue des Saints-Pères, Paris)

2nd *Building at Sea,* by Bonniceau (at *Lacroix*)?

It seems as though I asked for these very long ago and yet they have never gotten here.

Please don't make me wait too long for news. I wish you a pleasant autumn and every prosperity.

Yours,

Rimbaud.

TO HIS FAMILY
Maison Viannay
Bardey and Co.
Aden.

Dear Friends,

I received today, November 7, three letters from you, from the 8th, 24th, and 25th of September. As for military service, I'll write immediately to the French Consul in Aden, and the general agent in Aden will attach a certificate for the Consul, and will then send that to you right away, I hope. I can't leave the branch here yet as it would bring everything to a halt, since I am in charge of everything right now and am provisional finance director. Anyway, I intend to explore the country more deeply still. It's impossible to say what will happen soon or at all: even your letter of September 8 arrived after your letter of September 25, so. Once, I received one of your May letters in September.

One thing stands out in what you told me: that the money I've had sent to you hasn't arrived, or hadn't by September 25. The order for payment left here on August 4 and arrived in Lyon no later than September 10. Why haven't you been paid yet? I'm sending along (below) a model of the letter of complaint you should send along to:

Messieurs Mazeran, Viannay and Bardey,
Rue de l'Arbre-Sec, Lyon

Sirs,

My son, Monsieur Rimbaud, an employee of your Harar branch, has alerted me by letter from Harar dated _____ that an order had been placed in the Harar mail of August 4, 1881, to your firm in Lyon to pay me the sum of one thousand one hundred sixty-five rupees directly in French francs, representing M. Rimbaud of Harar's salary from December 1, 1880, to July 31, 1881, and I am shocked that I have not as yet received any word concerning this matter. I would be very grateful to hear what you intend to do.

Respectfully etc.

If they don't write back, complain loudly; if they do respond, know that the sum is 1,165 rupees, and the exchange rate is 2 fr. 15, meaning:

$$\begin{array}{r} 215 \\ \hline 5825 \\ 1165 \\ 2330 \\ \hline 2,504,75 \text{ francs} \end{array}$$

That should be in your hands.

In any case, I won't get out of here until I hear that you've received the money or at least have word from you directly.

———

So it's winter there, and summer here. The rain has ceased; it has been beautiful and rather warm. The coffee trees are maturing.

I will soon make a major expedition, perhaps as far as Choa, a name you will see on your maps. Don't worry, I don't take stupid risks. There would be much to do and earn here, were the country not overrun with bandits who intercept all the best trade routes.

I trust you completely concerning these unfortunate funds. But what the hell do you expect me to do with land? I have other money I could send, another 1,500 or so; but let's wait to see the first bit arrive safely.

———

I'd like to think that this business of 25 days will work out fine; I've let the Aden office know not to drag its feet. How the hell do you expect me to put my work aside for four weeks?

Whatever happens, it makes me happy to know that your doings are proceeding unimpeded. If you need anything, feel free to take what you need of mine: it's yours. As for me, I have no one to worry about here except myself, who asks nothing of me.

Yours alone,

Rimbaud.
Harar, November 7, 1881

TO HIS FAMILY
Harar, December 3, 1881

Dear friends,

This represents my wishes for a happy new year in 1882. Good luck, good health, and good weather. I don't have time to write much more. I think that the declaration which I sent to Aden to the French Consulate should by now have been redirected and sent along to you, and that will be the end of the whole military service situation.

I complained to the firm over the sum of 1,160 rupees that they should have sent you, at an exchange rate of no less than 2 francs 12 centimes per. No one has yet responded. If they do not pay soon, I will lodge a formal complaint with the French consul in Aden.

I am feeling well.

Yours ever,

Rimbaud.

TO MONSIEUR ALFRED BARDEY
Harar, December, 1881

I would be very pleased to see you in person in Aden.

Rimbaud.

TO HIS FAMILY
Harar, December 9, 1881

Dear friends,

Just a note to say hello.

Don't write me anymore in Harar. I am about to leave, and it is very unlikely that I will ever return here.

As soon as I'm back in Aden, unless I hear from you first, I will telegraph the firm regarding the 2,500 francs they owe you, and I will apprise the French consul of the situation. Nonetheless, I think that they will have paid you by now. I expect to find another job, as soon as I'm back in Aden.

I wish you an easy winter and good health.

Yours,

Rimbaud.

I am about to put together a study of the parts of Harar and Gallas which I have explored and submit it to the geographical society. I have spent a year in these parts, working for a French concern. From Lyon, I have just ordered photographic equipment that will allow me to intersperse images of these strange landscapes into my report.

JANUARY 18, 1882

VI

ADEN REDUX

1882–1883

Les hôtes d'Hassan Ali, c. 1880, detail.

TO HIS FAMILY
Aden, January 18, 1882

Dear friends,

I received your letter of December 27, 1881, containing a letter from Delahaye. You tell me that you wrote twice regarding the matter of the money. How is it that I never received them? And I just telegraphed from Aden to Lyon, on January 5, demanding they pay what they owed! You also don't tell me how much they sent, which I need to know. I am at least happy that something arrived, after a six-month delay! I also wonder about the exchange rate. In the future, I'll use another means of sending money, because they way these people handle things is disgraceful. I have another 2,000 francs here, but will be using them soon.

I left Harar and returned to Aden, where I am in the midst of ending my tenure with the company. It will be easy to find something else.

As for the matter of military service, attached you'll find a letter from the consul to me, indicating which steps I've already taken and what information the minister already has. Show this letter to the military authorities; it will placate them. If you can send me a copy of my lost service record, I would be grateful were it soon, as the consul has asked me for it. So between what you already have and what I'm sending along, I think all of this will work out fine.

I've also attached a letter to Delahaye, which I'd ask you to forward. If he's still in Paris, all the better for me: I need to have some precision instruments purchased for me. I am about to undertake a commission for the geographical society, requiring maps and illustrations, concerning Harar and the Galician countries. I have ordered photographic equipment from Lyon; I will take it back to Harar, and will bring back views of these unknown parts. It's an excellent opportunity.

I also need instruments to enable my topographical survey of the area and to establish the latitudes. When the study is complete and in the possession of the geographical society, perhaps I will be able to receive further commissions from them to report on other regions. It's very easy work.

So I ask that you forward the request on to Delahaye, who will take it upon himself to secure my requests. You will only have to reimburse him for the total. It will all cost several thousand francs, but it will facilitate an excellent study. Of course I request that you make sure it all arrives here as quickly as possible, *directly*, to Aden. I beg that you send the complete order; if anything is missing from the order you will put me in an awkward position.

Yours,

Rimbaud.

TO ERNEST DELAHAYE
Aden, January 18, 1882

My dear Delahaye,

I read your letter with great pleasure.

Without preamble, I'll explain how, if you are still in Paris, you could do me an enormous service.

I am about to put together a study of the parts of Harar and Gallas which I have explored and submit it to the geographical society. I have spent a year in these parts, working for a French concern.

From Lyon, I have just ordered photographic equipment that will allow me to intersperse images of these strange landscapes into my report.

I am missing various instruments necessary for the creation of maps and would like to purchase them. I have a sum of money deposited with my mother in France; I would pay for what I need from that.

I need the following, and would be infinitely grateful were you to make these purchases for me with the help of someone who knew these items intimately, perhaps a professor of mathematics whom you know already, with whom you could visit the best supplier in Paris:

1) A pocket *Traveler's Theodolite.* Pay for it carefully, and wrap it carefully. They aren't cheap. If it costs more than 15 to 18 hundred francs, don't buy it and instead buy the two following items:
   A good sextant; a standard Cravet compass
2) Buy a *Mineralogical Kit with 300 Samples.* You can find this in a store.
3) *A pocket aneroid barometer*
4) *A hemp surveyor's line*
5) *A mathematics set* containing: a ruler, a T-square, a protractor, a reducing compass, a ten centimeter ruler, a ruling pen, etc.
6) *Drawing paper*

And the following:

Topography and Geodesy,[*] by Commander Salneuve (*librairie Dumaine,* Paris*);*

Trigonometry for high-school seniors
Mineralogy for high-school seniors, or the best book available from the Grande École of Mining Studies
Hydrography, the best book available
Meteorology, by Marie Davy (Masson, bookseller);
Industrial Chemistry, by Wagner (Savy, libraire, rue Hautefeuille);
Traveler's Manual, by Kaltbrünner (chez Reinwald)
Instruction for Travelers' Assistants (Librairie du Muséum d'Histoire naturelle)
The Sky, by Guillemin
And *The Department of Longitudes Annual,* 1882.

Make a bill for everything, add your shipping costs, and get reimbursed from my money deposited with Madame Rimbaud in Roche.

You have no idea how much help this will be. I will be able to complete my project and continue to work for the Geographical society.

I am not afraid of spending a few thousand francs, which I'll mostly make up with this one project.

So please, if you can do this, buy me what I ask as soon as possible; above all the theodolite and the mineralogical collection. Regardless, I need everything equally. Wrap everything carefully.

More details to come with the next mail delivery, which leaves in three days.

Cordial greetings,

Rimbaud.
Maison Mazeran, Viannay and Bardey,
Aden.

---

[*]And if not that, the best course book on topography.

TO HIS FAMILY
Aden, January 22, 1882

Dear friends,

Just confirming that you should have received my letter of the 18th a few days before this one, which left by British boat.

Today, a letter from Lyon informs me that you were paid only 2,250 instead of the 2,469 francs 80 that I'm owed, calculated at the rate of 2 francs 12 centimes specified in the letter. I'm about to send a letter of complaint to the firm and I will send a formal complaint to the consul, as this is a swindle, plain and simple; and, meanwhile, I have had to wait unreasonably, because these people are unscrupulous misers whose goodness is limited to their ability to take advantage of their workers' exhaustion. What I still do not understand is how your letters alerting me to your receipt of the payment of this sum continue not to arrive: did you send them care of the firm, in Lyon? In that case, I wouldn't be surprised were nothing to have gotten here, as these people arrange for their employees' correspondence to be scattered around and intercepted.

Make sure, in the future, to write me here directly, without their damned meddling. And be careful, particularly in the matter of sending things I've asked for in my letter of the day before yesterday and to the purchase of which I have decided to put the sum you received: so that nothing goes through them, as at this point anything would be infallibly ruined or lost.

You sent me a first shipment of books, which arrived here in May of 1881. Someone had the clever idea of wrapping bottles of ink in the crate, and, the bottles of ink having broken, all the books were bathed in ink.

Have you made another shipment apart from that one? Tell me, so that I can claim it if it is lost somewhere.

I suppose that you sent my letter along to Delahaye, and that he will be able to attend to what it asks. I have once again ordered that the precision instruments be carefully examined, before purchase, by competent individuals, and, next, carefully wrapped and sent directly to my address in Aden by the Parisian offices of the Messageries Maritimes.

I am holding out above all for the theodolite, as it is the best topographical instrument and the one which I can do the most with. Of course, the sextant and the compass can be used instead of the theodolite, if it's too expensive. Forget about the mineralogical collection if that helps with the cost of the theodolite; but, whatever happens, buy the books, which I ask you to look after.

I also need a telescope, or staff major's glasses: to be bought from the same manufacturer as the theodolite and the barometer.

In fact, forget about the mineralogical collection for the time being, I'll soon send you a thousand francs: I ask that *above all you buy the theodolite.*

Spend the money this way:

Telescope, 100 francs; barometer, 100 francs; compass and line, 40 francs; books, 200 francs; and the remainder for the theodolite and shipping to Aden.

My photographic equipment will arrive from Lyon in a few weeks: I sent the money, paid in advance.

I beg you to undertake all that I've asked and not to leave me without anything I've requested, if you see that you can really get me everything in good condition; because it is understood that all these instruments must be purchased only by someone who knows how to use them. If such an individual cannot be found, hold on to the money—it's unbearable to think of earning it only to spend it all on junk!

Please send the following letter to *Monsieur Devisme, gunsmith,* in Paris. It is a request for information regarding a special gun used for elephant hunting. I ask that you forward his response, in which I will find out whether I will then need to send you more money.

I am writing to have the outstanding 219 francs 80 centimes you are owed sent along, which I expect they will do upon my recommendation.

Ever yours,

Rimbaud.

—And make sure you buy the theodolite, the barometer, the compass and line, no matter what, under the advisement of someone aware of their particulars and from good manufacturers. Otherwise, it would be better that you save the money and buy the books.

—Didn't you receive money I had sent in November of 1880 and a second time in February of 1881? They have just written from Lyon with word. Please reconcile my account through today, so that I know what I do or do not have.

TO MONSIEUR DEVISME
Aden, January 22, 1882

Monsieur,

I am traveling through the Galla lands (East Africa), and, as I am currently putting together a troop of elephant hunters, I would be altogether grateful were you, as soon as possible, to send me information concerning the following subject:
Is there a special gun for hunting elephants?
If so, please describe it?
Specifications?
Where may it be obtained? At what price?
The nature of its ammunition, poison, explosives?
I would wish to purchase two sample guns, and, if they prove adequate, another half-dozen.
Thanking you in advance for your response, I am, Monsieur, your humble servant,

Rimbaud.
Aden (English colonies).

TO HIS FAMILY
Aden, February 12, 1882

Dear friends,

I have your letter of January 21, and I expect that you have received my two letters containing orders for books and instruments, and also the telegram of the 24th, canceling them.

As for the receipt of money: your letters arrived in Harar the day after my departure, such that they weren't able to reach me before the end of January in Aden. In any case, it seems they withheld a certain sum because of the exchange. But rest easy, and don't send complaints. I'll get my hands on it here, or I will have it sent to you in France.

You bought land with the money, and did well. As soon as I learned this, I cabled you to not buy what I ordered, and I hope you have understood.

When I have sent you a new lump of money, it may be used as I requested and explained; because I really need the instruments I mentioned. I will simply make use of them later. I don't expect to remain very long in Aden, as I need more intelligent activities than those I currently have. If I leave, and I expect to do so soon, it will be for Harar, or down to Zanzibar, where I will have excellent recommendations; in any case, if I find nothing there, I can always come back here, where I'll still be able to find better work than I currently have.

I sent you all the requested forms and certificates over a month ago, or at least to the minister of war, through the channels of the French Consulate in Aden.

The Consul wants to see my military record. I haven't told him it's lost. If it is possible to obtain a copy, please send it to me.

Good luck and good health. More news soon.

Rimbaud.

TO HIS MOTHER
Aden, April 15, 1882

Dear mother,

Your letter of March 30 arrived April 12.

I am happy to see that things are getting back to normal for you, and I should reassure you that things are fine here. No reason to think dark thoughts as long as one is alive.

As for my interests of which you speak, they are slight and I don't beat myself up over them at all. No one is going to bother with me, given I have nothing in the world but myself. A capitalist of my type doesn't fear such speculations, nor does he fear those of others.

Thank you for the hospitality you offered me, dear friends. Whether I take you up on it or not.

Sorry I've not written for a month. I have been exhausted from all sorts of work. I'm still in the same firm, the same situation; now, however, I work more and spend nearly everything, and I have decided not to stay in Aden. In a month I'll either go to Harar, or be en route to Zanzibar.

In the future, I will not forget to write you with each mail delivery.

Good weather and good health.

Yours,

Rimbaud.

TO HIS FAMILY
Aden, May 10, 1882

Dear friends,

During the course of April I wrote you twice, and my letters should have made it there. I received yours of April 23. Don't worry about me: my situation is not at all out of the ordinary. I'm still working for the same company, and I slave away like an ass in a country for which I have an invincible disdain. I'm working my fingers to the bone to try and get out of here and get a more enjoyable job. I really hope this sort of existence will be done with before I turn into a complete moron. What's more, I am spending a lot in Aden, and that has the advantage of tiring me out more than before. Soon I will send you a few hundred francs for some purchases. In any case, if I leave here, I will let you know. If I don't write more tonight it's only that I am very tired and, in fact, here, as there, nothing is new.

Above all, good health.

Rimbaud.

TO HIS FAMILY
Aden, July 10, 1882

Dear friends,

I have your letters of June 19 and thank you for your good advice.

I too hope my hour of rest comes before death. But anyway, right now I am very accustomed to every sort of annoyance; and if I complain, think of it as a kind of singing.

I will probably leave for Harar in a month or two if the Egyptian kerfuffle is settled. And this time I will go there to do real work.

It is in looking forward to this next trip that I ask you to send the attached letter to its destination, in which I request a good map of Harar. Please put this letter in an envelope addressed as indicated, stamp it, and include a stamp for the reply.

He will tell you the price and you will send the sum of a dozen francs or so via postal order. When it arrives send me the map.

I can't do without it, and no one has one here, so I'm counting on you. News soon.

Yours,

Rimbaud.

TO HIS FAMILY
Aden, July 31, 1882

Dear friends,

I received your letter of July 10.

You're all well, as am I.

You must have received a letter from me in which I requested that you send me a map of Abyssinia and Harar, a map from Peterman's Geographical Institute. I expect that you were able to find it, and that I will receive it. Above all don't send me any map but that one.

Work is still the same; and I don't know if I will be switching things around, or if I'll be kept here.

The upheavals in Egypt are upsetting businesses throughout the region; I'm taking it easy in my little corner of the world, for the time being, as I wouldn't be able to do any better elsewhere right now. If the British occupation of Egypt persists, things will improve. And if the British get as far as Harar, the good old days will be with us again.

Hoping for the future.

Yours alone,

Rimbaud.

TO HIS FAMILY
Aden, September 10, 1882

Dear friends,

I received your July letter with the map: thank you.

Nothing new here, my situation is the same. At the most, I have another thirteen months left on my contract with the firm; hard to say if I'll work them all. The official Aden agent leaves in six months; I might replace him. The salary would be about ten thousand francs per year. At that rate, it's better than my current position; at that rate I'd be willing to stay here for five or six years.

We'll see how the scales balance out, in time.

I wish you every prosperity.

Make sure your letters to me are entirely proper, as they are examining my correspondence here.

Yours alone,

Rimbaud.

TO HIS FAMILY
Aden, September 28, 1882

My dear friends,

I am still in the same place; but I expect to leave at the end of the year for the African continent, not for Harar anymore, but for Choa (Abyssinia).

I just wrote to the former agent of the Aden branch, Monsieur Colonel Dubar, in Lyon, that he should send a complete photographic outfit to me that I could carry to Choa, which is entirely undiscovered and which could net me a small fortune in little time.

This Monsieur Dubar is a very serious fellow, and he will send me what I need. He has to gather some information; and as soon as he has, he will request the required funds from you directly, which I ask that you send and which you will send him immediately without delay.

I am having a sum of 1,000 francs sent to you via that Lyon office. This sum should be used specifically for what I mention above: don't use it for anything else unless you hear it from me. And if it were to cost more, by 500 or 1,000 francs, please make up the difference and send it along all together. Then write me with details of what I owe you, and it will be sent immediately: I have 1,000 francs with me here.

This expenditure will prove most useful; even if I am regrettably delayed here, I will still be able to sell it at a profit.

At the end of October, you will receive the 1,000 francs from Lyon. As I said, they are only to be put toward the purchase. I don't have time to write anything else today. I can only hope you are all well and prospering.

Yours alone,

Rimbaud.

—Enclosed, a check for 1,000 francs to be drawn on the Lyon account.

TO HIS FAMILY
Aden, November 3, 1882

Dear friends,

A letter from Lyon, dated October 20, alerts me that my photographic paraphernalia has been purchased. It should be on its way here by now. So you should have been approached regarding the shipping costs. I expect that you received, some time ago, my check for 1,000 francs to be drawn on the Lyon account, and that they have already sent you the sum, with which you were able to pay for the purchases.

I await news on this front, and expect that all this will have transpired without difficulty.

When all of this is settled, I will send you further requests, if any money is left over.

I am leaving for Harar in January of 1883, on company business.

Good health. Yours alone,

Rimbaud.

TO HIS FAMILY
Aden, November 16, 1882

Dear friends,

I received your letter of October 24. I think that by now the check has been paid, and that my request is en route.

If I leave Aden, it will probably be on company business. None of this will be decided for a month or two; for now, they aren't making any of this very clear. As for France, were I to return, what would I find? I think it makes much more sense for me to be here socking it away; then we'll see. What is most important and urgent for me is to be independent no matter where I am.

The calendar says that the sun rises in France at 7:15 and sets at 4:15 in November; here, it's about 6 to 6. I wish you a bearable winter—and (as who knows where I'll be in two weeks or a month) a happy new year, or what one might call a happy new year, and every happiness in 1883!

When my African trip is underway with my photographic equipment, I will send you some interesting things. Here, in Aden, there's nothing of interest, not even a single leaf (unless someone brings one here), and no one visits it except if they have to.

In the event something remains of the 1,000 francs, I will give you a list of books I need, which will be indispensable where I'm going, as otherwise I'll have no means of learning anything about it.

If you could give the attached list to the Attigny bookstore, with the provision that they send everything along as quickly as possible (because if it doesn't get to Aden in time, it will slow me down considerably).

If there isn't any money left over, send the order anyway, and alert me: I'll send the difference. The most all of this could run is 200 francs. Crate them up with the customs declaration reading "Books" on the outside; send them to M. Dubar, with a note explaining that he take the bundle

---

Attigny bookstore: The list may well have been given to the bookstore, as no trace of it remains.

and address it with my name to Aden, via the Messageries Maritimes. If the package were to be sent via the Lyon office, I'd never get it.

I must take my leave of you. I thank you in advance.

Yours alone,

Rimbaud.

TO HIS MOTHER
Aden, November 18, 1882

Dear Maman,

I received your letter of October 27, in which you report having received the 1,000 francs from Lyon.

You say that the photographic equipment cost 1,850 francs. I am cabling you today: "Pay the difference with my money from the previous year." Which is to say make up the extra 1,000 francs from the 2,500 I sent the year before.

I have 4,000 francs here; but they are on deposit with the British Treasury, and I can't withdraw them without accruing fees. Anyway, I'll need to make use of them soon.

So take the 1,000 francs from what I sent you in 1881: there's no other way of me handling this now. I need to hold on to what I have here for the time being, as whatever I have I'll be able to triple in Africa. If this is a problem for you, I'm sorry. But I can't dip into my pockets right now.

As for the camera, if it's in good working order, there's no question that I'll be able to make it pay for itself in short order. I am sure of this. In any case, I will always be able to sell it at a profit if need be. What's done is done, let's see how it turns out.

I wrote you yesterday, and attached an order for books costing around 200 francs. Please do send them along, as asked, no matter what.

I will be returning to Harar as an agent of the firm, and I'll be working hard. I hope to have 15,000 francs saved by the end of next year.

Once again, I am sorry about all this trouble. I promise not to add to your worries. Please, just send the books.

Yours alone,

Rimbaud.

TO HIS MOTHER
Aden, December 8, 1882

Dear Maman,

I received your letter of November 24 indicating that the payment was made and that the shipment is on the way. Of course, the equipment wasn't purchased until it was certain that there were funds to cover it. For that reason, the transaction wasn't complete until the 1,850 francs were received.

You say they are robbing me. I know very well what a camera alone costs: a few hundred francs. But the chemicals, of which there are many and all are expensive, some are made of gold and silver, can cost as much as 250 francs a kilo, and then there's the cost of the mirrors, papers, basins, bottles, expensive packaging, all of which inflate the price. I ordered enough material for two years of work. So as far as I'm concerned, I got off cheap. My only worry is that something should break while en route, at sea. If it all arrives intact, I will be able to make a profit, and to send you interesting things.

So instead of being upset with me, be excited for me. I know how much money this has cost; and if I'm risking anything, I'm doing so advisedly.

Please pay for everything, equipment, wrapping, and shipping.

You have the 2,500 I sent you two years ago. Keep the land you bought in my name as yours, and pay the bill in exchange. Nothing could be more straightforward.

The most upsetting aspect of your letter is that you end it by saying you won't have anything further to do with my affairs. This is not the way to help a man who is thousands of leagues away from home, traveling among savage peoples and without a single correspondent where he resides. I hope that you will resolve toward a more charitable stance. If I can't even ask my family for favors, who the hell am I supposed to go to?

I just sent you a list of books to send me here. Please don't tell me to go to hell! I am about to reembark into the African continent for several years; and without these books, I will be without a heap of essential information. I will be like a blind man; and the lack of these things will problematize everything. So please send these works right away, every last one; put them in a crate marked "Books," and pay to have them sent to me here via M. Dubar.

Include these two works:

Compleat Treatise on Railroads, by Couch (chez Dunod, quai des Augustins, Paris)

The *Mechanical Treatise*, of the École des Châlons

Combined, the works run 400 francs. Pay for them as I've said above; I won't make you spend anything further, as I am leaving for Africa in a month. Hurry.

Yours,

Rimbaud.

TO HIS MOTHER AND SISTER
Aden, January 6, 1883

My dear Maman,
My dear sister,

A week ago I received your letter containing New Year's wishes. I wish you a thousandfold the same, and hope we'll all be happy this year. I still think about Isabelle; I think of her each time I write, and I wish particularly that all her wishes are realized.

I will be leaving for Harar at the end of March. All the photographic equipment will arrive here in two weeks, and I will quickly learn how to use it and to make it pay for itself, neither of which should be difficult, including making reproductions of this hitherto unknown landscape and the people locked within the land, reproductions that sell well in France, and so this whole bargain will offer immediate potential for income.

I would like to think that the costs associated with this matter have reached their end, but if there is anything more that needs to be spent I would ask that you spend it, please, and bring all this to a close.

And send me the books as well.

M. Dubar is also supposed to send me a scientific instrument called a graphometer.

I expect to make some profit in Harar this year, and I will send you the balance of anything I've made you spend. And I'll put my requests to you on hold. I ask your forgiveness, if I have inconvenienced you. The mail round-trip from Harar takes forever, and I have wanted to be better able to provide for myself for quite some time.

All best.

Rimbaud.

TO HIS FAMILY
Aden, January 15, 1883

Dear friends,

I received your last letter, with your new year's wishes. Thank you with all my heart, and believe that I remain always devoted to you.

I received the list of purchased books. As you say, the ones that are missing are indeed the most important of the batch. One is the treatise on topography (not photography, I have one of those here). Topography is the art of surveying a countryside: I need it. So please send the letter attached to the bookstore, and they will be able to find one easily enough. The other is a treatise on geology and practical mineralogy. To find one, the bookseller may do as I suggest.

These two requests were part of an older order; that is why I insist upon having them. They will be very useful to me.

I will not send you any more orders—without money. I am sorry for all the trouble.

. . . .

Isabelle is wrong to want to see me in this country. It's the bottom of a volcano, without a blade of grass. The only advantage here is that the climate is very clean and that business can be done easily. But from March to October, the heat is excessive. Right now, it's winter, and the thermometer is only at 30° in the shade: it never rains. I have been sleeping under the stars all year. I happen to like this climate; because I hate rain, mud, and cold. Meanwhile, I'll probably be leaving for Harar by the end of March. There, the terrain is mountainous, the elevation high; from March to October it rains continuously and the temperature is 10°. The vegetation is magnificent, as is the likelihood of fever. If I leave again, I'll probably stay there another year. All this will be decided soon. I will send you images of the land and people from Harar.

As for the British treasury of which I wrote before, it's just a special deposit box in Aden; it brings in about 4.5 percent. But the deposit maximum is limited. It's not very practical.

More soon.

A. Rimbaud.

TO M. DE GASPARY, FRENCH VICE-CONSUL, ADEN
Aden, January 28, 1883

Monsieur,

Excuse me for bringing the following matter to your attention.

Today, at 11 in the morning, I allowed myself to give Ali Chemmak—the warehouse supervisor at the firm where I am employed, having acted in an insolent manner toward me—a gentle slap.

The coolies and various Arab witnesses to the scene then grabbed and held me so that the aforesaid Ali Chemmak could strike me in the face, rip my clothes, and grab a stick with which he threatened me.

Other witnesses intervened, Ali withdrew, and then shortly after filed a complaint against me with the police, claiming I had struck and wounded him, presenting various false witnesses to back his claims that I threatened him, struck him with my fist, etc., etc., and other lies aimed at making it seem as though the matter were of my doing, with the goal of inciting the indigenous population against me.

Appearing before the municipal police of Aden in this matter, I took it upon myself to alert Monsieur le Consul de France concerning the attack and threats thereof on the part of the indigenous population to which I was exposed, and request its protection in the event that the outcome of the situation would require it.

I have the honor, Monsieur le Consul, to be,

Your humble servant,

Rimbaud
Employee of the Maison Mazeran,
Viannay and Bardey, Aden

TO HIS MOTHER AND SISTER
Aden, February 8, 1883

Dear Maman, dear sister,

I received a letter from M. Dubar, end of January, announcing the shipment of the aforesaid item and that the bill had gone up 600 francs. Pay this against my account, so that this whole thing can be completed. I have spent a large sum; but it will pay off, I am certain, and so I am not moaning over the costs involved.

Right now, we are going over the list of charges, items sent, etc.

Only send me the books I asked you for; don't forget.

I will be leaving Aden in six weeks without fail, and I will write you before then.

Yours alone,

Rimbaud.

TO HIS FAMILY
Aden, March 14, 1883

Dear friends,

I am leaving for Harar on the 18th, on company business.

I received everything you sent and which so inconvenienced you. Now all I need are those last three books.

You will be asked fairly soon, via Lyon, to pay 100 francs to cover a graphometer I ordered (a surveying instrument). Pay it; and, hereafter, I won't ask you to pay for something again that I haven't sent you money for in advance.

I expect to turn a small profit in Harar, and should receive, in a year, funding from the Geographical Society.

I will write you the day that I leave.

Good luck and good health.

Yours alone,

Rimbaud.

TO HIS FAMILY
[undated]

My dear friends,

I received your last letter, and the crate of books arrived yesterday evening. I thank you.

The photographic equipment, and everything else, is in excellent condition, despite having come here via île Maurice, and I expect to make the most of it.

As for the books, they couldn't be more useful to me here in this country where I can't manage to get the least information about anything, and without them I would otherwise become as dumb as an ass without brushing up on my studies. The days and above all the nights are long in Harar, and these books will make time pass much more pleasantly. Because there isn't a single public meeting place in all of Harar, you have no choice but to stay at home incessantly. I expect at least to put together an interesting album documenting all of this.

I am sending you a check for one hundred francs, which you should deposit and use to buy the books below. Money spent on books is essential.

You mention that a few hundred francs remain of my old money. When they ask you to pay for the graphometer (a leveling instrument) that I ordered from Lyon, pay it from that leftover money. The entirety of that sum has been given over to this enterprise. I have five thousand francs here, in the hands of the firm and held at 5% interest: so it isn't as though I am ruined. My contract with the firm ends in November; that's another eight months at 330 francs before me, around 2,500 francs, so I should have 7,000 francs on deposit by the end of the year, without including what I'm able to put together buying and selling from my account. After November, should they not fire me, I could still do a little business, which would bring in 60% in a year. I would like, in 4 or 5 years, to quickly make fifty thousand francs; I would get married thereafter.

I am leaving tomorrow for Zeila. You will not hear from me for two months. I wish you good weather, health, and prosperity.

Yours alone,

Rimbaud.

Keep writing me in Aden.

Aden, March 19, 1883
Dunod, 49, quai des Grands-Augustins, Paris:

Debauve, *Roadbuilding*, 1 Volume	30 francs
Lalanne-Sganzin, *A Summary of Earthworks Calculations*	2
Debauve, *Geodesics*, 1 v.	7.50
Debauve, *Hydraulics*, 1 v.	6
Jacquet, *Planning Arches*, 1 v.	6

Librairie Masson:

Delaunay, *Course in Elementary Mechanics*	8
Liais, *Treatise on Applied Astronomy*	10
Total:	69 francs 50 centimes

TO HIS FAMILY
Aden, March 20, 1883

My dear friends,

With this letter I am alerting you that I have renewed my contract with the firm through the end of December 1885. My salary is currently 160 rupees per month and a share of the profits, giving me an annual net of 5,000 francs per year, above all costs for lodging and expenses, which are always provided free of charge.

I am leaving the day after tomorrow for Zeila.

I forgot to tell you that the check for 100 francs is payable through the Marseille branch (Mazeran Viannay Bardey, Marseille), and not Lyon.

Add to the list of books:

Librairie Dunod:
Salin. *Practical Manual for the Laying of Railroad Tracks,* 1 Vol.   2 fr. 50 &:
Nordling. *Earthworks,* 1 Vol.   5
Debauve, *Tunnels and Underground Passages,* 1 V.   10

Send me everything together if you can.
Yours alone,

Rimbaud.

To what end these comings and goings, this exhaustion, these adventures among strange races, and these languages that fill my memory, and these nameless pains if I cannot, one day, after a few years, manage to rest in a locale that I more or less like and find a family, at least have one son whom I can spend the rest of my life raising as I see fit, adorning and arming with the most complete education one can currently imagine, and whom I will watch become a renowned engineer, a man made rich and powerful by his knowledge of science? But who can say how long my days amid these mountains will last?

MAY 6, 1883

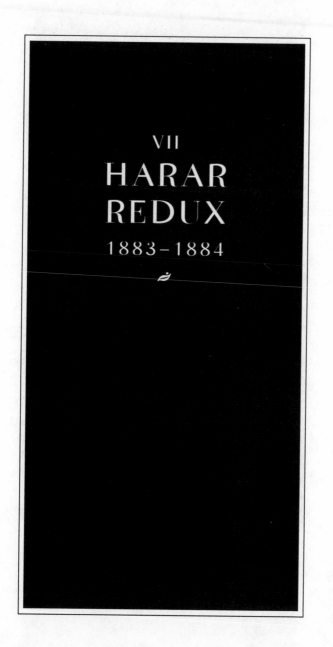

VII

HARAR REDUX

1883–1884

Self-portrait, Rimbaud, c. 1883.

TO HIS FAMILY
Mazeran, Viannay and Bardey
Lyon-Marseille-Aden
Harar, May 6, 1883

My dear friends,

April 30, I received your letter of March 26 in Harar. You tell me you sent me two crates of books. I received only one, in Aden, the one Debar says he paid 25 francs for. The other has probably arrived in Aden by now, with the graphometer. After all, I sent you, before leaving Aden, a check for 100 francs with another list of books. You must have cashed this check, and probably bought the books. As for now I have no idea when. Soon I will send you another check for 200 francs, as I need some mirrors for the camera.

This bill of goods was entirely worthwhile; and if I want to, I'll be able to earn back the 2,000 francs it cost me. Everyone here wants to be photographed, paying a guinea per picture. I am neither set up nor up to speed yet, but I will be soon, and I will send you some curious things.

I've included some photographs of myself I took:

I am happier here than in Aden. There is less work and more air, greenery, etc. I renewed my contract for three years here, but I think that the firm will shut down soon, salaries not being covered by earnings. So, it has been decided that the day they let me go, I will be given three months' severance. At the end of this year, I will have spent three full years in this company.

Isabelle is very wrong not to marry if a serious, educated fellow presents himself, someone with a future. Life is like that, and solitude is a bad thing here. Myself, I regret not being married and not having a family. But for the time being I am condemned to wander, affiliated with a far-flung firm, and every day I lose my taste for the climate and the customs

---

some photographs of myself: In addition to the image opposite, Rimbaud's self-portraits appear on pages 194 and 226.

and even the languages of Europe. Alas! To what end these comings and goings, this exhaustion, these adventures among strange races, and these languages that fill my memory, and these nameless pains if I cannot, one day, after a few years, manage to rest in a locale that I more or less like and find a family, at least have one son whom I can spend the rest of my life raising as I see fit, adorning and arming with the most complete education one can currently imagine, and whom I will watch become a renowned engineer, a man made rich and powerful by his knowledge of science? But who can say how long my days amid these mountains will last? And if I might disappear, in the midst of these peoples, with news of my disappearance never being heard.

You mention political news. If you only knew how little I cared! I haven't read a newspaper in more than two years. Now all those debates seem incomprehensible. Like the Muslims, I know that what happens happens, and that is all.

The only things that interest me are bits of news about the house, and I am always happy to recline into the image of your pastoral labors. It's too bad that it's so cold and sad in winter where you are. But it's spring there now for you, and your climate happens to match my own here at Harar right now.

These photographs are of me, the one standing on the terrace of the house ... the other standing in the café garden, another with arms crossed in a banana garden. All of these are a little washed out because of the dirty water I'm forced to use to clean them with. The next ones will be better. They're only sent as a reminder of my face, and to give you some idea of the landscape here.

Au revoir,

Rimbaud.
Maison Mazeran, Viannay and Bardey
Aden.

TO HIS FAMILY
Harar, May 20, 1883

My dear friends,

I expect that you will have received my first letter from Harar by now.

My last order of books should be en route: you will have paid for them, as I asked you to, including the graphometer, which you must have sent me at the same time.

The photography is going well. It turns out it was a good idea I had. Soon I'll send you some successful examples.

The next time the mail leaves, I will have a check sent to you for a few small new orders.

I am well, business is good; and it makes me happy to imagine that you are healthy and prosperous.

Rimbaud.

TO HIS FAMILY
[August 12, 1883]

Dear friends,

I am sending you, attached, a copy of my agent's papers in Harar. They feature a visa from the French consulate in Aden.

I suspect that this will prove sufficient.

The only thing is that you absolutely have to send it back to me here, or I will find myself in a difficult position should my agency be contested. This document is indispensable in my business.

So please do return it to me after you have made use of it as required.

There is a new consul in Aden and he is on a trip to Bombay right now.

If they should tell you that the effective date of the papers is old (March 20), you need only observe that, were I not still in the same position, the papers would have been returned to the firm and voided.

So I think that will do, for the last time.

—It is true that I received all the books, with the exception of the last crate, which I am still awaiting.

Yours alone,

Rimbaud.
Harar, August 12, 1883

TO MM. MAZERAN, VIANNAY AND BARDEY
Harar, August 25, 1883

Harar market has never been worse than this season, this year, according to everyone here.

—No coffee. The Bewin and Moussaya agency is selling ¼ fraslehs of filth that amounts to ground-up bits of floor from Harar houses: they're asking 5 thalers a ½.

—The skins are prohibitively expensive, for the reasons given earlier; and anyway there aren't any. 2,600 hides belonging to the government got 70 paras at auction; we were thinking we could then repurchase them for 1.5 paras and put together a caravan. They are the same quality as the last ones.

—Goat skins. 3,000 in the store already. With purchase price and the cost of their freight here, their average price is 4 dollars. But we put together their purchase, and each month we can get another 2,500 to 3,000 without going over that price.

—Ivory. Trying to put something together; we're short on specialist labor and special merchandise.

M. Sacconi, along with three servants, was killed during an expedition parallel to our own into Ogadine, in the land of the Hammaden tribe, which neighbors Wabi, on August 11, 250 kilometers from Harar. This news arrived in Harar on the 23rd. The causes of this misfortune were the sorry state of the members of the expedition, the ignorance of the guides, who led them poorly, down exceptionally dangerous routes, braving belligerent populations. Lastly, the poor behavior of M. Sacconi himself, going against (out of ignorance) the manners, religious customs, and rights of the indigenous population.

The Bewin and Moussaya agency: a competitor in the coffee trade. *fraslehs:* units of measure weighing around 37 pounds. *thalers:* Emblazoned with the face of Empress Marie-Thérèse of Austria, a thaler was the most prevalent coin throughout Abyssinia of the era. It was worth about 4 francs 50. *paras:* Turkish currency. *M. Sacconi ... was killed:* Pietro Sacconi, merchant. Killed in Carnagott, near Harar. Rimbaud attended his funeral in Harar on August 24, 1883.

The source of the massacre was a quarrel with the Abbans: M. Sacconi hired a guide of his own and wanted to have him lead his expedition rather than the indigenous Abbans whom he was offered. So M. Sacconi took to the trail wearing a European suit, made his bearers dress as Christians, dined on ham, emptied little glasses in the presence of sheiks, cooked for himself, and forged ahead making his suspicious geodesic surveys, twirling his sextants, etc., wherever he went.

The indigenous peoples who escaped the massacre were three Somali bearers and the Indian cook Hadj-Sheiti, who took refuge two days east of here chez M. Sotiro.

M. Sacconi wasn't buying anything and his only goal was to reach the Wabi, for his greater geographical glory. M. Sotiro stopped at the first place he thought he might be able to trade his merchandise for that of others. Anyway, he took the correct route, a very different one from that of Sacconi. I had a good Abban who stopped where Sacconi should have. The Abban traveled wearing Muslim clothes, under the name Adji-Abddallah, and adopted all the political and religious formalities of the indigenous people. Wherever he stopped, he became a sort of point of pilgrimage like a wodad or sherif. News comes fairly frequently, and we expect more by the end of the month.

New expeditions are already in the planning stages. Will return your funds via M. Sotiro, via Ogadine. The mail, which had been sending our funds in increments of 3,000 thalers, won't work right now. We regret having to make our employees undertake such unproductive routes, given we need them for work in the exterior. The Marseille importers lost our orders.

Now we've reached the point where we're disgusted to have to complain about the situation they've put us in. The only thing we hold to is that we aren't responsible in the least for any damage that was done. Nonetheless we request once again, for the last time, all our merchandise orders, made in the quantities and qualities ordered. We are ordering them all one by one and have called for the fulfillment of said orders.

Abbans: Abban is a local name for a caravan guide. *Wabi:* a river he wished to be credited with discovering. *wodad:* a man of letters. *sherif:* religious nobleman of the blood of Mohammed.

Should no one attend to our orders, no matter. The same may be said for all the local products of Aden: in the future we will go buy them ourselves. Whatever ends up arriving is considerably different in every way from whatever it is we ordered in the first place and ends up being not at all as we would have wished. This month we won't even sell 200 thalers worth of merchandise, and as a result our expenses will begin to weigh on us. If our suppliers could supply us, and this seems too simple I know, with what we ask of them, then we would be able to cover, easily, these expenses, while awaiting more favorable economic times. Others got us into this mess, and they are also responsible for the damage that was done to us *personally*.

We are awaiting the new governor, who, it seems, has a European education. The elephant hunter you had sent to us from Aden is parading around the gorges of Darimont seemingly indefinitely, and will pop out around here once he's decimated his stores of cured pig and preserved milk among the Guerris and Bartris.

Attached find the July crate forgotten somewhere in the last mail and a survey of merchandise available throughout Harar.

Rimbaud.

7th SURVEY OF MERCHANDISE
[1883]

For the land of *Harar Sirwal Habeschi.* Find or have made a coarse cotton fabric with a tight weave of the weight of light sail material, with red or blue stripes five centimeters wide and twenty centimeters apart.

Have 500 Surwall made like the sample attached (not of the same fabric). It should do well in the Abyssinian and Gallas tribes, where there are already some interesting examples of items of this kind.

Kamis. Of the same fabric, a simple shirt that cinches at the chest, falls to the hips, arms only reaching the elbows. Make 500.

Sperraba. 50 red wool or green braided tassels, to attach to bridles and saddles, destined for the Gallas and the Somalis, and 20 meters of long fringe, same color and wool, worn above the chest—all from an upholsterer or tapestry maker.

We have sent a team of tiger, leopard, and lion hunters into the exterior, with flaying instructions.

4 or 5 hours from Harar, there is a forest (Bisédimo) filled with wild animals, and we have alerted the people in the neighboring villages that we would be happy to have them hunt for us.

We believe that a type of steel trap used specifically for trapping wolves is available in France; it might work very well for Leopards. I'm sure you could find them through a wolfery association, and upon their evaluation send us two of these traps.

Rimbaud.

Surwall: article of clothing.

TO ALFRED BARDEY
Maison Viannay and Bardey
Lyon-Marseille-Aden
Harar, August 26, 1883

I received your letter where you acknowledge the receipt of the photographs. I thank you. None of them was very interesting. I set that pursuit aside because of all the rain, not having seen the sun in three months. I'll start up again when good weather returns, and then I'll really be able to send you some interesting things.

If I have anything to ask you at all, it is only that you keep your eye on the progress of the items I've asked be manufactured for sale in Harar. I will need them to set up and see flourish a Gallas branch. I have chosen those items by hand as ordered; above all, I need the *zâbouns*, the leather jewelry. But everything is needed. And why not even the harari robes (the expensive ones, at 15 thalers per)? The path to success here is to attend to such details.

I imagine that all this is being taken care of.

—M. Sacconi died near Wabi on August 11, massacred because of his own ignorance and stupidity.

Would you like anything else from Harar? The history of Guirane Ahmed is into its second volume, I am told, and offers more geographical interest.

—On that account, I received a note from M. Pierre Mazeran announcing his return to Harar in October.

I hope that we won't be blamed for the new expenses of late, and that our situation will not be further problematized by the arrival here of anyone incapable of anything more than squandering what we currently have and contradicting what we have been doing, ridiculing us, and ruining everything we've set up. —Lastly, personally, we are willing to endure every privation here without complaint, and every boredom without impatience, but we will not suffer the company of a [...].

Best wishes.
Rimbaud.

[...]: The word is crossed out on the original of the letter.

TO MM. MAZERAN, VIANNAY AND BARDEY, ADEN
Mazeran, Viannay and Bardey.
Lyon-Marseille-Aden.
Telegrams: Mazeran-Lyon. Maziba-Marseille.
Harar, September 23, 1883.

Received your letter of September 9. Confirming the one of September 9. We are sending, on this September 23, with caravan 46: 42 camels loaded with steer leather. We are preparing, for caravan 48 of October 20, 5,000 goat skins. The same caravan will probably also bring you feathers and ivory from Ogadine, from which our expedition will have returned no later than the end of September. We have made a fledgling expedition to the Itous of Djardjar; the expedition carried gifts to the important chiefs and some merchandise; from the information the expedition gathered, we will try to establish something on a regular basis with the tribes. So things bode well from there.

The men we use for the expeditions to Danakil and Haawache come from Zeila, and we also plan to include that interesting area in our pursuits.

Two other expeditions among the Wabi, one via Ogadine, the other via Ennya, are also in the works. The rivers are receding right now and we will inform ourselves definitively as to everything that we can pursue in the region surrounding greater Harar. A commercial and geographical survey will follow from these investigations and we will see that you receive it in Marseille.

According to specific information, we believe that Itou will be invaded again and definitively annexed by the Ménélik empire at the beginning of 1884. We even expect an imperial residence there. The Egyptian and Abyssinian borders will be determined and agreed upon. Access to the Galla, Itous, and Oroussis should prove easier. As for Harar, it isn't a part of Abyssinia's plans.

Djardjar: near Harar, major coffee producers in the region.

It brings us pleasure to see your orders gradually arriving. We never meant to make it seem as though the blame lay with the Aden agency and its delays. There is little therefore that we can do but complete the supporting documents you are preparing. In the future we'll have to go about things differently. Be so kind as to note the orders that remain unfulfilled, Guéset, Kéhas, Kasdir, Kahrab, Abbayas.

Pearls, among other things: and add the following: 100 pieces of Massachusetts shirting A (30 yards) first quality (like the last shipment). Try to buy it at a few anas cheaper by the piece. —100 pieces of Vilayeti Abou Raïa (Colabaland Smill and Co.), above and beyond the 50 en route.

Bring 12 maunds of the little pearls from the last batch and 12 maunds of the fat white ones as well.

2 new maunds of Assa fœtida (actite).

2 corja of the biggest aïtabanes (the *tobe* with blue and red stripes, as our order of May 20).

And some ammunition, which we have twice requested, and the aforementioned Somali grammar.

Sincerely,

Rimbaud.

---

anas: Indies currency worth one-sixteenth of a rupee. *Vilayeti Abou Raïa:* cotton ecru from Colaba in the English Indies. *maunds:* a unit of weight equal to 28 pounds. *corja:* unit of 20. *tobe:* a swath of cotton ecru worn as the principal article of clothing by many African peoples.

TO HIS FAMILY
Harar, October 4, 1883

Dear friends,

I received your worried letter.

As far as I'm concerned, I never pass a post office without writing you; but the two most recent times, I sent a letter to you via the Egyptian mail. From now on, I'll make sure they go in the regular mail.

I am in excellent health, and hard at work. I wish you the same good health and prosperity. This mail is about to leave, the next will bring you a long letter.

Yours alone,

Rimbaud.

TO HIS FAMILY
Harar, October 7, 1883

My dear friends,

I as yet have no word regarding your last shipment of books, which must be stuck somewhere.

I would be very grateful to you were you to forward the following note to the Hachette bookstore, 79 boulevard Saint-Germain, Paris; and, once they have sent you the work in question, you will pay for it and send it along promptly by post, by whatever means insures it against loss.

I wish you good health and good weather.

Yours alone,

Rimbaud.

TO M. HACHETTE

I would be most grateful to you were you to send me as soon as possible, at the address below, payable upon receipt, the finest French translation of the Koran (with the Arabic text on facing pages, if it is available as such), and even without.

With cordial greetings,

Rimbaud.
Roche, via Attigny (Ardennes).
October 7, 1883

SURVEY OF OGADINE
by Arthur Rimbaud
Agent of MM. Mazeran, Viannay and Bardey,
Harar (Oriental Africa). (Transmitted by M. Bardey.)
Harar, December 10, 1883

What follows is a summary of information collected during our first expedition into Ogadine.

Ogadine is the name of a group of formerly Somali tribes, as well as the land they inhabit, most often situated on current maps between the Somali tribes of the Habr-Gerhadjis, the Doulbohantes, the Midhertines, and the Hawïa to the north, east and south. To the west, Ogadine is bordered by the Galla—the shepherds of Ennyas—all the way to the river Wabi, which separates the great Oromo tribe from the Oroussis.

There are two routes from Harar to Ogadine: the first runs east of the city toward Boursouque and then south of Mount Condoudo via War-Ali; it includes three way stations heading to Ogadine frontier.

This is the route that was taken by our agent, M. Sotiro; and the distance from Harar to where he was stopped in the Rere-Hersi is equal to the distance from Harar to Biocabouba along the Zeila route—both around 140 kilometers. This route is the least dangerous and has drinking water.

The other route runs south and east of Harar across the river at the Herer crossing, and then on through the Babili market and the Wara-Heban, before crossing paths with the pillaging tribes of Somali-Galla, Hawïa.

The name Hawïa seems specifically to designate tribes formed by a mix of Somalis and Gallas, of which a small number exist in the northwest below the Harar plateau, a few others south of Harar on the Ogadine route, and then a third, much larger tribe to the southeast of Ogadine—Wotards Sahel—the three parts proving completely separate and unrelated.

Survey of Ogadine: Published in _Comptes rendus des séances de la Société de Géographie,_ 1884. Bardey, to whom Rimbaud presented the report and who was a member of the society, sent it in.

Like all the Somali tribes around them, the Ogadines are completely nomadic and their land is utterly without roads or markets. Even from the exterior, there are few roads that lead to the area, and the roads listed on maps of Ogadine and Barberah, Mogdischo (Magadoxo) or Braoua, do little more, really, than indicate the presence of traffic.

Ogadine is a stepped plateau almost without variation, inclining gently to the southeast. Its elevation must be barely half that of the Harar massif (1,800 m.).

Its climate is therefore hotter than Harar's. It would seem to have two rainy seasons; one in October, and the other in March. The rain is general then, but fairly light.

The rivers of Ogadine are of no significance. There are four, all flowing from the Harar massif; that one, the Fafan, has its source in Condoudo, and flows through Boursouque (or Barsoub), and makes an elbow in the middle Ogadine, and empties into the Wabi at a place called Faf, halfway to Mogdischo; this is the major river of the region. Two other smaller rivers are: the Herer, also sourced in Faro Condoudo, skirting Babili and joined, four days south of Harar in the Ennyas, by the Gobeiley and the Moyo coming from the Alas, then emptying into the Wabi in Ogadine, in the Nokob lands; and the Dokhta, born in the Wara Heban (Babili) and flowing into the Wabi, probably in the direction of the Herer.

The strong rains of the Harar massif and Boursouque must also occur in upper Ogadine, fleeting torrential downpours and light inundations which, when they arise, bring the families of shepherds called *goums* to the area. During dry season, there is, by contrast, a general retreat of the tribes toward the Wabi.

The general appearance of Ogadine is one of high grassy steppes with rocky breaks; its trees, at least those seen by our explorers in the regions reached by our expedition, are the same as those found in the Somali desert: mimosas, gums, etc. As one heads toward the Wabi, the population is sedentary and agricultural. They cultivate *dourah* almost exclusively and even make use of slaves, some Aroussis and Gallas from beyond the river. A fraction of the Malingours tribe in upper Ogadine has inadver-

---

dourah: sorghum.

tently planted dourah, and there are also a few Cheikhaches villages here and there that cultivate it as well.

Like all the shepherds of these parts, the Ogadines are always fighting with their neighbors and among themselves.

The Ogadines have traditions that date back to their origins. We have only been able to determine that they are descendants of Rere Abdallah and Rere Ishay (*Rere* means: children, family, house; in Galla, they say *Warra*). Rere Abdallah was followed by Rere Hersi and Rere Hammaden: these are the two main families of upper Ogadine.

Rere Ishay sired Rere Ali and Rere Aroun. These Reres subdivided then into innumerable subfamilies. The tribes as a whole whom M. Sotiro visited were descendants of Rere Hersi, and are called Malingours, Aïal, Oughas, Semntar, Magan.

The different divisions of the Ogadines are all headed by chiefs called *oughaz*. The oughaz of Malingour, our friend Amar Hussein, is the most powerful of upper Ogadine and he seems to have authority over all the tribes from Habr Gerhadji to the Wabi. His father came to Harar in the time of Raouf Pacha, who gave him arms and clothes. As for Amar Hussein, he has never left his tribes, where he is renowned as a warrior, and is content to respect the Egyptian authority from a distance.

As for the Egyptians, they seem to view the Ogadines, along with the Somalis and Danakils, as their subjects or natural allies, given they are Muslims, and have no plans to invade their territories.

The Ogadines, at least those we encountered, are tall, and more red in color than black; their heads are bare, and the hair short, and they wear clean frocks, wearing a *sigada* over their shoulders, a saber and a gourd of ablutions at their hips, a cane in hand, a large and a small lance, and walk in sandals.

Their daily activities include crouching beneath trees in groups, at some distance from their camps, and, weapons in hand, conversing indefinitely over the diverse topics of interest to shepherds. Apart from these sessions, and their horseback patrols while watering their animals or raiding their neighbors, they are completely inactive. The care of the animals is left to the women and children, as is the making of cooking utensils, the construction of their huts, and the organization of their caravans. These utensils are of the milk-pot variety known throughout Somalia, and the camel mats, mounted on sticks, form the houses of the *gacias,* their temporary villages.

A few blacksmiths wander between the tribes and make the iron for their lances and daggers.

There are no known ores within Ogadine.

They are fanatical Muslims. Each camp has its imam who calls the prayers at the designated hours. The *wodads* (men of letters) are also a part of every tribe; they know the Koran and Arabic writing and are improvisational poets.

The Ogadine families are large. M. Sotiro's *abbam* had sixty sons and grandsons. When an Ogadine woman gives birth, the spouse has nothing to do with her until the child can walk on its own. Naturally, he marries one or several others in the interim, but always with the same guidelines.

Their herds consist of humped cattle, shaved sheep, goats, horses of a lesser breed, milk camels, and ostriches, the keeping of which is a custom throughout the region. Each village has several dozen ostriches who graze on their own, under the watch of children, even sleeping near the fire in the huts, and, male and female, their legs hobbled, follow the caravans behind the camels, whose height they nearly attain.

They pluck the feathers three or four times a year, and each time manage to harvest about a half pound of black feathers and sixty white feathers. Ostrich herders greatly value their stock.

Wild ostriches are everywhere. Hunters cover themselves in the hide of a female, and then shoot arrows at the males when they approach.

Dead feathers are worth less than live ones. The tame ostriches were captured young, the Ogadines not allowing domesticated birds to breed.

There aren't many elephants, nor are they very tall, in the heart of Ogadine. Nonetheless, they are hunted on the Fafan, and their real meeting place, the place where they go to die, is all along the bank of the Wabi. There they are hunted by the Dônwes, a Somali people made up of Galla and Swahili farmers who live along the banks. They hunt on foot and kill with their enormous lances. The Ogadines hunt on horseback: when fifteen horsemen have the animal surrounded, a hunter with a saber tries to cut the hams of the animal's rear legs.

They also use poison arrows. This poison, called *ouabay*, and used throughout Somalia, is made from the crushed and boiled roots of a shrub. We are sending you a fragment. According to the Somalis, the ground around these shrubs is always covered with sloughed skins of snakes, and all the other trees are desiccated around it. This poison acts slowly, as the indigenous peoples wounded by these arrows (which are also used as weapons of war) cut away the wound and remain unharmed.

Savage animals are relatively rare in Ogadine. The locals speak of serpents, including one with horns, whose breath is believed to be mortal. The most common of the wild animals here are gazelles, antelopes, giraffes, rhinoceroses, the skins of which are used to make shields. The Wabi welcomes all the animals found around great rivers: elephants, hippopotamuses, crocodiles, etc.

A race of men considered inferior to others exists in great numbers among the Ogadines. They are called *Mitganes* (Tsiganes); they appear to belong to the Somali race, whose language they speak. They only marry among themselves. They are the ones who hunt elephants, ostriches, etc. They are scattered throughout the tribes and in times of war are requisitioned as spies and allies. The Ogadines eat elephant, camel, and ostrich, and the Mitganes eat ass and dead animals, which is a sin.

The Mitganes are also present among the Danakils of Haawache, where they also maintain well-populated villages, and are renowned for their hunting.

A political custom and an Ogadine festival takes place once a year on a particular day during which all the tribes gather together.

Justice is meted down within families by elders and generally by the oughaz.

During our time in Ogadine, no one we encountered could recall ever having seen as much merchandise as the few hundred dollars of items we had carried. It is true that what little we brought back from there cost us a great deal, because half of our merchandise was given away as gifts to our guides, abbans, hosts here and there along the route, and the Oughaz himself received a few hundred dollars of golden abbayas, immahs, and

---

immahs: cheap knockoffs of native goods.

gifts of all kinds that ingratiated us to them, which is the principal success of the expedition. M. Sotiro is really to thank for this, his wisdom and diplomacy having enabled it. While our competitors had been pursued, cursed, pillaged, and killed, and even been the cause of terrible wars between tribes, we were able to forge an alliance with the Oughaz and made ourselves known throughout Rere Hersi.

Omar Hussein wrote us in Harar and is waiting for us only a few days from our first post, to go back to the Wabi with him and all his *goums*.

That is essentially our goal. One of us, or some enterprising local acting on our behalf, will be able to collect a ton of ivory, which we would be able to export directly via Berbera without paying a duty. Various Habr-Awal, setting off to the Wabi with a few wilayeti sodas or tobs over their shoulders, returned to Boulhar with hundreds of dollars of feathers. A few asses carrying ten or so pieces of sheeting brought back fifteen fraslehs of ivory.

We have therefore decided to establish a post on the Wabi, and this post will be approximately at the place called Eimeh, a large, permanent village situated on the Ogadine bank of the river, eight days from Harar by caravan.

TO HIS FAMILY
Harar, December 21, 1883

I continue to be well, and I hope that you are too.
At the same time, let me wish you a happy 1884.
Nothing new here.
Yours alone.

Rimbaud.

TO HIS FAMILY

Harar, January 14, 1884

Dear friends,

I only have enough time to say hello, and to let you know that the firm, finding itself short of money (and the war is causing repercussions here), is in the midst of making me liquidate the Harar agency. It is likely that I will leave here, for Aden, in a few months. As far as I'm concerned, I have nothing to fear as regards the affairs of the firm.

I am feeling well, and I wish you health and prosperity for all of 1884.

Rimbaud.

My life here is a real nightmare. Don't think I have it easy. Far from it: I have long been aware that it is impossible to live worse than I do. If work can get started again here in short order, if things can get back up to speed, I won't eat up my sad savings running around. In this case I would remain as long as I could in this unbearable pit, Aden, as sole proprietorships here are too dangerous in Africa.

Sorry for going on about my worries. But I see that I will be turning thirty (half a life!) and I am very tired of running around the world with little to show for it.

MAY 5, 1884

VIII

ADEN AGAIN

1884–1885

Self-portrait, Rimbaud, c. 1883.

TO HIS FAMILY
Aden, April 24, 1884

Dear friends,

After a six-week trip through the deserts, I arrived in Aden; this is why I have not written.

Because of the war, Harar, for now, is uninhabitable. Our firm has liquidated its presence in Harar, as in Aden, and, at the end of the month, I will be without work. Nonetheless, my salary is paid through the end of July, and here I will always find something to do.

I think, and hope, that our gentlemen will prove able to get something going here again.

I hope that you find yourselves well, and I wish you prosperity.

My current address:

Arthur Rimbaud.
Maison Bardey, Aden.

TO HIS FAMILY
Aden, May 5, 1884

My dear friends,

As you know, our firm has been completely liquidated and the Harar agency I had been directing is closed; the Aden agency is also closed. In France, the losses of the company are nearly a million francs, losses sustained in other affairs than these, which were going fairly well. So I found myself dismissed at the end of April, and, according to the terms of my contract, I received a severance of three months' salary, up until the end of July. I am therefore currently unemployed; however, I remain housed in the former building of the company, which is paid for through the end of June. Mr. Bardey departed for Marseille ten days ago to seek new capital with which to continue our activities here. I hope he succeeds, but I fear the contrary. He told me to wait here, but by the end of this month, if the news isn't good, I will look at finding other work elsewhere.

There's no work here for the time being; the large firms sponsoring agencies here have all jumped to Marseille. Another thing is that for those not working here, the cost of living is untenable, and existence intolerably boring, particularly with summer having begun, and you know that summer here is the hottest on the planet!

I really have no idea what I can find within a month. I have between 12 and 14 thousand francs with me, and, as I trust no one here, I'm bound to drag all my savings with me wherever I go and to keep one eye on it at all times. And this money, which would be able to give me a small but sufficient income to allow me to live without having to work, now brings nothing but constant annoyance!

What depressing circumstances I drag through these ridiculous climates and insane conditions! My savings would allow me the guarantee of a small revenue, I could rest a little after all these years of suffering, and not only can I now not rest for a day without work, but I can't even

---

Mr. Bardey: Alfred Bardey.

enjoy what I've saved. The Treasury here only takes interest-free deposits; and the commercial firms offer no kind of security!

I can't give you an address to which you can respond, as I am not sure where I will find myself dragged to next, and by which routes, and for whom, and why, and how!

It is possible that the English will occupy Harar next, and in that case I might return. Then one could make some money there; I could perhaps buy some gardens there and a few plantations and try to live there like that. Because the climates of Harar and Abyssinia are excellent, better than those of Europe since hard winters never come and life costs nothing. There's good food and delicious air; whereas a stay along the coast of the Red Sea upsets even the hardiest of people, and one year there ages them like four years elsewhere.

My life here is a real nightmare. Don't think I have it easy. Far from it: I have long been aware that it is impossible to live worse than I do. If work can get started again here in short order, if things can get back up to speed, I won't eat up my sad savings running around. In this case I would remain as long as I could in this unbearable pit, Aden, as sole proprietorships here are too dangerous in Africa.

Sorry for going on about my worries. But I see that I will be turning thirty (half a life!) and I am very tired of running around the world with little to show for it.

Good that you don't have to deal with these sorts of bad dreams. It does me good to bring your tranquil existence to mind, your untroubled endeavors. May they remain so!

As for me: I am condemned to live a great deal longer still, perhaps forever, in these parts, where I am now known and where I will always find work, whereas in France I will be a stranger and won't find a thing. So hope for the best.

Prosperous hellos
Arthur Rimbaud
General delivery
Aden-Camp
Arabia

TO HIS FAMILY
Aden, May 29, 1884

My dear friends,

I still don't know if work will start up again. They cabled me to stay put, but I am beginning to find this is taking too long. I haven't had any work here for six weeks; and because of the heat we've had here, it's absolutely intolerable. But still, it is clear that I did not come here to be happy. And yet I can't leave these parts, since now I'm known here and can find a way to get by—whereas elsewhere I would only find ways of starving.

If work starts up again here, I will probably re-up for a few years, two or three, until July of '86 or '87. I will be 32 or 33 by then. I will be starting to grow old. Perhaps then will be the time to pack up the twenty thousand francs or so I will have managed to save here, and to go marry back home, where I will be looked at as an old man, and there will only be widows left to take my hand!

May a day only come when I will be released from slavery and have sufficient income not to work any more than I should like!

But who knows what will happen tomorrow or the day after that!

Is there anything left of the 3,600 I sent you last year? If there is, let me know.

I never received your last crate of books. How could it have gotten lost?

I would send you the money I have; but if work doesn't start up again soon, I will be forced to organize some business of my own and will then need my resources, which could disappear quickly. Such is the way of the world, most of all here.

Do I still have to do my military service, after age 30, and if I return to France will I still have to serve the time I haven't? According to the law, it seems to me that in the instance of a voluntary absence, one's service is put on *hold,* and still remains to be served should one return.

I wish you good health and prosperity.

Rimbaud.
Maison Bardey, Aden.

TO HIS FAMILY
Aden, June 16, 1884

Dear friends,

    I remain in good health, and I expect to start work again soon.
Yours,

Rimbaud.
Maison Bardey, Aden

—Don't write "Mazeran and Viannay" on the address anymore, as it's
care of Bardey for the time being.

TO HIS FAMILY
Aden, June 19, 1884

Dear friends,

This just to let you know that I have been rehired for another 6 months in Aden, from July 1 to December 31, 1884, under the same terms. Business will return, and, for the moment, I remain at the same Aden address.

As for the box of books that didn't come last year, it must still be at the office of the Messageries in Marseille, from which, of course, it would not have been sent to me without a correspondent there to arrange a bill of lading and to pay the freight. So if it turns out that it was sent to the Messageries office, claim it and try to have it re-sent, in separate bundles, by mail. I don't understand how it could have been lost.

Yours,

Rimbaud.

TO HIS FAMILY
Aden, July 10, 1884

My dear friends,

I started my new job ten days ago, which I'll have through the end of December 1884.

I am thankful for your offers. But, as I have found work and I seem to be able to bear it, it would be better that I stick with it and gather a few pennies.

I would have liked to have sent you ten thousand francs; but, as our business is doing next to nothing right now, there is the chance that I might have to leave the job suddenly and would find myself in need of money. As it is at least safe for the time being, I will wait a few more months.

I wish you a good harvest and a cooler summer than we've got here (45° indoors).

Rimbaud.
Maison Bardey, Aden.

---

ten thousand francs: Berrichon says forty thousand.

TO HIS FAMILY
Aden, July 31, 1884

My dear friends,

So a month has passed with me at the new job; and I hope I have another five as good. I even hope to have my contract extended.

The summer will be over in two months, which is to say the end of September. Winter here runs six months, from October to the end of March; they call winter the season where the thermometer sometimes reaches 25° (above zero). Winter is therefore as warm as your summer. It nearly never rains during the course of this so-called winter.

Whereas summer is always 40°. It's very enervating and debilitating. Also, I am taking every opportunity to find employment elsewhere.

I wish you a good harvest, and hope that cholera remains far from you.
Yours,

Rimbaud.

TO HIS FAMILY
Aden, September 10, 1884

My dear friends,

It has been a long time since I have had word from you. Nonetheless I must assume that all is well, and wish you good harvests and a leisurely autumn. I expect you are in good health and living tranquilly, as usual.

So a third of my six-month contract is soon to have passed. Business is bad; and I think that, end of December, I will have to look for another job, which I will find easily, I hope. I haven't sent you my money because I don't know where I'll be; I don't know where I'll be next, nor whether I'll need to use these funds for some sort of lucrative trade.

In case I were to have to leave Aden, I would go to Bombay, where I would be able to put the money I have at high interest in secure banks, which would allow me for the most part to live off the dividends: 24,000 rupees at 6% makes 1,440 rupees per year, or 8 francs per day. And I could live on that while waiting for work.

Anyone here who isn't a talented merchant, who isn't well-funded or able to dispose of reasonable credit, is at greater risk of losing what he has than seeing it grow; because you're surrounded by a thousand perils, and life, if one wishes to live somewhat comfortably, costs more than you earn. Because the employees, in the East, are as poorly paid as in Europe; and their fate is more precarious because of fatal climates and the ener-vating existence one leads.

Myself, I'm pretty much able to manage no matter the climate, cold or hot, wet or dry, and I am not at risk of catching fevers or other maladies relating to acclimation, but I think that I am aging myself terribly, quickly, with these stupid jobs and savages or idiots for companions.

So, like me, think of the moment when I will be able to earn my living here, and how each man is a slave to this miserable fatalism, as much in Aden as anywhere else; better the same in Aden than elsewhere, where I am unknown, where I have been completely forgotten, and where I would be forced to start over! As long as I make my daily bread here, shouldn't I stay? Shouldn't I stay, as long as I don't have what it would take to leave easily? But it is more likely that I will never have what it takes, and I will neither live nor die at ease. So, as the Muslims say: So it is written! That's life: and there's nothing funny about it.

Summer ends with September; and from then on, it will be no worse than 25 to 30° centigrade during the day, and 20 to 25° at night. That's what we call winter in Aden.

The entire coastline of this dirty Red Sea is equally tortured by heat. There is a French warship at Obock, where, of the 70 men who make up the crew, 65 are sick with tropical fevers; and the commander died yesterday. And Obock, which is four hours from here by steamboat, is cooler than it is in Aden, where it is very clean but still enervating because of the excess of heat.

Yours,

Rimbaud.

So it is written!: the Arabic *mektoub.*

TO HIS FAMILY
Aden, October 2, 1884

Dear friends,

It has been some time since I have had news from you.

As for me, my business is the same. I am neither better nor worse than before or since; and I have nothing interesting to tell you this time.

I wish you only good health and prosperity.

Yours,

Rimbaud.
Maison Bardey, Aden.

TO HIS FAMILY
Aden, October 7, 1884

My dear friends,

I received your letter of September 23; your news saddened me; what you reported of Frédéric is very annoying and could make others think ill of us. It bothers me enough, for example, that people would think I have such an oddball for a brother. Not that his behavior surprises me: he is a total idiot, and we've always known it, and we have always marveled at his thick skull.

You didn't need to tell me not to write to him. As for giving him a handout, what I earn is done so with such difficulty that the idea of giving it as a gift to a Bedouin like him who is better-rested than I is highly unlikely. Nonetheless, I hope for all of our sakes that he puts an end to this silliness.

As for him running his mouth about me, my actions are well established here as elsewhere. I can send you the attestation of exceptional satisfaction that the bankrupt Mazeran Company gave me after my four years of service, from 1880 to '84, and I can tell you I have a very good reputation here, which allows me to earn my keep rather easily. If I have known moments of adversity in the past, I have never sought to live off of others, nor to make my living dishonestly.

It is now winter here: the temperature averages 25° above zero. All is well. My contract, which concludes at the end of December, will, I hope, be renewed to my advantage. I will always prove able to make an honest wage here.

Very nearby, there is a very sad little French colony called Obock, where they are trying to make a go of it; but I think that nothing will come of it. It's little more than an empty beach; burned, barren, untouched by commerce, the only utility of which is as a place to deposit coal for warships destined for China and Madagascar.

The Somali coast and Harar are in the midst of passing from the hands of the poor Egyptians to those of the English, who nonetheless haven't sufficient forces here to maintain all of these colonies. The English occupation is ruining the coastal trade routes, from Suez to Garafui. England's hands are dirty with Egypt's business and it is likely that it will all end badly.

Yours,

Rimbaud.

TO HIS FAMILY
Mazeran, Viannay and Bardey,
Telegraphic address:
MAVIBA-MARSEILLE
Aden, December 30, 1884

My dear friends,

I received your letter of December 12, and I thank you with wishes for prosperity and good health, which I also wish you for all the days of the coming year.

As you say, my vocation will never be concerned with plowing, and I have no objection to see my land rented out: for your sakes I hope that you see it rented soon and at a good price. Keeping the house remains a good idea. The idea of me coming to visit you sounds very appealing: I would be very happy, in essence, to rest a bit; but I can't begin to see when that might be. For some time, I have been able to make my living here: if I leave, what will I find in return? How could I busy myself in an area where no one knows me, where I wouldn't be able to find the least opportunity to earn anything? As you say, I could only go there to rest; and to rest one needs income; to marry, one needs income; and that sort of income I don't have. For the foreseeable future, I am therefore condemned to follow the trails where I know how to live, until the time when I manage to scrape together, through force of fatigue alone, the means by which I may briefly rest.

Right now I have thirteen thousand francs. What would you have me do with this in France? What marriage would you have me buy? Poor, honest women are available the world over. Were I to marry back home I would still have to travel to make my living.

So I've spent thirty years finding no end of difficulty and I don't see its clear end in sight, far from it, or even how it could likely improve.

Of course, if you have any ideas, let me know.

---

thirteen thousand francs: Berrichon says 43,000. The precise sum has been debated endlessly by scholars to no definitive conclusion.

Business is terrible here right now. I don't know if they are going to keep me on past my current contract, or under what conditions they might keep me. I have been here four and a half years; I don't want to be demoted, and yet business is terrible.

Summer will be back in three or four months, and life here will once again be miserable.

It's the English, and their ridiculous politics, that are ruining trade throughout the area. They want to change everything, and they are managing to do a worse job than the Egyptians and Turks they ruined. Their Gordon is an idiot, their Wolseley an ass, and all their business an endless stream of stupidity and illegality. As for news from the Sudan, we know nothing more than you have heard in France, no one arrives here from Africa anymore, everything is disorganized, and the English administration in Aden is only interested in disseminating lies: it is very likely that the expedition from Sudan will not succeed.

France isn't without its own dumb moves in the area: a month ago, we occupied the whole Tadjoura bay, in order also to occupy the ends of the roads from Harar and Abyssinia. But these coasts are completely desolate, and the money they spent on the campaign a total waste unless we soon visit the plateaus in Harar's interior, which are beautiful, clean, and full of people.

We also see that Madagascar, which is a good colony, is nowhere near to falling into our hands; and yet we are spending hundreds of millions on Tonkin, which, according to everyone who has been there, is a miserable area impossible to defend against invasion.

I'm certain that no country has a more inept colonial policy than France. —If England makes mistakes and costs us money, at least they have serious interests and important perspectives. But no single power in all the world better knows how to utterly waste its money in perfectly impossible places than France.

Gordon: Charles Gordon (1833–85), the English official whose responsibility, by governmental decree, had been to pacify the equatorial provinces. *Wolseley:* Sir Joseph Garnet, aka Count Wolseley (1833–1913), commander in chief of British forces in Egypt, most responsible for the "success" of their colonial endeavors in the area.

In a week, I will let you know if my contract has been extended or what I have to do.

Yours alone,

Rimbaud.
Aden-Camp.

TO HIS FAMILY
Aden, January 15, 1885

My dear friends,

I received your letter of December 26, 1884. Thank you for all your good wishes. May your winter be short and your year happy!
I am still feeling well in this dirty country.
I was rehired for another year, which is to say until the end of 1885; but it is possible that, this time too, business will be suspended before then. These countries have become terrible, since everything happened with Egypt. Everything remains the same here. I make 300 francs per month net, not including my other expenses, which are covered and come to another 300 francs per month. This job earns around 7,000 francs per year, of which I keep 3,500 to 4,000. Don't think of me as a capitalist: all my capital amounts to about 13,000 francs right now and should be around 17,000 francs by the end of the year. I will have worked five years to earn that amount. But what would I be doing elsewhere? Better that I wait here, where at least I can live some sort of life while working; because what are my options elsewhere? But it's the same, the years pass, and I save nothing, and I never manage to reach the point where I can live off my income.
My work consists of buying coffee. I buy around two hundred thousand francs' worth per month. In 1883, I bought more than 3 million during the year and my profit from that was nothing more than my miserable salary, three or four thousand francs per year: you see that work is poorly paid everywhere. It is true that the old firm was nine hundred thousand francs in debt, but that had nothing to do with its Aden business, which, while not profitable, wasn't losing anything either. I buy many other things: rubber, incense, ostrich feathers, ivory, dried leathers, cloves, etc., etc.
I am not sending you my photographs; I am trying to limit my nonessential expenditures. And anyway I am poorly dressed; the only thing one can wear here is very light cotton garments; people who have spent a few years here can no longer bear the winters in Europe. They

end up collapsing of pleuropneumonia. If I come back, it will only be in summer; and I will have to go south again, at least in winter, to the Mediterranean. In any case, I wouldn't count on my becoming any less of a vagabond; on the contrary, had I the means of traveling without having to work and earn my way, I would never be in one place more than two months. The world is very big and full of magnificent lands that a thousand lifetimes wouldn't allow one to visit. But, in another way, I wouldn't want to bum around in poverty; I would like to have a few thousand francs in profits which I could spend each year in two or three different lands, living modestly and trading here and there to cover my expenses. But to live in the same place all the time, I find that miserable. So, what is most likely is that I'll end up going where I don't want to go, and that I'll end up doing what I don't want to do, without hope of any other sort of life.

As for the Korans, I got them long ago, a year ago, in Harar. As for the other books, someone must have sold them. I had wanted to have you send me a few books, but I've already lost money at that. But I haven't any sort of distraction here, where there are no newspapers or libraries, and where we live like savages.

But if you would, nonetheless, write to the Hachette bookstore, I think, and ask which is the most recent edition of the *Dictionary of Navigation and Trade*, from Guillaumin. —If there is a recent edition, after 1880, you can send it to me; there are two fat volumes, it costs a hundred francs, but you can get it at a discount at Sauron. But if there are only old editions I don't want them. —Wait for my next letter on that.

Yours,

Rimbaud.

TO HIS FAMILY
Aden, April 14, 1885

My dear friends,

I received your letter of March 17 and see that your affairs are going exceptionally well.

If you're going to complain about the cold, then I'm going to complain about the heat, which just started up again here. It is already stifling, and it will so be through the end of September. I have a gastric fever, I can't digest a thing, my stomach has become weak here and makes me feel awful all summer; I don't know how I'll manage to get through this summer here, and strongly worry that I will have to leave this place; my health is run down: one year here is like five elsewhere. In Africa, however (in Harar, and in Abyssinia), the weather is excellent, and I am much happier there than I am in Europe. But since the English got to the coast, trade along all these coasts has been destroyed.

My salary is still the same, and I *don't spend a penny.* At the end of the year, I will have every one of the 3,600 francs I earn, or nearly, since in four years and four months, I still have 14,500 of what I earned. To my great disappointment, I sold the camera, but not at a loss. When I was telling you that my job earned 6,000 francs, I was including living expenses that they pay on my behalf. Because everything is very expensive here. I only drink water, and it costs me *fifteen francs* per month! I never smoke, I wear cotton clothing, and my various personal hygiene products run me no more than 50 francs a year. One lives terribly here, and it doesn't come cheap. We sleep outside every night of the year, and nonetheless pay 40 francs a month rent on a house! And so it goes. The life one leads here is the worst in the world, and there is no question that I won't be here next year. Not for anything in this world would you want to be living the life I am here: I came here thinking I would gain something, but a franc anywhere else requires five here.

There are no newspapers, no libraries, and the only Europeans are the few trading employees foolish enough to find themselves here and who consume their salaries at the billiards table before leaving and cursing the place as they do.

Just a few years ago business was good. The main product is a coffee called Mokha; all of the Mokha comes from here because Mokha has been deserted. There are a raft of other things, dried leathers, ivory, feathers, rubber, incense, etc., etc., etc., and imports are also varied. All we do here is coffee, and I am in charge of purchasing and expeditions. I bought 800 thousand francs over the last six months, but Mokhas are dead in France; it falls in value day by day, and profits barely cover shipping charges, which are always steep.

Doing business has grown very difficult here, and I am living as frugally as possible in order to leave here with something. Every day I'm busy from 7 to 5 and don't even get a day off. When will this life end?

Who knows? Perhaps we'll be attacked soon. The English are putting all of Europe on their back.

War has begun in Afghanistan, and the English will end up having to give it to Russia on a provisional basis; and Russia, a few years later, will be responsible for them.

In Sudan, the expedition to Khartoum retreated in defeat; and, as I know those parts, it must have mostly collapsed. In Souakim, I think that the English aren't advancing for the time being, until they learn how things have gone in India. Anyway, these deserts are uncrossable from May to September by marching armies.

In Obock, the little French administration is preoccupied with the throwing of banquets and drinking of government money, which won't end up netting a penny from that horrible colony, colonized by nothing more than a dozen freeloaders.

The Italians have gotten into trouble in Massaouah, though no one knows how. They will likely have to evacuate, given England can't really do anything to help them.

In Aden, expecting war, all of the fortifications are being rebuilt. It would make me happy to see this place reduced to dust—but not while I'm here.

Anyway, I hope very little of my remaining existence will have to be devoted to spending time in this filthy place.

Yours,
Rimbaud.

TO ERNEST DELAHAYE
Aden, 3/17 1885

Dear Delahuppe,

Attached, you'll find my portrait and that of my employer after our naturalization.

A handshake in thought.

Your

A. Rimbaud.

TO HIS FAMILY
Aden, May 26, 1885

Dear friends,

I am as well as ever, and wish you far better.

Vernal ovens beckon; skins stream, stomachs sour, heads cloud, business is horrible, news is bad.

Whatever may have been said recently, we are very worried that the Anglo-Russian war will soon be declared. Elsewhere, the English are arming themselves in India, and in Europe they are trying to make up with the Turks.

The war in Sudan ended shamefully for the English. They abandoned everything to focus their efforts on Egypt alone: there will probably soon be stories arising from the matter of the Canal.

Poor France is in a situation as ridiculous as Tonkin, where it is very likely that, despite promises of peace, the Chinese will cast the remaining troops into the sea. And the war in Madagascar seems also to have been abandoned.

I have a new contract here through the end of 1885. It is very possible that I will not see it through: business here has become so petty that it would be better simply to abandon it. I've saved 15,000 francs as of now; in Bombay, I can get 6% from any bank and yield 900 francs a year, on which I can live while looking for decent work. But we'll see about all that around the end of the year.

Awaiting your news.

Rimbaud.
Maison Bardey, Aden.

TO MONSIEUR FRANZOJ
[undated]

Dear Monsieur Franzoj,

Forgive me, but I have sent home that woman for good.
I will give her a few thalers and she can leave for Obock by the dhow
at Rasali where she can go where she wishes.
I have seen quite enough of this masquerade.
I would not have been so stupid as to bring her to Choa, I will not be
so stupid as to feel responsible for returning her there.
Yours,

Rimbaud.

Franzoj: Augusto Franzoj (1849–1911), Italian journalist and merchant. *I have sent home that woman for good:* The woman in question, according to various sources, lived with Rimbaud for at least eighteen months. The precise nature of their relationship is uncertain, but it has been inferred, not unwisely, that their involvement was romantic.

TO HIS FAMILY
Aden, September 28, 1885

My dear friends,

I received your letter of the end of August.

I didn't write because I wasn't sure whether I would still be here. This will be decided by the end of the month, as you will see yourselves according to the contract I've attached, three months before the expiration of which I must alert them. I am sending you this contract in the event you were to have to present it in reference to my military situation. If I remain here, my new contract will begin October 1. I would extend it at most another six months, but by next summer, I won't be here anymore, I hope. Summer ends around the 15th of October. You have no idea what it's like here. Not a single tree, even a desiccated one, nor blade of grass, nor fertile ground, nor drop of fresh water. Aden is an extinct volcanic crater filled to the brim with sand from the sea. One sees and touches nothing here but lava and sand, neither of which will allow the paltriest vegetable to grow. The surrounding area is desert that is invariably dry. But here the crater's walls won't allow any air to enter the city, and we roast inside this hole as if inside a lime kiln. The only reason you would work in a hell like this is because you need the money! There's no one to speak to here beyond the Bedouins, and so you become a total idiot in the span of a few years. So I just have to manage to save a sum here that, used elsewhere, would give me guaranteed interest that would be approximately what I need to live.

Unfortunately, that exchange rate for rupees into francs in Bombay goes down every day; *silver* is depreciating everywhere; what little capital I have (16,000 francs) loses its value, since it's in rupees; all of this is abominable: horrible countries and deplorable business are poisoning existence.

The rupee had been worth 2 francs 10 centimes in trade; now it's worth 1.90! This in three months. If monetary conventions stabilize, the rupee might climb back up to 2 francs. Right now I have 8,000 rupees. In

India, this amount will yield 480 rupees per year at 6%, on which I could live.

India is more pleasant than Arabia. I could also go to Tonkin; there must be jobs there now. And if there were nothing there, I could go as far as the Panama canal, which is still far from being completed.

I would like to send this sum to France, but to do so would bring so little; if I buy 4%, I lose two years' interest; and 3% isn't worth the trouble. Anyway, the actual exchange from rupees will have to wait; for now, as I can only get 1.90 from France, a 10% loss after five years of work sounds great!

If I sign a new contract, I will send it to you. Send back this one when you no longer need it.

Yours,

Rimbaud

TO HIS FAMILY
Aden, October 22, 1885

Dear friends,

When you receive this, I will probably be in Tadjoura, on the Danakil coast annexed by the Obock colony.

I quit my job in Aden, after an angry discussion with the vile oafs who were endlessly trying to turn me into an idiot. I did many things for these people; and they thought that I, to make them happy, was going to spend the rest of my life with them. They did everything they could to keep me there; but I told them to go to hell, with their benefits, and their trade, and their awful firm, and their dirty city! Without even going into how much boredom they brought me or how they tried to make me lose something. So to hell with them! They nonetheless gave me excellent letters of recommendation for the five years I was with them.

A few thousand guns are on their way to me here from Europe. I am putting together a caravan and bringing these wares to Ménélik, the king of Choa.

The road to Choa is a long one: two months march to Ankober, the capital and the country that has to be crossed after that is nothing but horrible deserts. But up above, in Abyssinia, the climate is wonderful, the population is hospitable and Christian, and the cost of living is next to nothing. There are only a few Europeans here, a dozen or so, and they are involved with the sale of arms, which the king buys at a good price. If all goes well, I expect to arrive there, get paid right away, and leave with a profit of 25 to 30 thousand francs in less than a year.

Once the deal is successful, you will see me back in France, toward autumn of 1886, where I will purchase new merchandise. I hope that all of this will work out well. Hope the same for me: I need it to work.

If I could, after three or four years, add a hundred thousand francs to what I already have, I would happily leave this unfortunate place.

I sent you my contract, in the last mail, with which to plead before the military authority. I hope that will settle everything. With all that, I never mentioned precisely what sort of service I am due to serve; meaning if I had to go before a consul here for some sort of visa, I would be incapable of filling in the blanks in my situation, as even I don't know what they are! It's ridiculous!

Don't write me at the Bardey address anymore; these animals are cutting off my mail. For the next three months, or at least two and a half, after the date on this letter, which is to say just until the end of 1885 (including the fifteen days from Marseille here), you can write me at the following address:

> Monsieur Arthur Rimbaud
> In Tadjoura
> French Colony of Obock

Happy new year, good health, rest, prosperity.
Yours,

Rimbaud.

TO HIS FAMILY
Aden, November 18, 1885

My dear friends,

I did receive your last letter dated October 22.

I told you already that I am leaving Aden for the kingdom of Choa. My plans have been held back unexpectedly; I think that I can't leave Aden until the end of this month. I hope you haven't already written me in Tadjoura. I have changed my mind about this: only write me at the following address: Monsieur Arthur Rimbaud, Hôtel de l'Univers, Aden. They will forward my mail from there, and it will be easier, as I believe that the Obock/Tadjoura postal service isn't very well organized.

I am happy to be leaving the horrible pit that is Aden, where I have been suffering for so long. It is also true that the route I have planned is awful: from here to Choa (which is to say from Tadjoura to Choa) is fifty days' march on horseback, through burning deserts. But in Abyssinia the climate is wonderful, it is neither hot nor cold, the population is Christian and hospitable; life is easy there, it is a place of pleasant relaxation for those who have been beaten into stupidity by many years on the white hot shores of the Red Sea.

Now that this initiative has begun, I can't turn back. I am not fooling myself about how dangerous this is, nor am I blind to the exhausting nature of these expeditions; but, given my time in Harar, I already know the manners and customs of these parts. However it should turn out, I do hope that the trip is a success. I expect that my caravan should reach Tadjoura around the 15th of January, 1886; and then arrive in Choa around March 15—Easter for the Abyssinians.

If the king pays me quickly, I will leave for the coast directly with around 25,000 francs profit.

Then I will return to France to buy merchandise—if it seems that business will be good. You could expect to see me toward the end of the summer of 1886. I strongly hope that things turn out this way: wish the same for me.

Now: you must track something down for me that I need, and which I would never find here.

Write to the Director of the Oriental Languages bookstore in Paris: "Monsieur,

I would ask that you send me C.O.D. at the address below the *Dictionary of the Amhara Language* (with a guide to pronunciation in Roman letters) by M. d'Abbadie, from the Institute.

With the greatest thanks,

Rimbaud, Roche, Attigny township, the Ardennes."

Pay whatever it costs, twenty francs or so, more or less. I need this book to learn the language of the country where I am going, as no one knows any European languages, given there are nearly no Europeans there, for now.

Send the aforementioned work to the following address:

M. Arthur Rimbaud, Hôtel de l'Univers, Aden.

Buy this for me as soon as you can, as I need to study this language before heading off. From Aden, they will forward everything to Tadjoura, where I will be spending a month or two gathering camels, mules, guides, etc., etc.,

I don't expect to set out until January 15, 1886.

Do whatever you must regarding the matter of military service. I want everything to be in order when I return to France next year.

I will write you several times before I leave.

So, au revoir, and yours alone,

Rimbaud.

Dictionary of the Amhara Language: spoken in Abyssinia. Rimbaud will refer to this book repeatedly in the following letters, alternately calling it the "Amhara Dictionary" and the "Amarinna Dictionary."

The people from the city are leaving, the Gallas are no longer growing. In just a few months, the Abyssinians have devoured the provisions of dourah left by the Egyptians and which could have lasted for several years. Famine and plague are imminent.

AUGUST 1887

IX

TADJOURA

1885–1886

Self-portrait, Rimbaud, c. 1883.

TO HIS FAMILY
Tadjoura, December 3, 1885

My dear friends,

Right now I am in the midst of forming my caravan for Choa. It is coming along slowly, as expected, but I expect to be out of here by the end of January 1886.

I am well. —Send me the dictionary I asked for, to the address I gave you. To the same address all communications with me should go. Everything will be forwarded.

For a year, Tadjoura has been under annexation by the French colony of Obock. It is a little Danakil village with a few mosques and a few palm trees. There is an old fort the Egyptians built where six French soldiers are now sleeping under the orders of a sergeant who is commander of the post. The country was left its little sultan and his local administration. It is a protectorate. The main trade of the area is the trafficking of slaves.

European caravans bound for Choa leave from here, practically empty, and one makes the trip with considerable difficulty, the locals of all these coasts having become enemies of all Europeans since the English Admiral Hewett made Emperor Jean du Tigré sign a treaty abolishing the slave trade, the only local commerce that was flourishing. Nonetheless, under the French protectorate no one is attempting to disturb the treaty, and things are going better.

Do not think that I have become a slave trader. We are importing guns (old hammer-fire guns that have been reconditioned and which would sell for 7 or 8 francs each in France) to the King of Choa, Ménélik II, who pays around forty francs apiece. But there are enormous costs in getting them here, without even beginning to speak of the dangers one can encounter on the route here and back; it's the Danakils one encounters, Muslim fanatic Bedouin shepherds—they're the ones to fear. It is true that we are armed, and that the Bedouins only have lances: but all the caravans are attacked.

Once the Haawache river is crossed, you're in the domain of the powerful king Ménélik, and there one finds Christian farmers; the country is at a higher elevation, 3,000 meters above sea level; the climate is wonderful, the cost of living next to nothing; everything that grows in Europe grows there; and the population is welcoming. It rains six months of the year, as in Harar, which is one of the foothills of this great Ethiopian massif.

I wish you good health and prosperity for the year 1886.

Yours,

A. Rimbaud
Hôtel de l'Univers
Aden

TO HIS FAMILY
Tadjoura, December 10, 1885

My dear friends,

I find myself delayed here until the end of January 1886; I'll even probably have to spend half the month of February here too.

I'll remind you about the *Amhara Dictionary* by M. d'Abbadie, which you must have already ordered. I absolutely need it if I am to study the language. Thinking about it, my only worry is that the weight of this volume not exceed the maximum weight for parcels. If it does, send it to:

MM. Ulysse Pila and Co., Marseille

With a letter begging these gentlemen to have the parcel sent by the Messageries Maritimes to:

MM. Bardey, merchants, Aden.

These men, with whom I got back in with before leaving, will get the package to me in Tadjoura. In the letter, ask MM. Ulysse Pila and Co. to tell you the freight and the charges they pay in Marseille for the forwarding of the aforesaid parcel to Aden, and you will reimburse them by mail.

Do not delay the expedition of this parcel as you did on the earlier occasion with the case of books. If you sent it by the post office it will reach me; if it was too heavy for the post office, I suppose that you wouldn't have sent it by rail to Marseille without a ship-to address. Someone has to be there to send the merchandise from Marseille and to pay the freight on the Messageries Maritimes steamship, or else it becomes an unclaimed parcel.

I hope, however, that you were able to send it by the post office. In the opposite case, I have told you what to do. I do not want to leave here at the end of January without this book, because without it I cannot study the language.

It is winter here, which is to say it isn't above 30°; and summer starts in again in three months.

MM. Ulysse Pila and Co., Marseille: which bailed out Bardey.

I won't repeat what of my business I've already explained to you in my recent letters. The way I've planned things, I expect, in any case, to lose nothing; and of course I hope to gain something, and as I told you, I expect to see you in France next autumn, before the winter of 1886–7, in good health and prosperity.

Yours,

Rimbaud.

—The mail in the French colony of Obock is as yet disorganized, so do not send the letters here, continue to send them to Aden at the above address.

TO HIS FAMILY
Tadjoura, January 2, 1886

Dear friends,

I received your letter of December 2.

I am still in Tadjoura and certainly will be for a few more months; everything is proceeding very slowly, but I hope that it will all work out anyway. A superhuman patience is required in these parts.

I have not received the letter you say you sent me in Tadjoura, via Obock. The mail service is still very disorganized in this filthy colony.

I am still waiting for the book I requested. I wish you a happy new year, free of the worries that torment me.

My departure is already quite a bit delayed; so much so that I now doubt that I will be able to come to France this autumn, and it would be dangerous for me to arrive in the middle of winter.

Yours,

Rimbaud.

TO HIS FAMILY
Tadjoura, January 6, 1886

Dear friends,

Today I received your letter of December 12, 1885.

Write me as you normally do: they will always forward my correspondence, no matter where I am. Everything else goes badly: it seems that the route through the interior has become impractical. It is true that I am putting myself in harm's way and, above all, exposing myself to indescribable inconveniences. This is all about earning ten thousand francs in the space of less than a year, which would ordinarily take me three. Moreover, I have left myself the means of accessing my capital whenever I need to; and if these ordeals exceed my ability to endure them, I will pay myself back and return to Aden to look for a job there or somewhere else. In Aden, I will always find something to do.

Anyone prone to saying how difficult life is should come and spend some time here to really know what they're talking about.

In Tadjoura, there is only one post: six soldiers and a French sergeant. They are relieved every three months, sent on leave to recuperate in France. There isn't a person posted here who spends three months without being overrun by fever. But fever season isn't for a month or two, and I expect to get through it.

So, man can expect to spend three quarters of his life suffering so that he may rest for the final quarter; and, most often, he dies of misery before getting there.

You embarrass me while embarrassing yourselves. This book is taking forever! This is the right one:

"D'Abbadie, *Amarinna Dictionary,* in one vol."

Send it, without any further delay, to my regular address: Hôtel de l'Univers, Aden, if the post office will take it; and should they not, if it has to be sent by rail, send it, as I explained, to:

MM. Ulysse Pila and Co., Marseille
For
MM. Bardey Brothers, Aden.

They will forward it to Tadjoura.

I can't find a stamp in this horrible country; I am sending you this unstamped, with apologies.

Rimbaud

TO HIS FAMILY
Tadjoura, January 31, 1886

Dear friends,

I have received nothing from you since the letter in which you sent me the title of the book I requested, asking me if that was the one. I responded in the affirmative, in the earliest days of January, and I repeat, in case this did not reach you:

"*Amarinna Dictionary,* by d'Abbadie"

But I suppose that the work is already en route, and it will reach me, because, at the speed at which things work, I see that I will still be here until the end of March. My merchandise has arrived; but the camels for my caravan have yet to be found, and I will have to wait a while still, perhaps until May, before leaving the coast.

Then the trip will last two months, arriving in Choa either by the end of June or thereabouts; even with everything going well, I wouldn't be back in Aden before the very end of 1886 or the beginning of '87; so that, if I go to Europe, it wouldn't be until spring of '87. The least initiative in Africa is subject to senseless setbacks and requires extraordinary patience.

Yours,

Rimbaud.

TO HIS FAMILY
Tadjoura, February 28, 1886

My dear friends,

This time, nearly two months have passed without word from you.

I am still here, with the idea that I will remain here another three months. It's very unpleasant; but this will all nonetheless end by ending, and I will hit the road to arrive, I hope, without a hitch.

All my merchandise is here, and I am awaiting the departure of a large caravan to join mine.

I worry that you did not attend to the particulars required concerning the mailing of the *Amhara Dictionary:* nothing has arrived yet. But maybe it's in Aden; because the first time I wrote you regarding this book was six months ago, and you see how adept you have been at making sure that I receive the things I need: six months for a book!

In a month, or six weeks, summer will begin again along the cursed coasts. I hope not to spend a large part of it here and instead, in a few months, refuge myself among the mountains of Abyssinia, the Switzerland of Africa, an area without winter or summer: spring and perpetual green, and life without cost or care!

I still expect to come back at the end of 1886, beginning 1887.
Yours,

Rimbaud.

TO HIS FAMILY
Tadjoura, March 8, 1886

Dear friends,

I am still waiting for the aforementioned volume. I find that my delay
grows worse. I am not leaving here before *May.*
Continue to write me at the address below.
And two months without word from you.

Arthur Rimbaud.
Hôtel de l'Univers, Aden

TO THE MINISTER OF FOREIGN AFFAIRS, PARIS
April 15, 1886

Monsieur le Ministre,

We are French merchants who have been in the court of King Méné-lik, in Choa, for the past ten years.

In August of 1885, the king of Choa, Ras Govana, and many of our contacts in Abyssinia placed an order with us for arms and ammunition, tools, and various merchandise; they advanced us monies, and, moreover, gathering together most of our capital available to us in Choa, we went down to the coast of Obock. There, having requested and obtained authorization to debark to Tadjoura from the honorable governor of Obock and to send the exact number of arms and ammunition we wished to buy via caravan, having also obtained from the governor of Aden, with the intervention of M. le Consul of France, the authorization to transport the aforementioned arms to Aden destined for Tadjoura, we ended up making our purchases in France with the help of our affiliates, one of us remaining in Aden for the shipment, the other in Tadjoura to prepare the caravan under the wing of the French presence there.

Toward the end of January 1886, our merchandise, having been shipped to Aden, was unloaded in Tadjoura as we were assembling our caravan, with the sort of difficulty one expects in Tadjoura. So our departure was to have taken place toward the end of April.

On April 12, the honorable governor of Obock came to tell us that a dispatch from the Government ordered an immediate halt to the importation of arms to Choa! Orders were given to the sultan of Tadjoura to stop the formation of our caravan! As such, with our merchandise on hold, our capital spent on the costs of the caravan, our personnel living indefinitely at our expense, and our supplies deteriorating, we were left waiting in Tadjoura for further explanation of the motives and consequences of this utterly arbitrary measure. All the while, we have remained in complete compliance with all regulations, as the colonial

---

Ras Govana: one of Ménélik's allies, a governor from the Wallaga province.

authorities can corroborate. We hadn't brought arms except those requested by the Choa government, and, having received the necessary authorization, we began the process of speeding them to their destination as quickly as possible; we can prove that we never sold, gave, or even entrusted a single weapon to the locals at any time or place. Our arms must be delivered to Ménélik in their export packaging, and we never lost sight of them for an instant, either on the coast or in the interior.

Whatever decisions the ministry may undertake in the future, we ask to establish in advance that it would be absolutely impossible for us to legally or normally liquidate our order: 1) because these weapons and ammunition have been ordered by the Choa government, and 2) because it is impossible for us to recoup the expenses lost.

The only place these arms would be able to recoup their value *is Tadjoura*. Those who are aware of these operations know that the moment the arms arrive at the coast, triple their original cost is spent on unloading, on the supplies and salaries of an entire population of Abyssinian servants and camel drivers assembled for the caravan, on the not inconsiderable bribes and gifts destined for notables, on the extortions by Bedouins in neighboring territories, on lost advances, on payment of rent on the camels, on surveying rights and taxes on movement, on the cost of housing and food for the Europeans, on the purchase and the upkeep of a mass of equipment, on meals, and lastly on pack animals for a route that lasts fifty days in one of the driest of deserts! As a caravan comes together in Tadjoura, the local population lives off of it for the three, six, and even ten months that one inevitably finds oneself held up in hell.

We would also have to list—on the first line of our accounting—the years lost in Choa waiting for these orders, the cost of going down to the coast, and the salaries of those people hired in Choa who have worked for us for years on the prospect of this operation. We have invested everything in this one undertaking, all our equipment and personnel, all our time and our very existence.

It should be understood that no one undertakes such a slow, dangerous and painstaking task but in the pursuit of large profits. The prices these arms bring in Choa, where they are as scarce as they are here, are in effect extraordinarily high, and all the higher given the king's payment is made in merchandise at its cost in Choa and which when sold in Aden yields a profit of 50 percent. This explains why French traders work in Choa with funds borrowed at 50, 75, and 100 percent annual interest.

It is therefore the absolute value of the arms in Choa by which we must now evaluate the stock of our Tadjoura caravan, given the expenses incurred and the labor exerted, and therefore all that remains is for us to embark, make the delivery, and collect our payment.

In detail, the worth of our operation which the French authority sanctioned and then prohibited from undertaking:

2,040 shotguns with primer, priced in Choa at 15 Marie-Thérèse dollars each, total dollars therefore: 30,600.

60,000 Remington cartridges at 60 dollars per thousand: 3,600.

Return: dollars, 34,200
30,600
3,600
Bid 34,200

Along with the arms and ammunition is an order of tools for the king which would be impossible to send alone. Value in dollars: 5,800

The total worth of the caravan upon delivery is therefore, in dollars, 40,000.

Adding fifty percent upon return, which is to say the profit of the sale in Aden of the merchandise given in payment in Choa by the king, we assert that this operation must result in a sum of 60,000 dollars net within 18 months. 60,000 dollars, at the average Aden exchange rate (4 francs 30), equals 258,000 francs.

We consider the Government to be our debtor, responsible for this sum as long as the current interdiction endures, and if it is maintained, the aforesaid will be the amount of the indemnity that we will demand of the government... And in any case, the fact of the interdiction of the importation of arms destined for Choa will have the singular, immediate, and unambiguous result of radically suppressing the commercial contacts between the Obock colony and the rest of Abyssinia.

Whereas the Assab route, under Italian protection, will remain particularly open to the importation of arms (just as the excellent Zeila route, under English protection, will monopolize the importation of piles of local merchandise), no French trader will dare venture into the Obock-Tadjoura gap, and there will no longer be any reason to continue to support the Tadjoura chiefs and the sinister route that links it with Choa.

We cannot help but reflect upon the following political reasons that might have motivated that measure that disturbs us:

1) It would be absurd to suppose that the Danakils could arm themselves from this traffic. The extraordinary fact—which will not happen again, of a few hundred guns having been stolen during the attack on the Barral caravan, guns now shared by one million Bedouins—does not constitute any danger. Meanwhile, the Danakils, as any population along this coast, have so little taste for firearms that one won't find a scrap of one along the coast;

2) We cannot say if there is a correlation between the importation of arms and the exportation of slaves. This traffic has existed between Abyssinia and the coast since antiquity in unchanging proportions. But our affairs are completely independent of the uncertain trafficking of the Bedouins. No one would dare suggest that a European has ever sold or bought, transported or helped transport a single slave, to the coast or the interior.

Hoping for better of the French we have honorably and courageously represented in these lands,

We beg you accept, Monsieur Minister, our most distinguished salutations.

Labatut and Rimbaud.
Tadjoura, April 15, 1886

TO HIS FAMILY
Aden, May 21, 1886

Dear friends,

In Aden, where I went to spend a few days, I find the book that you sent me.

Without question, I believe I will leave at the end of July.

I am still well. Business goes neither better nor worse.

Send your letters in large envelopes.

Yours,

Rimbaud.

RECEIPT
June 1, 1886

    We the undersigned affirm our debt to Monsieur J. Suel, in the sum of (11,518 rupees, 8 annas) eleven thousand, five hundred eighteen rupees, eight annas, the amount of various sums put in our trust through May 1886.

The above said sum will bear 12 percent interest beginning June 1, 1887.

Aden, June 1, 1886.
Pierre Labatut
A. Rimbaud.

$$11,518.8$$
$$\underline{115.3}$$
$$11,633.11$$

RECEIPT TO A. DESCHAMPS
June 27, 1886

I the undersigned A. Rimbaud will pay M. Deschamps upon the presentation of the present paper the sum of one hundred fifty thalers against the sale of rifles delivered to me.

Good for one hundred fifty thalers.

A. Rimbaud.

Tadjoura
June 27, 1886
Payable in Choa

Paid in Aden 150 thalers.

Pay to the order of M. Audon
Tadjoura, June 27, 1886
A. Deschamps
B. M. Audon

TO HIS FAMILY
Tadjoura, July 9, 1886

My dear friends,

Up until now I have only received your letter of May 28.

I do not understand anything about the postal service here in this cursed colony. I write you regularly.

There have been some unpleasant incidents here, but no massacres on the coast: a caravan was attacked en route, but it was because they were poorly guarded.

My business on the coast has yet to be settled, but I expect that I will be en route in September without fail.

The dictionary has long since arrived.

I am feeling well, as well as one can here, at fifty to fifty-five in the shade.

Yours,

A. Rimbaud
Hôtel de l'Univers,
Aden.

TO HIS FAMILY

Tadjoura, September 15, 1886

My dear friends,

I have heard nothing from you for the longest time.

I am expecting to leave without fail for Choa at the end of September.

I have been held up here for a very long while, because my associate here fell ill and returned to France, where I hear that he is on death's door.

I have power of attorney over all the merchandise; so I must leave no matter what; and I will leave alone, Soleillet (the leader of the other caravan I was supposed to travel with) having died as well.

My expedition will last a year minimum.

I will write you to the last. I am feeling very well.

Good health and good weather.

Address: Arthur Rimbaud,
Hôtel de l'Univers,
Aden.

---

he is on death's door: Labatut had throat cancer. *having died as well:* Labatut wasn't dead yet. Soleillet died of a heart attack on September 9 in Aden.

*I must therefore spend my remaining days wander-
ing, in exhaustion and hardship, with nothing to
look forward to but death and suffering.*

AUGUST 23, 1887

X

CHOA
AND CAIRO

1887

TO HIS FAMILY
Southern Abyssinia
Entotto (Choa), April 7, 1887

My dear friends,

I find myself in good health; my business here will not be complete until the end of the year. If you want to write me, the address is as follows:

Monsieur Arthur Rimbaud,
Hôtel de l'Univers, Aden.

From there, things will reach me as they can. I hope to have returned to Aden by October; but things take a very long time in these dirty countries, so who knows?
Yours,

Rimbaud.

OPPOSITE: *Hôtel de l'univers, c. 1880.*

TO M. DE GASPARY
Aden, July 30, 1887

Monsieur le Consul,

I have the honor of detailing the liquidation of the estate of the late Labatut, an undertaking in which I was involved according to the agreement made with the consulate in May of 1886.

I did not hear about the death of Labatut until the end of 1886, at the moment when—initial costs paid—the caravan began to move and could not be stopped, I could not renegotiate with our creditors.

In Choa, the negotiations surrounding this caravan were made in disastrous conditions: Ménélik seized all the merchandise and forced me to sell it to him at a reduced price, prohibiting me from selling it at retail and threatening me that he would have it all shipped back to the coast at my cost! He gave me the sum of 14,000 thalers for the whole caravan, cutting 2,500 thalers from this lump as payment on the 2nd half of the rent on the camels and other costs of the caravan established by the Azzaze, and another sum of 3,000 thalers, supposedly in payment of a debt Labatut owed the king, but which everyone here says was a debt the king owed Labatut.

Pursued in this manner by Labatut's supposed creditors, with whom the king always sided, whereas I couldn't recover a thing of what Labatut's debtors really owed him, and harassed by his Abyssinian family, who claimed they were his heirs and who denied my power of attorney, I believed I would soon be penniless and decided to leave Choa, and was able to obtain a bond from the king underwritten by the Harar governor, Dedjazmatch Makonnen, for payment of approximately 9,000 thalers, which were all that remained to me after the theft of 3,000 thalers Ménélik manufactured, and the ridiculous prices he paid.

The payment of Ménélik's bond was neither simply nor costlessly settled in Harar, quite the contrary, as several of the creditors followed me

---

Azzaze: or hazage, the chief of the household staff.

there. In all, I returned to Aden, July 25, 1887, with 8,000 thalers in drafts and 600 thalers in cash.

In our agreement with Labatut, I agreed to pay, aside from all the caravan costs:

1) In Choa, 3,000 thalers by the delivery of 300 rifles to Ras Govanna, a matter brokered by the king himself;
2) In Aden, a debt to M. Suel, settled just now with a reduction agreed to by all parties;
3) A note from Labatut to M. Audon, in Choa, a debt of which I already paid, in Choa and Harar, more than 50%, as the documents in my possession attest.

I have paid every debt which could have been associated with the operation. The cash balance was roughly 2,500 thalers, and Labatut remained in my debt in the amount of 5,800 thalers: so I end up with a loss of 60% of my capital, without mentioning twenty-one months of horrible exhaustion that led to the end of this miserable affair.

The Europeans in Choa were witness to the unfolding of this affair, and I have their attestations available for the Consul's perusal.

With the greatest respect,

A. Rimbaud.

TO THE DIRECTOR OF THE *BOSPHORE ÉGYPTIEN*
Cairo, August, 1887

Monsieur,

Having returned from an expedition in Abyssinia and Harar, I permit myself to forward the following notes on the state of things in that region to you. I believe that they will contain some information previously unavailable; and, as for the opinions articulated here, I have come to them via the experience of seven years spent in Abyssinia.

As this concerns a circular expedition between Obock, Choa, Harar, and Zeila, allow me to explain that I went to Tadjoura at the beginning of last year with the goal of assembling a caravan destined for Choa.

My caravan was made up of several thousand shotguns with primers and an order of tools and miscellaneous supplies meant for King Ménélik. It was held up in Tadjoura for a year by the Danakils, who did the same thing to all travelers in the area, not opening the road until they plucked everyone very nearly bare. Another caravan, the merchandise of which was leaving from Tadjoura with my own, had only succeeded in setting out after fifteen months, and the thousand Remingtons brought by the late Soleillet on the same date were still lying around nineteen months later in the only palm grove of the village.

Six short stops from Tadjoura, roughly 60 kilometers, the caravans descend to the salt lake along treacherous roads that one could imagine recalling lunar landscapes. It seems that a French company is currently forming to capitalize on this salt.

Certainly there's salt there, visible all across a wide area, and perhaps at some depth, although no one has yet charted just how deep. Analysis should prove it to be chemically pure, though its lakeside deposits remain unfiltered. But one doubts strongly that the sale will cover the costs of establishing a rail for the light train required to transport the product between the lake's beach and that of the gulf of Goubbert-Kérab, or to pay

---

Bosphore Égyptien: The *Bosphore* was the main newspaper of Cairo, run by the brother of Rimbaud's business associate Jules Borelli.

the costs of personnel and labor, which will be very high, given all the workers will have to be imported, because the Danakil Bedouins won't work. Then there's the need of an armed force to protect the site and its workers.

To return to the question of markets, one might note that the main saltworks of Sheik Othman—built near Aden by an Italian company and in exceptionally favorable conditions—has yet to find a market for the mountains of salt which it has in stock.

The Minister of the Navy has authorized this mining operation on behalf of its petitioners, who are also trading in Choa, on the condition that they obtain the acquiescence of the interested chiefs along the coast and throughout the interior. The government has stipulated a fee per ton, and has allotted a portion to be freely mined by the locals. The interested chiefs include: the sultan of Tadjoura, who would be the hereditary proprietor of several rocky massifs bordering the lake (he is very inclined to sell his land rights); the chief of the Debné tribe, who has hold of our route from the lake to Herer; the sultan Loïta, who receives a monthly payment of five hundred thalers from the French government in return for agreeing to limit his interaction with travelers; sultan Hanfaré of Aoussa, who could find salt elsewhere, but claims rights over much of the Danakils; and of course Ménélik, to whom the Debné tribe, and others, bring an annual supply of thousands of camels loaded with this salt, perhaps just under a thousand tons. Ménélik protested to the Government when he was made aware of the company's activities and of the mining concession. But the part set aside in the mining concession is sufficient to supply the trading requirements of the Debné as well as culinary needs throughout Choa, since granulated salt is not accepted as currency in Abyssinia.

Our route is called the Gobât, from the name of its fifteenth station, and along which pass gaggles of our allies through the Debné. There are approximately twenty-three stops on the way to Herer, cutting through the most unappealing landscape on this side of Africa. It is also very dangerous, as the Debné—one of the more miserable tribes and who are responsible for these transports—are forever at war with the Moudeïtos and Assa-Imara tribes to the east and the Issas Somali to the west.

In Herer, where pastures are at an elevation of roughly 800 meters, the Danakils and Issas graze their herds in a state of general neutrality 60 kilometers from the foot of the Itous Gallas plateaus.

From Herer, one reaches Haawache in eight or nine days. Ménélik decided to establish an armed outpost in the Herer plains to protect the caravans; this post is linked to those of the Abyssinians in the Itou Mountains.

The king's agent in Harar, Dedjaz Matche Mékounène, sent three million Remington cartridges and other munitions to Choa that the English stewards had abandoned after the Egyptian evacuation from Harar. These were sent by the Herer rail, to the profit of Emir Abdoullahi.

This entire route was surveyed using stellar referencing, for the very first time, by Jules Borelli, in May 1886, using topographical referencing via a line paralleling the Itou Mountains, and done during his recent trip to Harar.

Arriving at the Haawache, one is shocked to recall the canal projects of certain explorers. Poor Soleillet had a special dock under construction in Nantes! Haawache is like a bad joke, blocked at every turn by rocks and trees. I have crossed it at various points, various hundreds of kilometers apart, and it is simply impossible to travel, even during floods. Moreover, it is bordered by forests and deserts, is at a remove from all commercial centers, and does not intersect with a single road. Ménélik had two bridges build across the Haawache, one on the Entotto road to Gouragné, the other the Ankober route from Harar through the Itous. These are little more than basic footbridges made of tree trunks, useful for the traffic of troops during rains and floods, and which nonetheless remain remarkable constructions for Choa.

—Arriving in Choa with my expenses paid, the transportation of my merchandise—one hundred camel loads—ended up costing me eight thousand thalers, or eighty thalers per camel, *for just 500 kilometers.* This rate is unequaled anywhere in Africa: this despite every economy on my part, learned from many years of experience. Every report will tell you this route is a disaster, and now, happily, has been replaced by the road from Zeila to Harar and from Harar to Choa through the Itou Mountains.

—Ménélik was still off on his Harar campaign when I reached Farré, an arrival and departure point for caravans, and the frontier of the Danakil peoples. News of the king's victory soon reached Ankober, as did his entry into Harar, and the announcement of his return, which was projected to take place three weeks later. He arrived in Entotto heralded by musicians found in Harar blowing Egyptian trumpets as though their lives depended on it, and followed by his troops and his spoils, among which were two Krupp cannons, each carried by eighty men.

Ménélik had long planned on seizing Harar; he believed he would find a formidable arsenal there, and had warned agents of the French and English government along the coast. In the last few years, the Abyssinian troops regularly robbed the Itous; they ended up taking over. Elsewhere, emir Abdullaï, since Radouan-Pacha's departure with the Egyptian troops, had put together a small army and dreamt of becoming the Mahdi of the Muslim tribes around Harar. He wrote to Ménélik demanding the Haawache border and ordering him to convert to Islam. With an Abyssinian battalion having advanced to within a few days of Harar, the emir sent a few cannons and Turks that remained under his control to disperse the battalion: the Abyssinians were beaten, but Ménélik was so annoyed that he set off himself, from Entotto, with thirty thousand warriors. The confrontation took place at Shalako, sixty kilometers west of Harar, where Nadi Pach had, four years earlier, beaten the Gallas tribes of Méta and Oborra.

The confrontation lasted barely fifteen minutes; the emir had only a few hundred Remingtons, the remainder of his troops fighting with blades. His three thousand warriors were sabered and crushed in the blink of an eye by those of the king of Choa. Around two hundred Sudanese, Egyptians, and Turks, who had remained with Abdullaï after the Egyptian evacuation, perished with the Galla and Somali warriors. And when they returned, the Choan soldiers, who had never killed white men before, were said to have carried the testicles of all the Franguis from Harar with them.

The emir fled to Harar, from which he fled the same night to hide with the chief of the Guerry tribe, east of Harar, toward Berbera. Ménélik ar-

---

Franguis: Frenchies.

rived in Harar a few days later without local resistance, and, having camped his troops outside the city, saw to it that no pillaging occurred. The monarch decided to levy a seventy-five thousand thaler tax on the city and the land, allowing confiscation, according to the Abyssinian rules of war, of the various chattel of those dead who had been vanquished in battle, and removal of whatever pleased him from the houses of Europeans and others. He helped himself to all the arms and ammunition in the city storehouse—erstwhile property of the Egyptian government—and returned to Choa leaving three thousand of his riflemen on a hill adjoining the city and conferring the administration of the city to the uncle of the emir Abdullaï, Ali Abou Béker, whom the English had, during the evacuation, taken to Aden as their prisoner, only to release him later, and whose nephew was then held in slavery in his own house.

As things went on, it happened that the management of Ali Abou Béker was not to the taste of Mékounène, Ménélik's general agent, who went down into the city with his troops, put them up in the houses and the mosques, imprisoned Ali, and sent him to Ménélik in chains.

Once in the city, the Abyssinians reduced it to a horrible cesspit, demolishing houses, ravaging plantations, terrorizing the population as only the blacks know how. Ménélik continued to send reinforcements, followed by huge numbers of slaves, such that the number of Abyssinians now in Harar could be twelve thousand, of whom four thousand are riflemen armed with guns of every shape, from Remingtons to flintlock rifles.

Tax revenue from the surrounding Galla lands was no longer ensured but through raids where the villages are burned, the animals stolen, and the population sold into slavery. While the Egyptian government was able to levy eighty thousand pounds on Harar, the Abyssinian till is always empty. The revenues from the Gallas, from customs, from the post office, from the markets, and other sources are robbed by whosoever should happen to put their hands on them. The people from the city are leaving, the Gallas are no longer growing. In just a few months, the Abyssinians have devoured the provisions of dourah left by the Egyptians and which could have lasted for several years. Famine and plague are imminent.

The movement of this market—whose position is very important, as the nearest Gallas market to the coast—has ceased. The Abyssinians have prohibited the use of the old Egyptian piasters, which had been left in the country as a fractional currency for the Marie-Thérèse thalers, and have instead gone to the use of a sort of leather currency that has no value. At Entotto, however, I have seen a few silver piasters that Ménélik has had struck bearing his face and which he has sought to put into circulation in Harar, to end the question of currency.

Ménélik would like to keep Harar in his hands, but he knows that he is unable to administrate the country in such a manner as to be able to extract revenue in the deal, and he knows that the English have looked down upon the Abyssinian occupation. They say, in essence, that the governor of Aden, who has done his utmost to bolster the British influence along the Somali coast, would do all he could to encourage his government to occupy Harar were the Abyssinians to evacuate, which could, as a consequence, induce famine or complicate the Tigré war.

As far as they are concerned, the Abyssinians awake each morning in Harar expecting to see English troops coming through the mountains. Mékounène has written to the English political agents in Zeila and Berbera to send no more troops to Harar; the agents have been sending a few local soldiers to accompany their caravans.

The English government, as a result, levied a tax of five percent on the importation of thalers in Zeila, Boulhar, and Berbera. This measure helps to disperse what little cash remains in Choa and Harar, and it is uncertain whether it encourages the importation of rupees, which have never done very well in these parts and upon which the English have also, for reasons one can't imagine, levied a one percent import tax along the coast.

Ménélik was very annoyed by the interdiction of the importation of arms along the coasts of Obock and Zeila. Just as Joannès dreamt of his seaport at Massaouah, Ménélik, however far he was relegated to the interior, liked to think that he would soon make inroads to the Gulf of Aden. He had written to the sultan of Tadjoura, unfortunately, after the accession of the French protectorate, proposing to purchase the sultan's land. When he entered Harar, he declared himself sovereign of all the tribes

---

Joannès: Emperor of Tigré. One of Ménélik's rivals in the region.

along the coast, and authorized his general, Mékounène, not to miss the opportunity to take over Zeila; only after the Europeans spoke to him of artillery and warships were his designs on Zeila to change, and he last wrote to the French government to request Ambado's transfer.

We know that the coast, from the Gulf of Tadjoura to just beyond Berbera, had been shared between France and England in the following manner: France kept the coastal region from Goubbet Kératv to Djibouti, a cape ten miles northwest of Zeila, and a strip of territory that runs I don't know how many kilometers into the interior, whose border with the English territory is formed by a line drawn from Djibouti to Ensa, the third station along the road from Zeila to Harar. So we have a market along the road from Harar and Abyssinia. Ambado, which Ménélik wants as well, is a cove near Djibouti, where the Obock governor had long since raised a tricolor which the English agent from Zeila obstinately insisted upon removing, until negotiations came to a halt. Ambado has no water, but Djibouti has good springs; and of the three stops that fall along our road to Ensa, two have water.

In all, Djibouti could prove an excellent place for caravans to form, as soon as some sort of organization of local merchandise were established, and troops were stationed there. For now, the place is completely uninhabited. It goes without saying that a free port would be needed were one to wish to compete with Zeila.

Zeila, Berbera, and Bulhar remain in English hands, as well as the Bay of Samawanak, along the Gadiboursi coast, between Zeila and Bulhar, the place where the last French consular agent in Zeila, M. Henry, had planted the tricolor, the Gadiboursi tribe themselves having requested our protection, which is always enjoyed. All these stories of annexation or protection have been stirring up the minds along this coast these last two years.

The French agent's successor was M. Labosse, the French consul in Suez, sent as an interim measure to Zeila, where he smoothed out the

_____

Djibouti: As Enid Starkie first noted, Rimbaud was prescient about the role Djibouti would go on to play as a trading hub.

various disagreements. There are approximately five thousand Somalis under French protection in Zeila.

There is a considerable advantage to the route from Harar to Abyssinia. While one cannot go to Choa by the Danakil route except through a voyage of fifty to sixty days through a horrible desert rife with dangers, Harar, far down the Southern Ethiopian massif, is only fifteen days from the coast by caravan.

The route is excellent, the Issa tribe, accustomed to transportation, is entirely conciliatory, and one is not in danger from neighboring tribes.

From Harar to Entotto, Ménélik's current residence, is only a twenty-day march along the Itou Gallas plateau, at an average altitude of 2,500 meters, with supplies, means of transportation, and security guaranteed. It takes at most a month, then, to move between our coast and the middle of Choa, but the distance to Harar is just twelve days, and this last place, despite invasion, is doubtless destined to become the exclusive commercial market of Choa itself and of all the Gallas. Ménélik himself was so impressed by how advantageous a situation Harar represented that on his return, recalling the ideas for railroads that the Europeans had often tried to convince him to pursue, he sought someone to whom he could give the commission or the contract to lay railroad tracks from Harar to the sea; he soon changed his mind, recalling the fact of the English along the coast! It goes without saying that, in the instance where such an enterprise were realized (and of course it will be in the near future), the Choa government wouldn't contribute to the costs of its execution.

Ménélik has no money for such a project, as he has remained willfully ignorant (or unconcerned) about the exploitation of the region's natural resources, which he has stymied and continues to. His only interest is to gather enough guns to allow him to send his troops to commandeer Gallas. The few European merchants who have reached Choa have brought Ménélik, in all, ten thousand guns with cartridges and fifteen thousand guns with fuses, this in the space of five or six years. This was enough in the Amhara to subdue all the Gallas in the region, and the Dedjatch Mékounène, in Harar, offered to go down and conquer the Gallas as far as their southern border, near the Zanzibar coast. He had Ménélik's blessing in this, Ménélik who had been led to believe that he could establish a route in this direction for the importation of arms. It would also allow them to expand upon their borders, given the Gallas tribes are not armed. Above all, what compelled Ménélik to invade the South was the uncomfortable proximity and vexing suzerainty of Joannès. Ménélik had already left Ankober for Entotto. It is said he wanted to go to Djimma Abba-Djifar, the richest of the Gallas lands, to establish a residence there, and he also spoke of setting himself up in Harar. Ménélik dreams of a continual southward expansion of his domain, beyond the Haawache, and perhaps even thinks of himself emigrating from the Amhara lands to the center of the new Gallas lands, with his guns, his warriors, his wealth, to establish, far from the emperor, a southern empire much like the ancient kingdom of Ali Alaba.

One wonders what is and what will be Ménélik's position during the Italo-Abyssinian war. It is clear that his position will be determined by Joannès's will, since they are neighbors, and not by the diplomatic emissaries, whom he doesn't begin to understand and whom he never trusts. Ménélik cannot currently disobey Joannès, and Joannès, who is well up on various diplomatic intrigues concerning Ménélik, will know very well how to steer clear of any trouble. He has already called for Ménélik to single out his best soldiers and Ménélik must send them to the emperor's camp in Asmara. Even in the instance of a disaster, Joannès would go to Ménélik. Choa, the only Amhara land in Ménélik's control, isn't a fifteenth the size of Tigré. His other domains are all Gallas lands under precarious control, and he would have great difficulty quelling a general rebellion were he to commit himself one way or the other. One must also not forget that patriotic sentiment does exist in Choa and for Ménélik, however ambiguous it may be, and it is impossible that he should see either honor or advantage in listening to the advice of foreigners.

He will therefore conduct himself in such a manner as not to compromise his already precarious position, and, as in those cultures which one neither understands nor willingly accepts, he will act only as his nearest neighbor would have him act, and no one is his neighbor but Joannès, who has at least proven himself most able at avoiding temptation. Which does not mean that he will not politely listen to the diplomats; he will pocket what he can from them, and, the moment it's given, Joannès, alerted, will split it with Ménélik. And, once again, widespread patriotic sentiment and the opinion of Ménélik's people will prove to be worth something. For the time being, no one wants foreigners, their interference, their presence, under any circumstances, no more so in Choa than in Tigré or with the Gallas.

—Having quickly settled my account with Ménélik, I asked him for a bond payable in Harar, as I wanted to take the new route the king had opened through the Itou Mountains, a route that up until then remained unexplored, and which I had foolishly attempted to cross during the Egyptian occupation of Harar. On that occasion, M. Jules Borelli asked the king for permission to make a trip in that direction, and thus I had the honor to travel in the company of our amiable and courageous countryman, whose entirely unpublished geodesic treatises on the region I later sent to Aden.

This route includes seven stops beyond the Haawache and twelve from the Haawache to Harar on the Itou plateau, a region of magnificent pastures and splendid forests, all at an average altitude of 2,500 meters, and in a wonderful climate. There is little cultivated land; the area is sparsely populated, or perhaps it's just that they settle far from the roads to avoid the king's men. There are, however, coffee plantations, the Itous furnishing the majority of several thousands of tons of coffee that sell in Harar each year. These lands, very rich and very fertile, are the only ones in eastern Africa that have adapted to European colonization.

As for business in Choa, for now, nothing is being imported since the ban on the trading of arms on the coast went into effect. But whoever might appear with a hundred thousand thalers could use them during the year to buy ivory and other merchandise, the exporters having suffered these last few years and cash growing increasingly rare. An opportunity awaits. The new route is excellent, and the political situation in Choa will not be upset during the war. Ménélik intends, above all, to maintain order in his residence.

With the greatest respect,

Rimbaud.

TO HIS FAMILY
Cairo, August 23, 1887

My expedition to Abyssinia is done. I already told you how, my associate having died, I had considerable difficulties in Choa regarding his inheritance; I was made to twice pay his debts, and I had a horrible time trying to save what I had risked in this affair; if my associate had not died I would have earned thirty thousand francs; whereas I find myself with the fifteen thousand that I had after wearing myself out for two years. I have no luck!

I came here because the heat along the Red Sea this year was unbearable, 50 to 60 degrees all the time; and, finding myself weak after seven years of unimaginable exhaustion and the most abominable deprivation, I thought that 2 or 3 months here might set me to rights, but everything costs more here since there is nothing to do, and daily life is more European in style and therefore expensive.

These days I find myself troubled by a rheumatism of the small of the back that is driving me mad; I have another in the left thigh that paralyses me from time to time, pain when bending my left knee, a rheumatism (long felt) in the right shoulder, hair totally gray: I imagine my existence is on the decline.

Ask yourselves how one should feel after the following exploits: sea crossings and land crossing on horseback, in small boats, without clothes, without supplies, without water, etc., etc.

I am incredibly exhausted, I do not have work right now, I am afraid of losing what life I have, and given that I constantly wear sixteen thousand–odd gold francs in my belt, weighing eight kilos, I'm getting dysentery.

And yet, I can't come to Europe, for many reasons, above all, I would die in winter and am too accustomed to this free and wandering life, and finally, I don't have a job.

I must therefore spend my remaining days wandering, in exhaustion and hardship, with nothing to look forward to but death and suffering.

I will not be here long: I have no job and everything is too expensive, so I must return to the Sudanese coast of Abyssinia or Arabia. Perhaps I will go to Zanzibar, whence one may make trips to Africa, and perhaps China, Japan, who knows?

Finally, send me your news. I wish you peace and happiness.

Yours,

Address: Arthur Rimbaud,
General delivery, Cairo (Egypt)

TO HIS MOTHER
[undated]

My dea,

I have to ask you a favor, which I hope to be able to reimburse soon.

I put the money I had on me in the Crédit Lyonnais on deposit for six months at 4% interest.

But soon I must take the Zanzibar boat from Suez around the 15th of September, as I have been given recommendations there; here I spend too much and am too sedentary, whereas at Zanzibar there are expeditions to the interior, one lives on nearly nothing, and one reaches the end of the year with one's salary intact; here, lodging, food, and clothing (in the deserts one barely dresses at all) consume everything.

So I will go to Zanzibar and should have great opportunities there, without even mentioning the references I have on me.

I will leave my money here with the bank, and as there are merchants in Zanzibar who deal with the bank, I will be able to get ahold of my interest dividends.

If I withdraw the deposit now, I lose the interest, and I can't continue to carry this money on my back, it's foolish, exhausting, and too dangerous.

I ask you therefore, as I only have a few hundred francs left, to please lend me the sum of *five hundred francs,* while sending it to me here as soon as you receive this letter, or I will miss the steamboat, which only leaves once a month, between the 15th and the 18th. And another month here would be expensive.

I haven't asked a thing of you for seven years, be good enough to do this for me, and don't refuse me, as it would bother me a great deal.

Regardless, I must wait here until the 15th of September, and it must not arrive after that.

My dea: Ma che in Fr., abbreviation for *Ma chère mere,* in all probability.

This letter will arrive in eight days, and then another eight days for the response.

Send it to me by registered mail, addressed as follows:

> Monsieur Rimbaud,
> At the French Consulate,
> Cairo (Egypt).

TO HIS MOTHER
Cairo, August 25, 1887

My dear mother,

I write again to beg you not to refuse to send me the five hundred francs that I requested in my letter yesterday. I believe that something must remain of the money I once sent you. But, whether it does or not, you would put me in a very awkward position were you not to send me the aforementioned sum of five hundred francs, which I badly need; I hope to reimburse you by the end of the year.

But my money is tied up, and for the moment I am unemployed, am living off myself, and I have a trip to take, around the 20th of September.

Send it to me by registered mail addressed as follows:

> Rimbaud,
> at the French Consulate,
> Cairo.

I only have a few hundred francs at my disposal for the time being, and that won't be enough. Moreover, I must go to Zanzibar, where there's work, in Africa and Madagascar, where you can save money.

I'm not worried about any of this, I won't lose what I have, but I can't get at my money for six months; moreover, I can't stay here more than a month as I'm bored here and it's too expensive. So I look forward to receiving this sum by the 15th of September at the Consulate, and I will wait for it in the interim.

Yours,

A. Rimbaud.

For the registered letter:

> At the French Consulate,
> Cairo, Egypt

TO ALFRED BARDEY
Cairo, August 26, 1887

My dear Monsieur Bardey,

Knowing that you are always interested in matters African, I have decided to send you the few following notes on what is happening in Choa and Harar at present.

From Entotto to Tadjoura, the Danakil route is utterly impassable; Soleillet's rifles—which arrived in February of '86—are still there. The salt from Lake Assal, which a company had intended to mine, is inaccessible and would be unsalable anyway: it's a big swindle.

My business turned out badly, and I was afraid I would return without a thaler; I was assailed by a pack of Labatut's self-styled creditors, of whom Ménélik was at the head, and who robbed me, in Labatut's name, of 3,000 thalers. To avoid ending up completely cleaned out, I asked Ménélik to get me to Harar, which he had just annexed: he gave me a Choa draft, from his chargé d'affaires in Harar, Dedjatch Makonnen.

It was not until I had asked Ménélik to go this way that M. Borelli had the idea to join up with me.

Here's the itinerary:

1) From Entotto to the Akaki river farming plateau, 25 kilometers.
2) Abitchou village in Galla, 30 kilometers. Continuing along the plateau: 2,500 meters. Marching with Mount Herer to the south.
3) Following the plateau. Descent to the Mindjar plain via Chankora. Mindjar has rich, carefully cultivated soil. The altitude must be 1,800 meters (I am estimating altitude on the basis of vegetation; one can't be wrong, however little one may have traveled in these Ethiopian lands). Length of this stage: 25 kilometers.
4) Following Mindjar: 25 kilometers. Same terrain. Mindjar lacks water. Rainwater is saved in pits.
5) Mindjar ends. The plains ends, the land grows bumpy; the soil worsens. Fields of cotton. —30 kilometers.
6) Descent into Cassam. Agriculture ends. Mimosa forests crossed by a road ten meters wide, cleared by Ménélik. —25 kilometers.

7) In Bedouin country, Konella, or "hot land." Undergrowth and mimosa forests populated by elephants and ferocious animals. The king's road leads to a hot-water spring called Fil-Ouah, and to the Haawache. We camped this way, 30 kilometers from Cassam.

8) From there to the Haawache, very steep in this leg, for 20 kilometers. The region extending two days from either side of the Haawache is called Cateyon. Bedouin Gallas tribes, tenders of camels and other creatures, at war with the Aroussis. The high-water point of the Haawache: around 800 meters. 80 centimeters deep.

9) Beyond the Haawache, 30 kilometers of brush. Walking in the path of elephants.

10) Climbing rapidly to Itou through shady paths. Beautiful wooded country, mostly uncultivated. Soon at 2,000 meters again. Halt at Galamso, Abyssinian outpost with three or four hundred soldiers loyal to Dedjatch Woldé Guibril. —35 kilometers.

11) From Galamso to Boroma, outpost of a thousand soldiers of the Ras Dargé—30 kilometers. Beautiful cultivated land. A few coffee plantations. Abyssinia's crops are replaced by sorghum. Altitude: 2,200 meters.

12) Following Tchertcher, magnificent forests. A lake called Arro. You walk along the crest of a chain of hills. Aroussi to the right and parallel to our route, higher than the Itou; these great forests and beautiful mountains offer a panoramic view. Camp at a place called Wotcho. —30 kilometers.

13) 15 kilometers to the house of sheik Hahia, in Goro. Many villages. At the center of the Itous the merchants of Harar and Abyssinia come to sell *channuas*. There are many Abyssinian Muslim families there.

14) 20 kilometers, Herna. Splendid valleys crowned by forests in whose shade we walk. Coffee trees. There, Abdullahi, Emir of Harar, sent some Turks to root out an Abyssinian outpost, which set Ménélik's advances in motion.

---

channuas: candles.

15) Bourka, a valley named for its river, which reaches to Ennya. Forest expanses. —30 kilometers.
16) Obona, wooded lands, uneven terrain, chalky, poor. —30 kilometers.
17) Chalanko, the Emir's battlefield. Meta, pine forests. Wara-belly-Meta must be the highest point on the whole route, perhaps 2,600 meters. Length of stage: 30 kilometers.
18) Lake Yabatha, Harramoïa lakes, Harar. —40 kilometers.

General direction: between NNE. and SSE., it seemed to me.

The route carries convoys of fully loaded mules; but the postmen cover it in ten days.

In Harar, the Amara confiscate, extort, and raid, as we know; the downfall of the country. The city has become a cesspit. The Europeans were confined to the city when we arrived. All this because of the fear Abyssinians have of the English. The Issa road is very good, and the Gueldessey to Herer as well.

There are two types of business to conduct in Choa right now.

1) Bring sixty thousand thalers and buy ivory, musk, and gold. —You know that all the merchants, except Brémond, have left, and even the Swiss. —There isn't a thaler left in Choa. I left the ivory, 50 thalers retail; with the king, 60 thalers.

The Ras Govena alone has more than forty thousand thalers of ivory he wants to sell: no buyers, no money! He also has a thousand okiètes of musk. —No one wants it at two thalers per three okiètes. —There are also many other holders of ivory from whom one might buy, without counting the individuals who sell it on the sly. Brémond tried to get the Ras to give him the ivory for free, but the Ras wanted to be paid in cash. —Sixty thousand thalers can be used to make these purchases over six months, without any expenses, along the route from Zeila, Harar, Itou, and can lead to a profit of twenty thousand thalers; but it must be done soon, as I believe that Brémond will soon seek cash.

2) Bring two hundred camels with one hundred armed men (the

Brémond: the most senior French trader in Ethiopia.

Dedjatch will provide all of this for nothing) from Harar to Ambado, and, at the same time, leave with a boatful of eight thousand Remingtons (without cartridges, the king asks without cartridges: he found three million in Harar) and head straight for Harar. France now holds Djibouti with sea access at Ambos. There are three Djibouti stations in Ambos. —Here Remingtons are being sold for eight francs.

—The only question is about the boat; but it will be easy enough to rent in Suez.

As a gift to the king: a machine for making Remington cartridges.

—Metal plate and chemical products and supplies for the manufacture of war cartridges.

I came here to see if an idea might form. But here is too far away; and, in Aden, one finds oneself filled with nothing but disgust for these matters, partly because of misconduct, partly because of mischance, and as a result ending up without success. —And yet there is much that can be done, and those who hurry and are thrifty will be able to make things happen.

My situation ended up badly because I was associated with that idiot Labatut, who, compounding my misfortune, died, and who left me to deal with his family in Choa and all his creditors; such that I exited this affair with very little, less than I brought. I can't undertake anything else myself, I don't have financing.

And now there isn't a single French merchant left in all of Sudan! In Souakim I learned that caravans make it all the way to Berbera. Rubber is starting to arrive. When the Sudan reopens, and bit by bit it will, there will be much one can do there.

I won't stay here, and will instead leave as soon as the heat, which was unbearable during the summer, diminishes along the Red Sea. I am at your service should you have need of me for any venture you might organize. —I can't stay here any longer, because I am accustomed to the free life. Think of me.

Rimbaud.
General delivery, Cairo.
Until the end of September.

A photograph by Rimbaud of a trading colleague, Constantin Sotir.

Think of me as a new Jeremiah, with my endless lamentation; there's nothing fun about my situation.

OCTOBER 8, 1887

XI

ADEN ALAST

1887–1888

TO HIS FAMILY
Aden, October 8, 1887

Dear friends,

Thank you so much. I see that you haven't forgotten me. Do not worry. If my business dealings aren't extraordinary for the moment, at least I'm losing nothing; and I hope that a less precarious period will soon present itself to me.

So, for two years, my work has been going badly, I exhaust myself purposelessly, I have great difficulty holding on to what I have. I would very much like to be done with these damned countries; but I still hold on to the hope that things will be better while still wasting my time surrounded by deprivation and suffering of the sort you and anyone else wouldn't begin to be able to understand.

And what would I do in France? There is no doubt that I can no longer live a sedentary life; and, above all, I am terrified of the cold—and then there's the matter of not having enough income, or work, or support, or connections, or profession, or resources of any kind. To come back would be to request my burial.

The last trip I took in Abyssinia, and which was terrible for my health, could have earned me 30,000 francs; but the death of my associate and other problems led to the situation ending up badly and I ended up poorer than I was in the beginning.

I will stay here a month, before leaving for Zanzibar. I don't make this decision lightheartedly, as I have only seen people return from there in terrible shape, despite others telling me that one can find business down there.

Before leaving, or even if I don't leave, I will perhaps decide to send you the money which I deposited in Egypt; because, with the awkward position Egypt is in, with the blockade in Sudan and the blockade in Abyssinia, and also for other reasons, I see that one can only lose by hold-

OPPOSITE: *Steamer Point, Aden, 1880.*

ing on to the money in these desperate regions, however much or little matters not.

So you can reach me in Aden at the following address:

Monsieur Arthur Rimbaud, general delivery.

If I leave, I will have them forward everything.

Think of me as a new Jeremiah, with my endless lamentation; there's nothing fun about my situation.

I wish you the opposite, and am your affectionate,

Rimbaud.

TO THE FRENCH CONSUL IN BEYROUTH
Aden, October 12, 1887

Monsieur,

Excuse me for having to ask you for the following information: to whom should one address oneself in Beyrouth or otherwise along the Syrian coast regarding the purchase of four donkey studs, in top condition, of the best breeding, used for the breeding of the largest and most powerful saddle mules in Syria? What would the price be, and also the cost of freight with the Messageries and insurance from Beyrouth to Aden?

This concerns an order by King Ménélik of Choa (Southern Abyssinia), where there are only small asses; he would like to create a superior race of mules, given the huge number and low price of fillies.

Awaiting your response, I am, Monsieur le Consul,
Your dutiful,

A. Rimbaud
At the French Consulate,
Aden,
English possessions

TO MONSEIGNEUR TAURIN-CAHAGNE
Aden, November 4, 1887

Monseigneur,

May the present find you in peace and good health. Secondly, forgive me for requesting your intercession in the following matter.

You know that Ménélik sent me to Harar with a bond for 9,866 thalers. Whereas a M. Audon at Ankobe had a note in his possession for 1,810, un-dersigned by the late Labatut to M. Deschamps of Aden and payable to M. Audon, a correspondent of M. Audon's in Choa. Without money in Choa, I can't pay anything more against this note. Next, following my de-parture from Choa, the aforesaid Audon hired the azzaze Waldé-Thadik to write to Mékonnène in Harar to have my payment of the sums I owed stopped. To free myself from this forced halt, I said to Mékonnène that he should hold on to 866 thalers, and I made it clear to him that he should make certain that this money reached Audon personally, and not merely his European or Abyssinian creditors. Mékonnène gave me a receipt for the aforesaid 866 thalers in the name of M. Audon, and even wrote to the consul in Aden about the affair, attesting to the receipt of the aforemen-tioned sum for the aforementioned individual in Choa.

But now M. Deschamps refuses to give me control of Labatut's ac-count (which I balanced with a discount) before he receives news that the aforesaid 866 thalers were paid to M. Audon; nor will he write to MM. Moussaya in Harar giving them the right to handle the aforesaid sum of 866 thalers with the Dedjatch in Harar, nor send him back to Aden so the Dedjatch doesn't send the sum to M. Audon.

I worry that the Dedjatch hasn't thought to pay a debt due of one of M. Audon's Abyssinian creditors from this sum. Should that be the case, my payment will be nothing, and that will prevent me from settling my account here. But what is most likely is that Mékonnène let the matter drop, and isn't giving the 866 th. another thought, any more than, having

---

a correspondent of M. Audon's in Choa: Rimbaud meant Deschamps was the correspondent, and thus miswrote.

received a receipt from him for the aforesaid 866 th. destined for M. Audon, I of course released him completely from the sum of 9,866 thalers that the king had me cash in Harar and, if it was done in bad faith, which is always the case with them, my only recourse against him with the King would be to send the receipt for 866 th. signed by him, which I have—as he would take my release for 9,866 th. and say he knows nothing of the rest.

As it is likely that he will consult you in this matter, you will help all by reenlightening him, by reminding him that he received this sum from me, or at least that I relinquished this sum to my account, so that he could see to it personally that M. Audon got it in Choa.

If he decided to make use of this sum by crediting one of M. Audon's regular creditors (I mean one of the Abyssinians), I will feel that the Dedjatch has robbed me to the tune of 866 th., and at the same time robbed M. Audon, because I asked him to pay M. Audon and no one else.

In this instance, the settling of my account with M. Deschamps would be finished, and I would have no recourse to the Dedjatch but to seize his merchandise through consular channels, which is hardly possible.

I would like you to make him understand that he is nonetheless responsible for the aforementioned sum as far as the consulate is concerned, since he wrote to the consul here, acknowledging having received the sum for the purpose indicated.

—If the sum remains in his possession in Harar, he should do as M. Deschamps requested and return it to MM. Moussaya. As far as I'm concerned, it is almost certain that he sent nothing. In any case, he had no right to send it to anyone but Audon.

—M. Savouré wrote us yesterday that he has bought the Soleillet caravan, and he will return to Aden in a month.

—M. Tian returns to Aden end of November.

—They say that troops have set off from Naples, but England is still trying to settle the Italo-Abyssinian affair, and it seems that the expedition is less and less a fait accompli, or at least that the scale of it will not be anywhere as large as originally imagined, the will just not being there. The Italian newspaper correspondents are still in Massaouah. Here they are buying some mules and horses, but, at this rate, it would take three years to make the preparations, since the Italians in the Red Sea only manage to rouse themselves in winter!

—As for the Russian religious mission, that's all done with.

—Monseigneur Toucier, bishop of Massaouah, is leaving for France as soon as things have come to their conclusion.

—As far as I'm concerned, I'm looking for a chance to return to Ethiopia, but not on my tab, and it is possible that I will return with M. Savouré's caravan.

—I don't need to tell you that I cashed your note for 500 th. with M. Riès right away.

—Say hello, if you would, to M. Sacconi on my behalf. Here we've heard he is gravely ill. I hope that he's back on his feet.

—I have been asked to tell the Dedjatch that Bénin is very unhappy with his Harar agent's delay in payment. But these commercial matters have no bearing on you. —I have only asked for your involvement in my situation with M. Audon because in that case it has to do with raising his awareness, and to prevent him from committing a theft if he has yet to. I too am eager to see this matter done with, and that is how I will obtain the release of the final account related to the Labatut affair.

I am, Monseigneur, your humble servant.

Rimbaud.
General Delivery,
Aden Camp.

Monseigneur Taurin,
Apostolic Vicar of Gallas
Harar

TO HIS FAMILY
Aden, November 5, 1887

My dear friends,

I am still waiting. I am awaiting responses from different places, to learn where I must go.

There may be something for me to do in Massaouah, with the Abyssinian war. So it shouldn't be long now before I make a decision or find the work I want; and there's always the chance I won't leave for Zanzibar or anywhere else.

It's winter here, which is to say that it's never hotter than 30° above zero during the day, 25° at night.

Write me with news. What are you doing? How are you? It's been a long time since I've heard anything from you. It isn't pleasant to feel so abandoned.

Don't worry about me: I am feeling better, and I expect to improve on my losses; losses! After spending two years without earning a thing, it seems one either loses one's money or one's time.

Tell me: which newspaper is the most influential in Ardennes?

Yours,

Rimbaud.

TO M. DE GASPARY
Aden, November 9, 1887

Monsieur,

I have your letter of the 8th and I thank you for your observations.

I am sending along a copy of the accounting of the expenses of the Labatut caravan, while retaining the original in my possession, because the head of the caravan who signed it stole some of the money that the Azzaze had included in the money used to pay the camels. Essentially, the Azzaze insisted on never paying the caravan expenses directly to the Europeans, who would be able to settle everything without difficulty: the Danakils take that as an opportunity to mix up the Azzaze and the Franguis at the same time, and every European here has seen himself ripped off by the Bedouins to the tune of 75% above the actually cost of the caravan, the Azzaze and Ménélik themselves invariably having the habit—before the opening of the Harar route—to side with the Bedouins over the Franguis.

Aware of this, I had the idea to make the chief inventory his caravan's expenses. This didn't prevent him, the moment I left, from bringing me before the king to demand some 400 thalers above the amount he accepted! In this instance, his lawyer was *the redoubtable bandit Mohammed Abou-Beker,* the enemy of European merchants and travelers to Choa.

But the king, without looking at the Bedouin's signature (as documents mean nothing in Choa), understood that he was lying, insulted Mohammed, who was doing his furious best against me, and ruled that I should pay the sum of 30 thalers and a Remington rifle: but I paid nothing. I learned that the chief of the caravan had already taken these 400 thalers against the monies deposited into his hands by the Azzaze to pay the Bedouins, and which he had used to purchase slaves, which he sent off with the caravan belonging to MM. Savouré, Dimitri, and Brémond, who all died en route; he himself went to hide in Djimma Abba-Djifar, where I'm told he died of dysentery. So one month after my departure, the Azzaze had to reimburse 400 thalers to the Bedouins; but, if I had been present, he most certainly would have made me pay them.

No matter what, the most dangerous enemies to Europeans are the Abou-Beker, given the ease with which they can access the Azzaze and the king: they heap calumny on us, denigrate our manners, misrepresent our intentions. They set a horrible example for the Danakil Bedouins by stealing, killing, pillaging. Their impunity is assured by the Abyssinian authority and by the European authority along the coasts, each of which they are able to hoodwink outrageously. There are even some French in Choa who will nonetheless tell you, despite having had their belongings pillaged by Mohammed along the way, "Mohammed is a fine fellow!" But the few Europeans in Choa and Harar who know the politics and customs of these people—hated by all the Issa Danakil tribes, by the Gallas and the Amharas—run from them as if from the plague.

In Sajale, before the departure, the thirty-four Abyssinians in my retinue signed a bond stating they would be paid 15 thalers apiece for the trip and two months of back pay, but in Ankober, annoyed by their insolent demands, I grabbed the bond and tore it up before them; next came complaints to the Azzaze, etc. Never, by the way, are receipts given for wages paid to Choan domestics: they would find such an action strange, and would think that they were in grave danger, of what who can say.

I would never have paid the Azzaze the 400 thalers due Labatut had I not discovered myself, in an old notebook found in Mme. Labatut's shack, an annotation in Labatut's hand acknowledging receipt of five okiètes of ivory less a few rotolis. Essentially, Labatut was preparing his *Memoirs:* I gathered up thirty-four volumes, which is to say the thirty-four notebooks at his widow's house, and, despite her curses, threw them into the fire—which, I am told, was unfortunate, given that they contained, stuck between their confessional pages, various deeds to property, which I missed in the face of such an overflow of banality unworthy of consideration.

Anyway, barely having said "hello," this sycophant, leaving Azzaze for Farré with his mules just as I was leaving with my camels, begins to insinuate that the Frangui, in whose name I had come, owed him a huge debt,

---

Abou-Beker: In this case, the whole family.

and he demanded my entire caravan as a security against it. I calmed him down, briefly, by offering him a pair of my glasses and some laxatives; and afterwards I sent him, with hindsight, what it seemed he was owed. He was bitterly disappointed, and reacted very hostilely; among other things, he kept the other sycophant, the *Aboune,* from paying me what was owed of a shipment of grapes I had brought him to make his holy wine.

The various debts I paid in Labatut's name went as follows:

A Dedjatch would come to me, sit and drink my tedj, while talking up the noble qualities of the late Labatut and expressing his hope that I would prove to be his equal. When a mule grazing the grass would wander into view, the fellow would shriek: "That's the mule I gave Labatut!" (They wouldn't mention that the burnouses they wore on their backs had come from Labatut.) "Anyway," they would add, "he was in debt to me to the tune of 70 thalers (or 50, or 60, or...).". And they would insist on this matter being settled, to the extent that I would end up dismissing the brigand by saying: "Tell it to the King!" (Which is pretty much like saying *go to hell!* —But the king made me pay a part of the claim, adding hypocritically that he would pay the rest!)

But I did pay legitimate claims to their wives, wages to servants who died on the return trip with Labatut, or the reimbursement of 30, 15, or 12 thalers that Labatut had taken from farmers, promising he would return with rifles, fabric, whatever. These poor people were always honest, I couldn't help but be touched by them, so I paid them. A debt of 20 thalers was brought to my attention by a M. Dubois: I saw that he was in the right and I paid him, adding, as interest, a pair of my shoes, since this poor devil was complaining of having to go around barefoot.

But news of my decency spread far and wide and awakened, here and there, a range, a gang, a horde claiming to be Labatut's creditors, with sob stories that would make you blanch, which altered my generous predisposition; and I decided to make for Choa as quickly as possible. I recall that the morning of my departure, setting out on a NNE. course, I witnessed the representative of the wife of a friend of Labatut's burst from a

---

Aboune: head of the Coptic orthodox clergy. *tedj:* a mead.

bush, demanding 19 thalers in the name of the Virgin Mary; farther along the road, a fellow wearing a sheepskin cape leapt from a ridge, asking if I had paid his brother the 12 thalers Labatut borrowed, etc. To such requests I gave the answer that now wasn't the time!

Labatut's widow, complaining to the Azzaze, had, as soon as she saw me, intended to sue me over the touchy matter of the claims on the estate. M. Hénon, the French explorer, had nobly taken it upon himself to serve as her lawyer in this matter; and it was he who had me cited and who prepared the widow's claim, with the help of two old Amharan lady lawyers. After an endless back and forth in which I was both winning and losing, the Azzaze granted me a seizure order over the houses of the decedent. But the widow had already hidden away the few hundred thalers of merchandise, various effects and oddities he had left behind, and during the seizure which I undertook, not without resistance, I only found a few old pair of underwear, which the widow clutched with fiery tears, a few bullet molds, and a dozen pregnant slaves, all of which I left there.

M. Hénon planned on appealing, and the Azzaze, stunned, gave the case over to the Franguis there in Ankober. M. Brémond decided, given that my situation was already pretty disastrous, that the only thing I owed the shrew was the property, gardens, and animals of the decedent, and that, when I left, the Europeans would take up a collection among themselves to the tune of one hundred thalers for the widow. M. Hénon, the plaintiff's prosecutor, took responsibility for the operation and remained in Ankober himself.

The day before I left Entotto—when I went up to see the monarch with M. Ilg to collect the bond payable by the Dedjatch at Harar—I noticed Hénon's helmet in the mountains behind me: having learned of my departure, he had hastily made the 120-kilometer trip from Ankober to Entotto; behind him was the frenetic widow's burnoose, snaking along the cliffs. At the king's, I had to wait in the antechamber for a few hours, and *they* made a desperate effort to convince him. But when I was introduced, M. Ilg quickly told me that *they* had not succeeded. The monarch declared that he had been friends with Labatut, and that he planned on continuing that friendship with his descendants: and as proof, he withdrew the use of the lands he had given to Labatut from the widow!

It turns out that Hénon just wanted me to pay the hundred thalers that he himself was supposed to collect from the Europeans. Only after I left did I discover that the collection hadn't been made.

M. Ilg, who because of his knowledge of languages and his honesty is usually used by the king to settle disputes between Europeans and the court, explained that Ménélik claimed Labatut had huge debts to him. In essence, the day I was told how much I owed, Ménélik said he was owed a great deal more; to which I said: prove it. It was a Saturday, and the king said the accounts would be reviewed. Monday the king declared that, having unrolled the scrolls they use as archives, he had discovered the sum of 3,500 thalers, and that he had subtracted that from my account, and that besides that, all of Labatut's profits should revert to him; all of this said in a tone that did not admit of debate. I invoked my European creditors, and as a last resort displayed my debt. M. Ilg reprimanded the king, got him to reverse himself and abandon three eighths of his claim.

As far as I'm concerned, I am convinced that the Négou robbed me, and as this merchandise is now circulating on the very routes I am condemned to travel, I hope to take it all back one day at the value I am owed; just as I must bargain with Ras Govana over a sum of 600 thalers should he continue to demand it, even though the king told him to drop it, which is what the king always tells others as long as he himself has been paid.

Such is, Monsieur le Consul, the story of my payment of debts to locals relating to Labatut's caravan. Sorry to have related it in this style, but it at least serves to distract me from the nature of these events, which are, on the whole, very unpleasant to recall.

Know I remain, Monsieur, your humble servant.

Rimbaud.

TO HIS FAMILY
Aden, November 22, 1887

My dear friends,

I hope that you are well and happy, and I am well too, but not exactly happy, because I still haven't found anything to do, although I think I will soon get something.

I haven't heard any news from you, but I am not worried. Do answer the following questions for me: what are the names and addresses of the Ardennes representatives, particularly those of your arrondissement? It may be that I will soon have to make a request of one of the ministers regarding a contract with the Obock colony, or for permission to import firearms destined for Abyssinia through the aforesaid coast, and I would make my request through your representative.

—How do I set up a retirement fund? With the government? Could I qualify for a pension at my age? What interest would I earn?

Yours,

Rimbaud.
General delivery, Aden Station.
British Colonies

TO HIS FAMILY
Aden, December 15, 1887

My dear friends,

I received your letter of November 20. I thank you for thinking of me.
I am fairly well; but I have yet to find anything decent to do.

I would like you to do me a little favor, which won't compromise you
in the least. I would like you to try to find out if I could obtain ministerial authorization to find some capital.

Send the adjoining letter to the representative of the Vouziers arrondissement, adding his name and that of the arrondissement to the top
of the letter. This letter to the representative should contain the letter to
the Minister. At the end of the letter to the Minister, in the space I've left
blank, carefully write the name of the representative whose assistance I'm
asking. That accomplished, send the whole thing to the representative's
address, making sure you take care to leave the envelope containing the
letter to the Minister unsealed.

If M. Corneau, the iron merchant, were still the Charleville representative, it would perhaps be better if it were sent to him, as it concerns a
metallurgical business; and then his name would go in the blanks left in
my letter at the end of the request to the Minister. If not, and as I am not
at all up to speed on current political intrigue, get in touch as soon as you
can with your local representative. You have nothing more to do than
what I just told you; and then nothing further will be sent your way, because you see that I am asking that the Minister respond to me through
the representative, and that the representative respond to me here, at the
Consulate.

I doubt that this attempt will work, because of current political conditions in this part of the African coast; but, nonetheless, this, as a beginning, costs only as much as the paper it's made on.

Do kindly send this letter to the representative (containing the request
to the Minister) as soon as you can, and without any corrections. The
matter will move forward all by itself if it moves forward at all.

I ask for your intervention in all of this because I do not know the representative's address, and I can't write to the Minister without my request coming with a recommendation. I hope that the representative will do something.

So now there is only the waiting. I will tell you, naturally, what they say, if they say anything: which is my hope.

I wrote an account of my travels in Abyssinia for the Geographical Society. I sent articles to *Temps, Figaro,* etc.... I am planning on sending some to the *Courrier des Ardennes,* just a few interesting tales of my travels in east Africa. I suspect that this couldn't do any harm.

Yours.

And write me only at the address below:

A. Rimbaud
General Delivery, Aden-Camp, Arabia.

TO THE VOUZIERS REPRESENTATIVE
Aden, December 15, 1887

Monsieur,

I am a native of Charleville (Ardennes), and it is my great honor to request that you might be so kind as to forward, in my name, with your considerable assistance, the attached request to the Minister of the Navy and the Colonies.

I have been traveling for the past eight years around the eastern coast of Africa, in the lands of Abyssinia, Harar, Danakil, and Somalia, in the service of various French commercial enterprises; M. le Consul of France in Aden, where I currently reside, can apprise you of the honor of my character and conduct.

I am one of a very small number of French merchants who does business with King Ménélik, king of Choa (central Abyssinia) and friend to all the European and Christian powers—and it is in his country, roughly 700 kilometers from the Obock coast, that I intend to try to develop the industry mentioned in my request to the Minister.

But as the sale of arms and munitions is prohibited on the eastern coast of Africa held and protected by France (which is to say the Obock colony and its coasts), I ask that the Minister give me the authorization to have the tools and supplies described shipped through the aforesaid Obock coasts, without interruption except to load those camels required to cross the desert.

As none of these tools or supplies can sit idle on the coast as the ban stipulates; as nothing of the aforesaid load will be misappropriated either en route or on the coast; as the importation of the aforesaid tools and supplies is destined exclusively for Choa, a Christian country that is a European ally; and as I must present myself, in order to fulfill the aforesaid order, exclusively to French investors and manufacturers: I hope that the minister will look kindly on my request and send me authorization along the lines of my request, which is to say: allow the entirety of the aforesaid order destined for Choa to make its way through the entirety of the

Obock coast and the adjacent Danakil and Somali coasts protected or administered by France.

Allow me, Monsieur, to ask you once again to pass along my request to the Minister, whose response I will be most grateful to have you forward directly to me.

Accept, Monsieur, my most respectful consideration.

Arthur Rimbaud.
Address: French Consulate,
Aden (British Colonies).

TO THE MINISTER
Aden, December 1887

Monsieur le Ministre,

It is my privilege herewith to request official authorization to unload the following merchandise on the eastern coast of Africa—comprising the Obock colony, the protectorate of Tadjoura, and the complete expanse of the Somali coast protected and held by France—destined for King Ménélik, king of Choa, and to be sent by caravans that would be organized along the aforesaid French coast.

The merchandise is:

1) All the materials, tools, and supplies required for the fabrication of flintlock rifles, Gras or Remington design.
2) All the materials, tools, and supplies required for the fabrication of cartridges and weapons of war.

To enable all of this, I will require French investment and manufacture in order to establish the aforesaid industry, which will be manned by French personnel. This boils down to an attempt to establish a French industrial concern some 700 kilometers from the coasts that would benefit a useful Christian power, allied with Europe in general and France in particular; and the requested authorization is only made in order to ensure the delivery of the caravan to the coast, where the trafficking in arms and munitions is prohibited.

French commercial agent and traveler throughout the eastern coast of Africa for over eight years; well respected by all the Europeans in the region; loved by the locals: I hope, Monsieur le Ministre, that you will deign to grant my request, which I also have the honor of making in the name of King Ménélik, and I will await the Minister's response care of representative Fagot of the Vouziers arrondissement of the Ardennes, whence I come.

With my deepest respect,

Arthur Rimbaud.
Address: French Consulate, Aden, Arabia.

TO HIS FAMILY
Aden, January 25, 1888

My dear friends,

I received the letter in which you tell me that you sent my outpourings to the Minister's address. Thank you. We will see what that brings. I'm not counting on anything; but he could grant the permission I seek, at least after the Italo-Abyssinian war, which doesn't seem to have reached its end.

Still, with authorization given, I'll need to find the capital; which is easier said than done. You must realize that my 40,000-odd francs won't be sufficient for such an endeavor; but I could manage to drum up some money with the fact of the authorization alone, were it given, and given with clear terms. I am already sure of a few investors' willingness to help, and who could be tempted by such possibilities.

Do be so kind as to let me know, should something come of this and you hear of it; although I told the representative to respond to me directly, here at the French consulate. —Don't involve yourselves in this in the least. It will take care of itself; or it won't at all, which is more likely.

There is nothing keeping me in Aden; summer is very nearly here, meaning I need to find a cooler climate soon, because this one drains me completely, and I've had more than enough of it.

Things have really changed around the Red Sea, aren't anything like they were six or seven years ago.

It's the European Invasion on every coast that is responsible: English in Egypt, Italians in Massaouah, French in Obock, English in Berbéra, etc. and they say that the Spanish want to occupy some port near the straits! All these governments are here to gobble up millions (and in some cases billions) along these godforsaken, desolate coasts, where the locals wan-

---

40,000-odd francs: Berrichon was in the habit of changing these numbers throughout his edition of the correspondence. Here, as no original manuscript of the letter exists, one would presume the figure to have been 16,000, as would be consistent with both the originals we have of the period and Berrichon's changes of the figure to 40,000 in his editions.

der around for months without food and water in the most abominable climate in the world; and the millions that have been cast into the bellies of Bedouins have brought nothing in return but war and disaster of every variety! Nonetheless, I will find something to do here.

I wish you a happy '88, in all shapes and forms.

Yours,

Rimbaud.

TO UGO FERRANDI
Monsieur Ugo Ferrandi
Steamer Point, Aden
Aden, April 2, 1888

My dear sir,

I am ready to leave by the "Tuna," which arrives Saturday. By avoiding unnecessary packages, you can do the same. I am delighted to make the trip together, and I expect that we will arrive quickly and easily.

Yours,

TO HIS FAMILY
Aden, April 4, 1888

My dear friends,

I received your letter of March 19.

I have just returned from a trip to Harar: six hundred kilometers, which I did in 11 days on horseback.

I am leaving again, in three or four days, for Zeila and Harar, where I will settle. I am going on business for some Aden merchants.

The ministerial response arrived long ago, in the negative, which I expected. Nothing to do about it, and anyway, for now, I have found something else.

So I will be living in Africa once again, and I won't be seen for some time. For me, hope that business will be good.

For the time being, write me at my employer's in Aden, avoiding the mention of anything that could be considered compromising.

Yours,

Monsieur Rimbaud
Chez Monsieur César Tian,
Aden,
English holdings,
Arabia

You can also, and even preferably, write me directly in Zeila, since it's a member of the postal union. (You'll have to find out the price of postage.)

Monsieur Arthur Rimbaud,
In Zeila, Red Sea, via Aden,
English holdings.

---

some Aden merchants: his old employers, Bardey and Tian.

TO UGO FERRANDI
Aden, April 10, 1888

My dear Hugo,

They tell me that the "Toona" isn't leaving until Monday afternoon.
Regardless, I expect that you are ready.

As I am leaving from Mallah, be so good as to bring *Mr. Rondant's two cases* with your luggage. They are beneath the Suel's veranda, and you should bring them along. I will pay the shipping.

Otherwise, I fear that the cases will remain there only another few years.

Yours,
Rimbaud

"*Toona*": same boat as before, new spelling; a 200-ton English ship of the era.

I am bored all the time; I've never met anyone as bored as I am. And if that weren't bad enough there's the matter of living without one's family, without intellectual pursuits, lost in the midst of all these Negroes whose lives one is trying to improve and who, themselves, are trying to take advantage of you and make it impossible for you to sell your wares without delays. Having to speak their gobbledygook, to eat their dirty food, to suffer a thousand boredoms as a result of their laziness, their dishonesty, their stupidity. . . .

AUGUST 4, 1888

XII

HARAR ONCE
MORE

1888–1891

A photograph by Rimbaud of a dwelling in Harar.

TO ALFRED BARDEY [EXCERPT]
May 3, 1888

I just arrived from Harar. The rain is incredibly heavy this year, and my trip took me through a series of cyclones; rain in the lowlands will end in two months.

TO HIS FAMILY
Harar, May 15, 1888

My dear friends,

I find myself resettled here, for the foreseeable future.

I have established a French commercial desk, modeled on the agency that I held long ago, with, nonetheless, a few improvements and innovations. I am doing some fairly important business, which is returning a profit.

Could you give me the name of the largest manufacturers of Sedan cloth in your region? I would like to ask them for some small supplies of their fabrics: they could be sold in Harar and Abyssinia.

I am feeling well. I am very busy, and all alone. It is cool here and I am happy to be able to rest, or at least to refresh, after three summers spent on the coast.

Be well and prosper.

Rimbaud.

TO HIS FAMILY
Harar, July 4, 1888

My dear friends,

I am settled here again for the long term and am doing business. My correspondent in Aden is Monsieur Tian, who has been there for the last 20 years.

I already wrote you from here once without having a response. Be so good as to share your news with me. I hope that you are all in good health and that your work is going as well as possible.

I have heard nothing from you. You are wrong to forget me like this.

I am very busy, very bored, but currently in good health since I left the Red Sea, where I hope not to have to go for a long while.

This land is currently under the governance of Abyssinia. We are at peace for now. On the coast, at Zeila, England governs.

So write me, and know I remain your devoted,

Rimbaud,
Address: chez Monsieur Tian, merchant
In Aden.

TO HIS FAMILY
Harar, August 4, 1888

My dear friends,

I received your letter of June 27. The delay in the mail shouldn't surprise you, as where I am is separated from the coast by deserts that take eight days for the mail carriers to cross; then there's the matter of the service between Zeila and Aden being very intermittent, the mail for Europe leaving Aden only once a week and then taking two weeks to reach Marseille. It takes three months round-trip for a letter sent to Europe to yield a response. It is impossible to write to Harar directly from Europe, because beyond Zeila, which is under English protection, there is only desert occupied by wandering tribes. It is mountainous here, and borders the Abyssinian plateaus: the temperature never rises past 25 degrees above zero, and is never less than 5 degrees above zero. So it never freezes, and you never sweat.

Right now it's rainy season. It is somewhat gloomy. The government is that of Abyssinian King Ménélik, which is to say a black-Christian government; but, above all, we are in a state of peace and basic security, and, as for business, it goes better some days than others. I am not living with the hope of becoming a millionaire any time soon. And so it seems to be my fate that I should have to live this way in these lands!

There are barely twenty Europeans in all of Abyssinia, including those here. And you can imagine how spread out they are in these vast spaces. Harar remains where the majority are located: perhaps ten. I am the only Frenchman. There is also a Catholic mission with three priests, one of whom is French and is educating the pickaninnies.

I am bored all the time; I've never met anyone as bored as I am. And if that weren't bad enough there's the matter of living without one's family, without intellectual pursuits, lost in the midst of all these Negroes whose lives one is trying to improve and who, themselves, are trying to take advantage of you and make it impossible for you to sell your wares without delays. Having to speak their gobbledygook, to eat their dirty food, to suffer a thousand boredoms as a result of their laziness, their dishonesty, their stupidity?

But that's not even the saddest part. It is the fear that little by little one is becoming a moron, given such isolation and a complete lack of intelligent company.

We import silks, cottons, thalers and other trinkets: we export coffee, rubber, perfume, ivory, gold from far away, etc., etc. Business, however much there is, isn't as much as I would like and, on top of that, is divided between the few Europeans stuck in these vast lands.

Sincerely yours. Write me.

Rimbaud.

TO HIS FAMILY
Harar, November 10, 1888

Dear friends,

Today I received your letter of October 1. I would have preferred to return to France to see you, but it is completely impossible for me to leave this African pit for the foreseeable future.

So, my dear Maman, rest, take care. Enough of all the overwork. At the very least, spare your health and get some rest.

· ·

Were there something I could do for you, I wouldn't hesitate to.

· ·

Know that my conduct here is irreproachable. In all my affairs, others have taken advantage of me, not the contrary.

My existence here—and I say this often, but I don't say it enough and I have hardly anything else to say—my existence is painful, my life being shortened by fatal boredom and exhaustion of every kind. But who cares! —I only want to know that you are happy and in good health. I have grown accustomed to this life. I work. I travel. I would like to do something good, something useful. What will come of it? I don't know yet.

So, I have been feeling better since I have been in the interior, and that's something.

Write me more often. Do not forget your son and your brother.

                                                            Rimbaud.

Dotted lines indicate sections of the letter edited out by Berrichon in his first edition. The manuscripts no longer exist.

TO HIS FAMILY
Harar, January 10, 1889

My dear Maman, my dear sister,

I did indeed receive your letter dated December ten, 1888. Thank you for your suggestions and your wishes. I wish you good health and prosperity for the year 1889.

Why are you always writing of illnesses, of death, of all kinds of disagreeable things? Let us put these things far from view, and strive to live as comfortably as we can, within our means.

I am well, better than my affairs, which provide me with ample trouble in exchange for little benefit. Given the various complications surrounding where I work, it is very unlikely that I will leave this country any time soon. And yet my savings barely increase. I may even be going backward more than forward.

I have every intention of making the donation of which you speak. It doesn't really make me very happy to think that what little I have taken such great pains to amass would serve to fatten those who haven't even written me a single letter! Were I ever to find myself seriously ill, I would do it, and there is a Christian mission in this area to which I would entrust my will, which would then be sent to the French Consulate in Aden a few weeks later. But what I have won't be released until I've completed the liquidation of the firm of César Tian in Aden. In any case, were I very ill, I would liquidate the agency here myself; and I would then go to Aden, which is a civilized country, and where one's affairs can be settled immediately.

Send me news, and know that I remain
Your devoted,

Rimbaud
Chez Monsieur César Tian
Aden

TO HIS FAMILY
Harar, February 25, 1889

My dear Maman, my dear sister,

Just a note to ask you what's new, since I haven't heard from you for so long.

I am feeling very well right now; and business isn't doing too badly either.

I like to think that everything is going as well as can be imagined with you.

Know I remain devoted to you, and do write me.

Rimbaud.

TO JULES BORELLI
Harar, February 25, 1889

My dear Monsieur Borelli,

How are you?
—I received your letter from Cairo of January 12.

A thousand thanks for all that you were able to do and say on my behalf in our colony. Unfortunately, God knows what continues to divert the Issas around our Djibouti; trouble along the road from Biocabouba to Djibouti (because you can't go from here to Ambos, which is too close to Zeila, without running alongside it all the way to Djibouti!); lack of a commercial installation in Djibouti or any sort of political organization; failure of navy communication between Djibouti and Aden; and, above all, the following question: how will merchandise arriving in Djibouti be handled in Aden (as there isn't a warehouse for our merchandise in Obock)?

It's relatively easy to find camels to go from Djibouti to Harar, and the customs exemption makes up or, really, exceeds the cost of renting the animals. As such we received M. Savouré's 250 camels, whose business finally succeeded: he arrived here a few weeks after you, with his associate. Dedjatch Makonnen left here for Choa on November 9, 1888, and M. Savouré went up to Ankober by the Herer route a week after Makonnen's departure through the Itous. M. Savouré stayed here with me; he even left twenty of his loaded camels here with me, which I sent along to him in Choa two weeks ago, along the Herer route. I have power of attorney to dispose of fifty thousand thalers in his name in Harar to buy rifles, as it seems that he didn't receive much of anything from King Ménélik. In any case, his partner leaves Farré for Zeila at the end of March, with their first return caravan. M. Pino will go to the coast when this happens.

---

the Issas: a Somali population located between Djibouti and Zeila. *M. Pino:* Éloi Pino was an arms trader.

You must know that M. Brémond arrived in Obock-Djibouti. I have no idea what he plans on doing. He does have an associate traveling with him. I haven't had a letter from him since he left Marseille; but I am awaiting mail from Djibouti. M. Ilg arrived here from Zeila at the end of December 1888 with forty-odd camels loaded with things for the king. He stayed with me for about six weeks: we couldn't find him any camels, our present administration being useless, and the Gallas being as unaccommodating as ever. Anyway, he was able to load up his caravan and leave for Choa on February 5, via Herer. He should be in the Haawache by now. —The two other Swiss are waiting for him there.

Our *choums* here are Alto Tesamma, Ato Mikael, and *gragnazmatche* Banti. Abd-Ullahi is *mouslénié* or tax collector. Life has never been so peaceful here, and we aren't in the least affected by the political convulsions that have hold of Abyssinia. —Our garrison has around a thousand Remingtons.

Naturally, since Makonnen's retreat, which was followed by those of Dedjatch Bécha of Boroma and even that of Waldé Gabriel of Tchertcher, the road is completely closed to us. —We haven't received any more *maggadies* for a long time.

And the only mail we receive comes from M. Savouré, despite the king sending orders to the choums here, and despite Makonnen continuing to send his orders to the aforesaid choums as if he were here, despite it not being certain that he will be renamed the local governor, given that he left considerable debts.

So, via the last courier, we learned that things appear to have settled down in Choa, that the Dedjatch Waldé Gabriel had returned to reoccupy Tchertcher: this would mean the reopening of commercial relations with Choa.

Surely you're up to speed on everything that has happened in Choa. The emperor dethroned Tékla Haïmanante of Godjam to replace him with, I think, Ras Mikael. The former king of Godjam rebelled, hunted

---

choum: chieftain. *gragnazmatche:* a military title; roughly "commander." *Waldé Gabriel of Tchertcher:* in central Ethiopia.

down his replacement, and fought the forces of the emperor; whence the initiative by Ato Joannès and his assault on Godjam, which he ravaged horribly and where he remains. We don't yet know if peace has been made with Tékla Haïmanante.

Ato Joannès had many grievances against Ménélik. Ménélik refused to return a number of Joannès's deserters who had sought asylum with the king. It is even said that he lent a thousand rifles to the king of Godjam. The emperor was also very unhappy with the various plots, sincere or otherwise, thickened by Ménélik and the Italians. So relations between the two sovereigns became bitter, and so one worried, and one still does, that Joannès might cross the Abbai to attack the king of Choa.

In a state of worry with respect to this invasion, Ménélik abandoned all the outer positions to redouble his fortifications in Choa, particularly along the Godjam road. Ras Govana and Ras Darghi still have control of Abbai crossings; it is also said that they have had to repel an attempted crossing by the emperor's troops. As for Makonnen, he went as far as Djimma, the food tax of which the unfortunate king already paid to a detachment of Joannès's troops moving west. Abba Couri paid a second food tax to Ménélik.

Aboune Mathios and a group of other people interceded between the two kings in the hope of restoring peace. They say that Ménélik, very upset, refused to propitiate them. But little by little the disagreement, it seems, subsided. The fear of the Derviches holds the emperor back; and Ménélik, who has hidden his wealth from God and the Devil, is, as you know, too prudent to make so dangerous a move. He remains in Entotto. Things remain very quiet here.

Antonelli arrived in Ankober on January 25 with 5,000 rifles and a few million Vetterli cartridges, which he was to have delivered, I think, some time ago. It seems that he brought back quite a few thalers. —They say that the whole thing is a gift! I think it's more likely a simple business transaction.

The count's assistants, Traverso, Ragazzi, etc., remain where they had been in Choa.

---

the Abbai: the Blue Nile. *Aboune:* Amharan religious title for Coptic orthodox leader.

We are still told that the honorable Viscardi has left for Assab with a new load of Remington rifles.

The Italian government has also sent Doctor Nerazzini to stay here (all these diplomatic doctors!) as an intermediary for the Antonelli station.

Just a few days ago, we had a visit from Count Téléki, who made an important mission to the unexplored regions of northwest Kenya: he claims to have made it as far as ten days south of Kaffa. He told us what you said of the Djibié river, which is to say that, instead of flowing into the Indian Ocean, it spills into a great lake to the southwest. According to him, the "Sambourou" one sees on maps doesn't exist.

Count Téléki is leaving for Zeila. The death of Prince Rodolphe calls him back to Austria.

I said hello to Bidault on your behalf. He sends you his very best. He has yet to find a home for his collection of photographs of the area, which he has completed. They haven't called him back to Choa or elsewhere, and he continues to live a life of contemplation.

Make use of me however you might need to around here, and know I remain devotedly,

Rimbaud.
c/o Monsieur Tian, Aden

Count Téléki: a Hungarian explorer.

TO UGO FERRANDI
Harar, April 30, 1889

Dear Monsieur Ferrandi,

I did indeed receive your bill from Geldessey, and sent it along to Naufragio, who says hello.

I imagine you must know that the Abyssinians occupied your house as soon as you left. I expect that doesn't surprise you.

The soldier will probably meet you in Biokaboba. Nothing new here: the gorgings of Easter Week are complete: now it's back to the same old shit, *Sm Joyés.*

Tomorrow or the day after, the Abyssinians will release a caravan bound for Choa, with which Khaouaga Élias and the imposing Mossieu Moskoff will also travel. —We haven't had any news from Choa for a month. The Greeks arriving from Zeila say that Joannès is dead, probably heard from Corazzini's telegrams, but here the locals don't know a thing.

Hello to your companion, tell him that up until now no one has taken care of things (4th day). I wrote to Tian's agent in Zeila to let him stay with him.

There is even a note for him.

Yours,

Rimbaud.

Biokaboba: a station along the Zeila Harar route. *Moskoff:* Vassili Moskoff, the Russian czar's representative to King Ménélik.

TO HIS FAMILY
Harar, May 18, 1889

My dear Maman, my dear sister,

I did indeed receive your letter of April 2. It makes me very happy to hear that, for you, all is well.

I am still very busy in this damned country; what I am earning is not worth the trouble it brings me, as we are leading a sorry existence surrounded by these niggers.

The only good thing about this country is that it never freezes here; it's never less than 10 above zero, and never more than 30. But it is raining torrentially right now, and as it is with you, that keeps us from being able to work, which is to say receive and send caravans.

Anyone who comes through here isn't at risk of becoming a millionaire—unless you're looking to become rich in lice by getting too near the locals.

You should have read in the papers that Emperor Jean (what an emperor!) died, killed by the *Mahdists.* We too depend indirectly on this emperor. We depend directly on King Ménélik of Choa, who himself pays tribute to emperor Jean. Ménélik rebelled last year against this unbearable Jean; they were at each other's throats when the aforesaid emperor had the idea to go beat the tar out of the Mahdists along the Matama coast first. And there he remains, may the devil take him.

Here, everything is peaceful. We depend on Abyssinia, but the Hawash river separates us from them.

It remains easy for us to communicate with Zeila and Aden.

I am sorry that I won't be able to make a trip to the exposition this year, but my profits are far from allowing me to do so, and anyway I am ab-

---

Mahdists: followers of a *mahdi,* or prophet, in this case, Sudan's fanatical Mohammed Ahmed Ibn Sayyid. *the exposition:* Rimbaud is talking about the 1889 Exposition Universelle in Paris, a sort of world's fair, visited by over 30 million people.

solutely alone here, and were I to leave, my agency would disappear completely.

So next time, perhaps, I'll be able to exhibit this country's products, and perhaps even exhibit myself, since I must have an exceedingly bizarre appearance after so long a stay in countries like these.

Awaiting news from you, I wish you good weather and good spirits.

Rimbaud
Address: chez Monsieur César Tian,
Merchant.
Aden.

TO HIS FAMILY
Harar, December 20, 1889

My dear Maman, my dear sister,

In asking you to forgive me for not having written more often, I write to wish you, for 1890, a happy year (as much as possible) and good health.

I am still very busy, and feel fairly well considering how bored I am, how very bored.

I have heard very little from you as well. Don't make yourselves so scarce, and know I remain

Your devoted,
Rimbaud.

TO HIS FAMILY
Harar, January 3, 1890

My dear mother
My dear sister

I received your letter of November 19, 1889.

You say that you haven't heard from me apart from a letter dated May 18! That's impossible; I wrote you nearly every month, I wrote you again in December, wishing you prosperity and health for 1890, which I have the pleasure to wish you here again.

As for your letters written every two weeks, know that I wouldn't not respond to a single one, but they haven't reached me, which makes me very upset, and I will ask for an explanation in Aden, where I am shocked that they would allow such a thing to occur.

Yours, your son and brother,

Rimbaud.
chez Monsieur Tian,
Aden (Arabia)
English colonies.

TO A. DESCHAMPS
Harar, January 27, 1890

Monsieur Deschamps,

M. Chefneux, passing through here, spoke to me on your behalf regarding the late Labatut's bill with you.

You know very well that I in no way endorsed that bill and I therefore shouldn't have any responsibility for it—any more than the other debts surrounding the inheritance—until my own interests are reconciled, interests I was wrong to overlook in the face of the conditions of my arrangement with Labatut.

I am shocked that you have forgotten, after my explanation of all this, your having accepted payment of 1,100 thalers against the aforesaid account, and after you promised the Consul himself to tear up the bill and send it to me, and yet the next day you refused without any justification.

So make your complaint to the Aden Consulate again, where all the accounts and evidence relating to the matter are deposed.

With my sincere attention,

Rimbaud.

Harar, February 25, 1890

Dear mother and sister,

I received your letter of January 21, 1890.

Don't be surprised that I rarely write: the recurring motif would only be that I have nothing interesting to say. Because when you're in country like this, you have more to ask about than to report! Deserts filled with stupid niggers, without roads, without mail, without travelers: and what would you have me write about that? That everyone is bored, annoyed, growing dumber by the day, that I've had enough, but that I can't get out of here, etc., etc.! As a result, that's really everything, everything I can say; and, as that isn't entertaining for anyone to hear, better not to speak. Essentially, we massacre and pillage the region. Happily I haven't been a part of any of that, and I expect to leave here in one piece when I do—what a waste otherwise! In the countryside and on the roads I enjoy a certain respect thanks to my reputation for decency, never having hurt a soul here. On the contrary, I do good when and where I can, which amounts to my only pleasure here.

I am working with Monsieur Tian, who wrote to you to put you at ease about my situation. Business would, at its root, not be terrible were, as you have heard, the roads not closed all the time by wars and revolts that imperil our caravans. Monsieur Tian is a major merchant in Aden, and he never travels in these parts.

The people of Harar are neither dumber nor more treacherous than the white niggers of the so-called civilized countries; they're just a different kind, that's all. They are, in fact, even less cruel, and can, in certain cases, exhibit gratitude and loyalty. One needs only treat them humanely.

Ras Makonnen, whose name you've read in newspapers and who led an Abyssinian delegation to Italy that made a lot of noise last year, is governor of Harar.

With the hope of seeing you again. Yours,

Rimbaud.

TO KING MÉNÉLIK

Letter from Monsieur Rimbaud,
Harar Merchant, to His Majesty,
His Majesty King Ménélik

Majesty,

How do you fare? Please accept my faithful greetings and my sincere good wishes.

The choums, or rather the Chouftas from Hararghé, refuse to give me the four thousand thalers that they ripped from my coffers in your name, under the pretext of a loan, now seven months ago.

I have already written you three times on this subject.

This money belongs to French coastal merchants; they sent it to me to do business here on their behalf and, as of now, have seized my possessions on the coast and wish to have me cease acting on their behalf.

I estimate a *personal* loss of two thousand thalers from this affair. What will you make up of this loss?

Moreover, each month I pay one percent interest on this money, which has already come to 280 thalers that I paid out of pocket for a sum you are keeping from me; each month the interest grows.

In the name of justice, I beg you to have these four thousand thalers returned to me as soon as possible; the good thalers I lent, as well as the interest accumulated at 1% per month, from the day of the loan to the day of repayment.

I am making a report of the matter to our choums in Obock and to our consul in Aden, so they can know how we are treated in Harar.

Please respond as soon as possible.

Harar, April 7, 1890

Rimbaud.
French Merchant in Harar

Hararghé: Harar.

TO ARMAND SAVOURÉ [FRAGMENT]
[undated]

[...]

I had no need of your revolting coffee, bought at the cost of incalculable annoyance at the hands of the Abyssinians; I only took it to bring your payment to an end, since you were in such a hurry. And anyway, I repeat, if I hadn't gone about things this way, you would *never have gotten anything, absolutely nothing, nothing of nothing,* and everyone knows it and would say as much! You know it yourself, but I see that the air in Djibouti gets the better of you!

So, after having assumed *the risks and dangers of shipping your garbage without any hope of profit,* I would have been utterly moronic, utterly stupid, to import thalers at 2% shipping for the whites' account at a 2 or 3% loss in the exchange, to reimburse against coffee that I never ordered, which earns me nothing, etc., etc. Would you believe that?

Once you spend time in Choa, you start to think like an Abyssinian!

Look over my accounts, cher Monsieur, make an honest accounting, and you will see that I'm perfectly in my rights, and you should consider yourself lucky it's ending here!

Please then do send me as soon as possible a receipt for *8,833 thalers* for the balance of the accounts; enough messing around; —because, as far as I'm concerned, I could easily present you with proof to the tune of a few thousand thalers in losses that your business has cost me, a business with which I should never have gotten involved.

Awaiting your receipt, sincerely.

Rimbaud.

This is a fragmentary letter that appeared in Berrichon's early biography of Rimbaud.

TO HIS MOTHER
Harar, April 21, 1890

My dear mother,

I received your letter of February 26.
. . . .

As for me, alas! I don't have the time to get married, or to look to get married. It is utterly impossible for me to leave my work any time soon. When one works in these damned countries, one never leaves.

I am feeling well, but my hair is turning white by the minute. All the time I've been here, I've been worried that I would soon have a head like a powder puff. It's distressing, this treasonous scalp; but what can one do.

Yours alone,

Rimbaud

TO HIS MOTHER
Harar, August 10, 1890

I haven't had any news from you in quite some time.

I like to think that you are in good health, just as I find myself these days.

. . . .

Could I get married at your house next spring? But I wouldn't be able to stay there, nor abandon my work here. Do you think I could find someone who would be willing to follow me in my travels?

I would like to have a response to this question as soon as possible.

All my wishes.

Rimbaud.

TO HIS MOTHER
Harar, November 10, 1890

My dear Maman,

I did indeed receive your letter of September 29, 1890.

Speaking of marriage, I always wanted to say that I intended to remain free to travel, to live abroad and even to continue to live in Africa. I am so unaccustomed to the European climate that I would find reacclimation difficult. I would probably have to spend the winters away to allow me to come back to France one day. And how would I make contacts again, what sort of work would I find? It remains a question. Anyway, the one thing that remains impossible is for me to live a sedentary life.

I must find someone who will follow me in my peregrinations.

As for my savings, I have it here, and it is available when I need it to be.

Monsieur Tian is a very honorable merchant, with thirty years of service in Aden, and I am his partner in this part of Africa. My partnership with him began two and a half years ago. I also work for myself on the side; and I am free, in any case, to liquidate my business whenever I should wish to.

I send caravans to the coast carrying products from these lands: gold, musk, ivory, coffee, etc., etc. In the business I do with M. Tian, we split the profits evenly.

Besides, for information, one need only ask Monsieur de Gaspary, French Consulate to Aden, or his successor.

No one in Aden has a bad word to say about me. On the contrary. I have been well known by everyone in this region for the last ten years.

Amateurs take heed!

As for Harar, there's no consul, no post office, no road; you go there by camel, and you live with the niggers. But you are free there, and the climate is pleasant.

That's the situation.

Au revoir.

A. Rimbaud.

TO HIS MOTHER
Harar, February 20, 1891

My dear Maman,

I did indeed receive your January letter.

I see that all is well with you, except the cold, which, after what I have been reading in the newspapers, is bad throughout Europe.

I am not well right now. At the very least, my right leg has varicose veins that hurt terribly. See what you get for working hard in these sad countries! And these veins are complicated by rheumatism. It isn't cold here; but climate is the culprit for my troubles. It's been two weeks since I slept a wink, because of the pain I've had in this damned leg. I'll get better, and I think that Aden's intense heat will do me some good, but I am owed a great deal of money and I can't go there now, or else I risk losing it. I asked for a stocking in Aden for my veins, but I doubt I'll find one.

So please do this for me: buy me a stocking for varicose veins, for a long slender leg—(the foot is size 41). This stocking has to reach above the knee, because there's a vein above the back of the knee. Stockings for varicose veins are made of cotton, or of silk woven with strands of elastic which compress the swollen veins. The silk ones are the best, the most durable. I don't think they are expensive. Anyway, I would reimburse you.

In the interim, I have my leg bandaged.

This infirmity was caused by too much time on horseback, and by long marches. Because in this country we have a maze of steep mountains, where one can't remain on horseback. All of this without roads or even paths.

The veins aren't in any way threatening to one's health, but they do prevent one from undertaking any sort of serious exercise. It is an incredible annoyance, because without the stockings they can develop sores, or worse! Lean, muscular legs won't tolerate stockings, particularly at night. In addition to that, I have rheumatic pain in my damned left knee, which tortures me at night! And you have to remember that this season, our winter never reaches below 10 degrees above zero (not below). But there are dry winds, which are very unhealthy for most whites. Even young Europeans from 25–30 suffer rheumatism after two or three years here.

The bad food, the unhealthy accommodations, the light clothing, the worries of every sort, the boredom, the unrelenting rage at being surrounded by niggers as dumb as devils, all this goes straight to one's morale and health in short order. A year here is like five anywhere else. You age very quickly here, as everywhere across the Sudan.

In your response, remind me of where I stand regarding military service. Do I have to serve? Make sure, and write me back.

Rimbaud.

Rimbaud's photo of a Harar horseman, c. 1883.

*I rented sixteen Negro porters, at 15 thalers each,
from Harar to Zeila; I had a stretcher made out of
a sail, and during the twelve days I spent on it I
crossed the 300 kilometers of desert that separate
the Harar mountains from the Zeila port. Useless
to detail the horrible suffering I experienced en
route.*

APRIL 30, 1891

XIII

FINAL
TRANSIT

1891

① Mardi 7 avril 1899

Départ de Harar à 6h du matin — Arrivée
à Degadallala à 9½ du matin — marécage
à Egon — Haut Egon 12h — Egon, Ballaoua
Fort 3h — Descente à Egon, Ballaoua très
pénible pour les porteurs qui tombent à chaque
caillou, et pour moi qui mange de chasie
à chaque minute, la civière est déjà à
moitié disloquée, et les gens commencent à rendre
je serai de monter à mulet la jambe attachée
au cou — je suis obligé de descendre en Brancard
de quelques minutes et de me remettre en civière
qui est déjà restée un kilomètre arrière
...
Arrivée à Ballaoua il pleut
Vent furieux toute la nuit

② mercredi 8
Attaché la grande journée avec ...
...
9e Levé de Ballaoua à 6½ entre
à Geldessey à 10½ — Les porteurs
se mettent au courant, et il n'y a
plus à souffrir qu'à la descente de
Ballaoua — — Orage à
4 heures à Geldessey — La nuit
rosée très abondante ...

③ Jeudi 9 Parti à 7 h matin
arrivée à Grawa à 9½. Resté à Ila de
l'abbaye les chameaux en arrière
3528

DIARY OF THE CROSSING

Tuesday, April 7 [1891]
Left Harar at 6 A.M. —Arrived Degadallal at 9:30 A.M. —Swamp to Égon. Upper Égon, noon. —Égon to Ballaouafort, 3 P.M. Difficult descent from Égon to Ballaoua for the bearers who reel at every pebble, and for me who reels at every minute. The stretcher is already half falling apart, and the bearers already exhausted. I already tried to ride a mule with the ailing leg attached to the neck—but I had to get down after a few minutes and lie back down on the stretcher which had already been left a kilometer behind. Night spent beneath the moon. Arrived in Ballaoua. It rained—furious wind all night—

Wednesday, 8
Attached [unreadable] to have [unreadable] and left at war with the whole body...
—Up in Ballaoua at 6:30. Enter Gueldessey at 10:30. Bearers begin to run, and no suffering until the descent from Ballaoua. —Storm at 4 P.M. in Gueldessey. Night, abundant dew, cold.

Thursday, 9th
Left 7 A.M. Arrived Glasley at 9:30. Waited for the Abban and the camels left behind. Lunched. Up at 1 P.M. Arrived Boussa at 5:30 P.M. Crossing the river impossible. Camped with M. Donald—his wife and 2 children.

Friday 10th
Rain. Rising before 11 impossible. Camels refuse to move. The stretcher leaves nonetheless and arrives Wordji in the rain, at 2 P.M. All evening and night we await camels which do not come. Rains 16 hours straight, neither food nor shelter. I spend this time underneath an Abyssinian skin.

Saturday 11th
at 6 A.M., sent 8 men to look for camels and rested with the others wait-

ing in Wordji. The camels come at 4 P.M., and we eat after thirty hours of complete abstinence, 16 hours of which in the open in the rain.

Sunday 12th
Left Wordji at 6 A.M. Cotto by 8:30. Stop at the river Dalahmaley, 10:40. Up again at 2 P.M. Camped at Dalahmaley at 4:30 [...] freezing. Camels don't arrive until 6 P.M.

Monday 13th
Up at 5:30. Arrived Biokabosba at 9 A.M. Camped.

Tuesday 14th
Up at 5:30. Porters proceed badly. At 9:30 stop in Arrouina. Throw me to the ground on arrival. I impose a 4 thaler fine. Up at 2 P.M. Arrived Samodo at 5:30 P.M.

Wednesday 15th
Up at 6 A.M. Arrived Lasman at 10 A.M. Up again at 2:30. Arrived Kombavoren at 6:30.

Thursday 16th
Up at 5:30. Passed Ensa. Stopped at Doudouhassa at 9 A.M. [unreadable]. Up at 2 P.M. Dadap, 6:15. At 5½ found 22 camels in 11 skins: Adaouel.

Friday 17th
Up at Dadap at 9:30. Arrived Warambot at 4:30.

TO HIS MOTHER
Aden, April 30, 1891

My dear mother,

I did indeed receive your two stockings and your letter, and I received them in unfortunate circumstances. Having seen the swelling of my right knee only increase along with the pain when bending it, and without finding any sort of remedy or opinion as to why (since in Harar we're surrounded by niggers and there aren't any Europeans there), I decided to leave. I had to abandon my business: which wasn't easy, because I had money scattered across the coast; but I managed to liquidate almost completely. For three weeks, I had been resting in Harar, unable to move at all, suffering incredible pain and not sleeping at all. I rented sixteen Negro porters, at 15 thalers each, from Harar to Zeila; I had a stretcher made out of a sail, and during the twelve days I spent on it I crossed the 300 kilometers of desert that separate the Harar mountains from the Zeila port. Useless to detail the horrible suffering I experienced en route. I was unable to take a single step away from my stretcher; my knee had visibly swelled, and the pain had only increased.

Upon reaching here, I registered at the European hospital. There is one room only for paying patients: mine. The English doctor, as soon as I showed him my leg, burst out that it was *a very dangerous stage of synovitis*, stemming from lack of proper care and rest. He immediately said that the leg would have to go; then he decided to wait a few days to see if the swelling decreased a little after treatment. I have been here for six days without improvement, but at the very least the rest has brought a decrease in the pain. You know that synovitis is a malady relating to the liquid that allows the knee to bend, and it can be hereditary, or can develop after an accident, or many other reasons. Undoubtedly, mine was caused by exhaustion from long marches on foot and on horseback to Harar. So, given the condition in which I arrived, there is little hope that I will be

---

synovitis: Rimbaud's younger sister, Vitalie, died of an illness not unlike this one.

better in any less than three months in the best case. And I am on my back, leg bandaged, tied, retied, chained, in such a way that I cannot move. I have become a skeleton: I frighten people. My back is raw from the bed; I don't sleep a wink. And here the heat has become intense. The food in the hospital for which I am nonetheless paying a great deal is terrible. I don't know what to do. On the other hand, I haven't settled my accounts with my partner, Monsieur Tian. That won't be settled for another week. I will leave with around 35 thousand francs. I would have had more; but because of my unfortunate departure, I lost several thousand francs. I would like to be taken to a steamboat and to have myself treated in France; the trip would help pass the time. And in France the medical care and medicines themselves are less expensive, and the air is good. It is therefore very likely that I will come. The steamboats for France right now are always full, because everyone is returning from the colonies this time of year. And I am a poor invalid who must be *transported* very carefully! So I should make my departure in about a week.

Don't be upset by all of this, regardless. Better days are coming. But it is a sad return on so much work, deprivation, and suffering! Alas, life is miserable!

With all my heart.

Rimbaud.

P.S. —As for the stockings, they are useless. I will resell them somewhere.

TO CÉSAR TIAN
Aden (Saint-Point), May 6, 1891

Monsieur,

I acknowledge receipt of your letter today returning the final accounting of our Harar partnership, with which I agree.

I also received your draft in my name on the Comptoir National d'Escompte de Paris and thank you for the sum of 37,450 francs or 20,805.90 rupees.

It remains understood that the balance of my account with you will not be settled until the liquidation of those remaining matters in Harar whose yields will be split between us.

You have my respectful greetings,

A. Rimbaud.

*Despair takes you again and you remain sitting
like a total invalid, sniveling until dark, darkness
that brings endless insomnia and a dawn sadder
than the dusk it preceded, etc., etc.*

JULY 15, 1891

XIV

AT REST

1891

Hospital of the Conception, Marseille.

TO HIS FAMILY
Marseille
[undated]

My dear Maman, my dear sister,

After terrible suffering, not having been able to get better in Aden, I took the Messageries boat to return to France.

I arrived yesterday, after thirteen days of pain. Finding myself too weak upon arrival here and overcome by the cold, I had to register at the *Hospital of the Conception,* where I pay ten francs per day, including the doctor.

I am doing very poorly, very poorly; I have been reduced to a skeleton by this disease in my left leg, which now has become enormous and looks like a great pumpkin. It's synovitic, hydro-arthritic, etc., a disease of the bend of the joint and the bone.

This will not be resolved for some time, particularly if complications force them to cut off my leg. In any case, I will remain crippled. I doubt I can wait that long. Life has become impossible. How unhappy I am! How unhappy I have become!

I have to cash a draft for 36,800 francs against the Comptoir National d'Escompte in Paris. But I have no one who can take care of the money for me. I can't take a single step from bed. I haven't been able to cash the money yet. What to do? What a sad life! Aren't you able to help me with anything?

Rimbaud.
Hospital of the Conception.
Marseille.

TELEGRAM TO HIS MOTHER
Marseille, May 22, 1891

Today, you or Isabelle, come to Marseille by express train. Monday morning, they amputate my leg. Risk of death. Serious matters to settle.

Arthur.

Reply to: Rimbaud, Conception Hospital

TO RAS MAKONNEN
Marseille, May 30, 1891

Excellency,

How are you? I wish you good health and great prosperity. May God grant you all you wish. May your life proceed in peace.

I write you from Marseille, in France. I am in the hospital. They cut off my leg six days ago. I am doing well now and in three weeks should be cured.

In a few months, I expect to return to Harar to get back to business as before, and I thought I would send you my greetings.

Accept the wishes of your humble servant.

Rimbaud.

TO ISABELLE
Marseille, June 17, 1891

Isabelle, my dear sister,

I received your note with my two letters returned from Harar. In one of these letters it says that they had returned a letter to Roche. Did you not receive anything else?

I have yet to write to anyone, I haven't yet gotten out of my bed. The doctor says that I'll be in bed for a month, and even afterward I will only be able to start walking very slowly. I still have a strong neuralgia where the leg was cut off, which is to say at the piece that remains. I have no idea what will happen. I am resigned to everything, I have no luck!

What's all this with you going on about burial? Don't busy yourself, be patient, get rest, be strong. Alas! I would so like to see you, what could be wrong with you? What illness? All illnesses are cured with time and caring. In any case, you must resign yourself and not lose hope.

I was furious when Maman left me, I don't know why. But for now it is better that she should be with you to take care of you. Ask her for forgiveness for me and wish her hello from me.

So au revoir, but who knows when?

Rimbaud.
Hospital of the Conception, Marseille.

TO ISABELLE
Marseille, June 23, 1891

My dear sister,

You haven't written; what has happened? Your letter scared me; I would like to have news from you. Let's hope that it has nothing to do with new problems, because, alas, we are already too experienced in these waters!

All I do is cry, day and night; I am a dead man; I am crippled for life. In two weeks' time, I will be better, I think; but I will only be able to walk with crutches. As for an artificial leg, the doctor says that I have to wait a very long time, at least six months! What will I do all that time, where will I stay? If I stay with you, the cold will chase me away in three months, perhaps even less, because, from here, I will not be able to move myself for six weeks, the time it will take for me to learn how to use crutches! So I won't be with you until the end of July. And then I'll have to leave again at the end of September.

I have no idea what to do. All these concerns are driving me mad: I don't sleep at all.

So our lives are misery, endless misery! Why do we exist?

Send me news of you. My best wishes.

Rimbaud
Hospital of the Conception.

TO ISABELLE
Marseille, June 24, 1891

My dear sister,

I received your letter of June 21. I wrote you yesterday. I didn't receive anything from you the 10th of June, neither a letter from you or from Harar. I only received the two letters of the 14th. I can't imagine where the letter of the 10th could be.

What is this new horror story you're telling me? What is the situation with my military service? When I was 26, didn't I send you, from Aden, a certificate proving that I was employed in a French firm, which is an allowable exemption—and later when I asked Maman she responded that everything was settled and that I had nothing to worry about. Barely four months ago, I asked you in one of my letters if there was anything else that needed to be done on this count, because I had wanted to return to France. And I didn't receive a response. I thought you had taken care of everything. Now it seems that you would have me believe I am down as a draft dodger, that they're after me, etc., etc. Don't look into this any further unless you are certain that it will not attract their attention. As far as I'm concerned, given my situation, there's no risk of me returning! Imagine prison after what I've been through. Death would be preferable!

And, actually, death would have been preferable to much of what I've been going through. What is a crippled man to do in the world? And now having to face the notion of permanent expatriation? For it is certain that I won't come back with all this going on—I'll be lucky if I can leave here by sea or ground for foreign soil.

Today I tried to walk with crutches, but I was only able to take a few steps. My leg has been severed very high up, and it is difficult for me to keep my balance. I won't be comfortable until I can try the artificial leg, but the amputation has caused *neuralgia in the remaining part of the leg,* and it would be impossible to use a mechanical leg until the neuralgia abates, and there are amputees for whom these neuralgias last four, six, eight, twelve months! I'm told they never take fewer than two months to pass. And if that's all it takes I'll be grateful. I would spend the time here at the hospital and would leave happily with two legs. As for leaving with crutches, I don't know what good that would do. You can neither climb up nor get down; it's awful. They leave you vulnerable to falling again and to crippling yourself further. I had thought I might be able to come stay with you to spend a few months waiting to have the strength to manage the artificial leg, but I see that for now that would be impossible.

So I am resigned to my destiny. I will die where I'm fated to. I hope to be able to return to where I had been; I have friends there I've known for ten years who will take pity on me, I will find work with them, I will be able to live as best I can. I will remain there for good, whereas in France, apart from you, I have no friends, no connections, no one. If I can see you, I will go back there. In any case, I must return there.

If you do get some information about my situation, don't let them know where I am. *I worry that they could get my address through the post office. Do not betray me.*

With best wishes,

Rimbaud

TO ISABELLE
Marseille, June 29, 1891

My dear sister,

I received your letter of June 26. The day before yesterday I received the letter from Harar. As for the letter of June 10, nothing new: it has disappeared, either in Attigny or here, but I suppose that Attigny is the more likely of the two. The envelope you sent me told who it was from. It must be from Dimitri Righas. He's a Greek living in Harar who I had contracted to do some work. I await news of your inquiry into the subject of military service: but, whatever the outcome, *I fear traps,* and I have no desire to go home right now despite whatever assurances you may have been given.

Otherwise, I am completely immobilized and can't take a single step. My leg is healed, which is to say a scar has formed, and, if I want, they will sign my release from the hospital tomorrow. But then what? I can't take a single step! I'm outdoors all day, in a chair, but I can't move. I try to use my crutches; but they're terrible, and I'm tall, my leg has been cut off up high, balance is very difficult to maintain. I take a few steps and stop, afraid of falling and crippling myself further.

To start things off, I am going to have a wooden leg made that you stick the cotton-padded stump into, and you walk with a cane. After time to practice with the wooden leg, one can, if the stump is well-padded, order an adjustable leg that bends so that one can more or less walk. When will this happen? Who knows what new catastrophe could befall me between now and then. But, this time, I would be quick to rid myself of this unbearable existence.

It's not wise for you to write me so often at the risk that my name could be recognized by the *postal service in Roche and Attigny.* That's where I'm at risk. Here no one bothers with me. Write me as little as possible—only when it cannot be avoided. Don't write "Arthur," write "Rimbaud." And tell me as soon as you can and *as clearly as you can* what the military authority wants with me, and, should they come after me, what penalty I have incurred. —But I'll be gone on the next boat should that occur.

I wish you good health and prosperity.

RBD.

TO ISABELLE
Marseille, July 2, 1891

My dear sister,

I did indeed receive your letters of the 24th and 26th of June, and that of the 30th. Only the letter of June 10 has been lost, and I suspect that it was diverted by the post office in Attigny. Here no one seems to bother with me at all. It's wise not to send your letters directly from Roche, so that they don't go through the Attigny bureau. That way you can write me as much as you like. As for the question of military service, it is essential I know my precise situation, so take the necessary steps to provide a decisive answer. You know I worry about being trapped and that is why I don't want to travel home no matter the situation. I suspect that you will never get a definitive answer, which would make it impossible to come and see you, since I could be caught in a trap.

My scar formed some time ago, but the neuralgia around the stump remains, and I'm still up, but my other leg has grown very weak. Whether through the long period in bed or through a lack of balance I don't know, but I find I can't move around on the crutches for more than a few minutes without exhausting the other leg. Do I have some sort of bone disease? Must I lose the other leg? I am very afraid; I fear I am exhausting myself and so I set the crutches aside. I ordered a wooden leg; it weighs only 2 kilos and will be ready in a week. I will try to walk very gently with it; it will take me a month minimum to get used to, and it remains possible that the doctor, because of my neuralgia, won't let me walk with it yet. A flexible leg would be too heavy for me just yet, the stump not yet able to bear it. That's for later. And a wooden leg does the same thing anyway: it costs fifty francs or so. Given all that, I'll still be in the hospital at the end of July. I pay 6 francs per day for board and sixty francs a minute for boredom.

I sleep no more than two hours per night. My insomnia has me thinking that this isn't the end of my illness. Thinking about my other leg makes me crazy: it's the only support I have in the world right now! When the abscess formed in my knee in Harar, it was preceded by two weeks of insomnia. Maybe it's my fate to become legless! For now, I guess the military authorities will be leaving me alone! Hope for the best.

I wish you good health, good weather, and every wish. Au revoir.

Rimbaud.

TO ISABELLE
Marseille, July 10, 1891

My dear sister,

I did indeed receive your letters of July 4 and 8. I am happy that my status has been resolved. As for my military folder, I must have lost it on my travels. When I can move around again I will see if I must get my discharge here or elsewhere. If Marseille, I think it would be best if I had the signed copy from your administration here in my hands. So it's best that I have that declaration: *send it to me.* With that no one can give me any trouble. I also have the certificate from the hospital and *with these two documents* I can secure my final discharge.

I'm still up and about, but not well. I haven't gotten any better at walking with crutches, and I still can't go up or down a single step. When I must, I have to be helped by someone. I had a very good, very lightweight wooden leg made, stuffed, and finished (for 50 francs). I put it on a few days ago and tried to practice with it while still on my crutches, but I inflamed the stump and put the damned thing aside. I can't try it at all for another two or three weeks, and still have to use the crutches for at least another month, and no more than an hour or two a day. The only advantage is in having three points of pressure rather than two.

So I've started to use the crutches again. Boring, exhausting, and so sad when I think about all my old travels, and how active I was only five months ago! Where are the paths between mountains, the cavalcades and promenades, the deserts, rivers, and seas? And now living a *legless existence*! Because I am beginning to understand that crutches, wooden legs, and mechanical legs are all jokes that do no better than to allow you to drag yourself around without managing to accomplish a thing. All this just when I had decided to return to France and marry this summer! Goodbye marriage, goodbye family, goodbye future! My life is over, I'm nothing more than an immobile lump.

I am far from even being able to move around with the wooden leg, which is nonetheless the lightest option. It will be another four months before I'll be able to manage even a few steps with a cane alone. Climbing and going down stairs remains hardest of all. It will be another six months before I'll be able to try a mechanical leg, and even then it will hurt a great deal and be almost useless. The biggest problem is how high up they had to make the amputation. Those who've been amputated at the knee fare far better. But all of this matters little right now: like life!

It's no cooler here than it was in Egypt. It's 30–35° at noon, 25–30° at night. —The temperature at Harar is more pleasant, above all at night, which never exceeds 10–15°.

I can't tell you what I am going to do; I am still *too down* to know myself. Things aren't going well, I'll say it again. I am worried by the prospect of another accident. My stump is thicker than the other leg, and riddled by neuralgia. Of course the doctor doesn't come to see me anymore; because, for the doctor, as long as the wound has scarred over, his work is done. He says you're better. He only deals with you if you have an abscess, etc., etc., or if there are any other complications that require the knife. The sick are only *cases*. It's perfectly clear. Above all in hospitals, because the doctor isn't paid. He takes the job only to acquire a reputation and to gather patients for a private practice.

I would like to go home, because it is cool there, but I doubt there is space there for my acrobatic exertions. And then I'm worried that the cool will turn cold. But the main reason is that *I can't move;* I can't now, nor will I be able to any time soon—and to tell the truth, I don't believe that I'm better inside and I am expecting some sort of explosion... I would have to be taken there in a carriage, carried in and out, etc., etc., it's too much trouble, expense, exhaustion. My room is paid until the end of July; I will think about it and I *will see what I can do* in the interim.

Still, I would prefer to think that things will be better as you would have me believe; —however ridiculous life becomes, man manages somehow to carry on.

Send me the letter from the administration. There happens to be a sick police inspector here whom I eat with and who annoys me endlessly with stories of military service problems and seems to want to amuse himself by toying with me.

Sorry for the bother, thank you, I wish you good luck and good health.
Write me.
Yours,

Rimbaud.

Mademoiselle Isabelle Rimbaud,
Roche, canton d'Attigny
Ardennes (France).

TO ISABELLE
Marseille, July 15, 1891

My dear Isabelle,

I received your letter of the 13th and find the opportunity to respond right away. I will see what steps I can take with the administrative note and the certificate from the hospital. Certainly it would please me to see this matter settled, but, alas! I don't see how I can manage it, let alone manage to put a shoe on my one remaining foot. In the end I'll just have to do the best that I can. At the least, with these two documents, I am no longer at risk of landing in prison; without them, the military administration would even imprison a cripple, were it only to a hospital. Whereas I don't know where or who to turn to for a declaration of return to France. No one around me can advise me; and the day remains far off when I will be able to go to one of these offices myself, with my wooden legs, to get the information myself.

I spend night and day thinking of ways I might manage to move around: it's torture! I would like to do this and that, go here and there, see, live, leave: impossible, impossible at least for the foreseeable future, if not forever! All I have around me are these damned crutches: without these sticks, I can't take a single step, I can't exist. Without the most unbearable gymnastics, I can't even get dressed. I have managed to reach the point where I can almost run with my crutches, but I can't go up or down stairs, and, if the surface is uneven, lurching from shoulder to shoulder is very tiring. I have neuralgia in the right arm and shoulder that hurts a great deal, and then there's the pain of the crutch cutting into my armpit—a neuralgia still in the left leg, and with all that I have to act like an acrobat all day to make it seem like I'm alive.

This is what I've come to think my illness springs from. The climate in Harar is cold from November to March. Usually I wear next to nothing: basic cotton pants and shirt. Add to that 15 to 40 kilometers traveled daily on foot, insane cavalcades through the region's steep mountains. I believe that fatigue, heat, and cold created an arthritic pain in my knee. In essence, all of this started with a hammer blow (so to speak) beneath the kneecap, which then banged away lightly all the time, and tightness in the bending and extending of the knee running through the nerves of my thigh. Then the swelling of the veins around the knee, which made me suspect varicose veins. I continued to walk and work, more than ever, believing all I needed was a little air. The pain inside the knee worsened. It felt as though a nail were being pounded in with each step. —I continued to walk, but with more pain; I felt crippled every time I mounted or dismounted a horse. —The upper part of the knee swelled up, the kneecap swelled up, the back of the knee too, circulation became painful, and the pain ran along the nerves from my ankle to my hips. —I no longer walked without limping badly and felt steadily worse, but I still had a lot of work to do, obviously. —So I started to wear my leg bandaged from top to bottom, to rub it, bathe it, etc., without improvement. During that time, I lost my appetite. A dogged insomnia gripped me. I weakened and lost weight. —Toward March 15, I took to my bed to get off my feet. I put a bed between my till, my desk, and a window through which I could see my scales at the edge of the courtyard, and I hired a group of workers to ensure that work continued unimpeded, while myself remaining laid out to rest my sick leg. But, day by day, the swelling of the knee made it look like a ball; I noticed that the internal side of the head of the tibia was much fatter than that of the other leg: the kneecap became immobile, drowning in the excretion that the swollen knee was producing, and which I watched with horror become, within a few days, like bone: at that moment, the whole leg stiffened, became completely stiff; in a week, I couldn't get anywhere except by dragging myself there. All the while the leg and the upper part of the hips grew thinner and thinner, the knee and the back of the knee swelled, solidified, or more accurately *ossified,* and the general physical and moral weakness worsened.

By the end of March, I resolved to leave. In a few days, I liquidated everything at a loss. And, as the stiffness and the pain kept me from using a mule or even a camel, I had a stretcher made, covered in a curtain, which sixteen men carried to Zeila in two weeks' time. The second day of the trip, having advanced far from the caravan, I was surprised in the desert by rain, which lasted for sixteen hours, leaving me without shelter or any means of movement. This did me no good. En route, I was never able to lift myself up from my stretcher; a tent was erected over it and me wherever we stopped, and, digging a hole with my hands near the edge of the stretcher, I managed with difficulty to put myself on my side and have a bowel movement in the hole I'd dug in the earth. In the morning, they lifted the tent from me and lifted me. I arrived in Zeila exhausted, paralyzed. I only rested there for four hours, a steamboat leaving for Aden. Tossed on deck on my mattress (I had to be hoisted on board on my stretcher!) I suffered through three days at sea without food. In Aden, another lowering of my stretcher. I then spent a few days chez M. Tian to settle our affairs and left for the hospital, where the English doctor, after two weeks, advised me to leave for Europe.

My belief is that this pain in the joint, if it had been treated when it arose, would have been easily managed and would have led to nothing. But I was ignorant of all that. I ruined everything by walking and working excessively. In school, why don't we learn what little medicine we would need to know how to avoid these sorts of stupidities?

Were someone to ask my advice, I would tell him: you've come this far: now don't let them amputate. Get hacked up, ripped apart, torn to pieces, but don't tolerate amputation. If death comes, it's a far better thing than life with too few limbs. Many have said as much; and if I had it to do over again, I would do it differently. Better to live a year in hell than to be amputated.

Look what it's got me: I sit, from time to time I get up and skip a hundred steps on my crutches, and I sit down again. My hands won't hold anything. While walking, I cannot turn my head away from my one foot and the two ends of my crutches. My head and shoulders bend forward, and I barrel ahead like a hunchback. You tremble at the sight of people and things moving around you, out of fear that you will be knocked down and have your other leg amputated. You cackle at seeing yourself skip. Seated again, your hands are completely drained and your underarms sawed raw, and your face contorted like an idiot. Despair takes you again and you remain sitting like a total invalid, sniveling until dark, darkness that brings endless insomnia and a dawn sadder than the dusk it preceded, etc., etc. More next issue.

With all best wishes. RBD.

TO THE RECRUITMENT MAJOR OF MARSEILLE
[July 1891]

Monsieur le Commandant for recruitment in Marseille,

I am a conscript from the class of 1875. I drew in Charleville, in the Ardennes; I was exempted from military service, as my brother was serving under the flag. In 1882, on January 16, during my 28 days of training, I found myself in Arabia, working as a merchant in a French firm: I made my declaration of stay abroad, and sent a certificate to M. le Commandant in Mézières, the aforesaid certificate attesting my presence in Aden. I was put in deferment, renewable until the time of my return to France.

This last May 22, I returned to France with the intention of completing my military service; but, arriving in Marseille, I was required to check into the Hospital of the Conception, and the following 25th May they amputated my right leg. I have here, available for viewing by Monsieur le Commandant for recruitment, certificates from the director of the hospital where I remain, as well as that of the doctor who took care of me.

I would ask Monsieur le Commandant for recruitment to sort out my situation with respect to military service, and to give me my discharge, as I am no longer capable of performing any duties.

Hospital of the Conception, Marseille

To the Recruitment Major of Marseille: the final permutation of Rimbaud's desire to see his draft status resolved.

TO ISABELLE
Marseille, July 20, 1891

My dear sister,

I write you this under the influence of violent pain in my right shoulder, almost keeping me from writing, as you see.

All of this indicates a constitution that has become arthritic following unsuccessful treatments. But I've had enough of this hospital, where I am exposed every day to smallpox, typhus, and other germs that live here. I am leaving, the doctor having said that I can leave and that it is better that I no longer stay in the hospital.

In two or three days, then, I will leave and will see about dragging myself to your house as best I can; because, without my wooden leg, I can no longer walk, and even with these crutches I can't do better for the time being than take a step or two, so that I don't worsen the state of my shoulder. As you have said, I will get off at the Voncq train station. As for accommodation, I would prefer to stay upstairs; useless therefore to write me here, I will be leaving very soon.

Au revoir.

Rimbaud.

TO THE DIRECTOR OF THE MESSAGERIES MARITIMES
Marseille, November 9, 1891

One lot   1 single tusk
One lot   2 tusks
One lot   3 tusks
One lot   4 tusks
One lot   2 tusks

Monsieur le Directeur,

I would ask you if I have anything left on your account. I would like to transfer off of this service, the name of which I don't even know, but in any case will call the Aphinar service. There are all sorts of services here, and I, unhappy and infirm, can't find a single one, the first dog in the street will tell you as much.

So send me the price for service from Aphinar to Suez. I am completely paralyzed: so I would like to leave plenty of time to board.

Tell me what time I should be carried on board...

Un lot . 1 dent seule
Un lot 2 dents
Un lot 3 dents
Un lot 4 dents
Un lot 2 dents

M. le Directeur,

Je viens vous demander si je n'ai rien laissé à votre compte. Je désire changer aujourd'hui de ce service ci dont je ne connais même pas le nom, mais en tous cas que ce soit le service d'Aphinar. Tous ces services sont là partout et moi impotent, malheureux je ne peux rien trouver, le premier chien dans la rue vous dira cela. Envoyez-moi donc le prix des services d'Aphinar à Suez. Je suis complètement paralysé donc je désire me trouver de bonne heure à bord dites-moi à quelle heure, je dois être transporté à bord.

Rimbaud's last known letter, dictated to his sister on November 9, 1891, the day before he died.

APPENDIX: LETTERS NOT INCLUDED IN THE PRESENT EDITION

LETTERS TO ALFRED ILG

February 1, 1888
March 29, 1888
April 12, 1888
June 25, 1888
July 1, 1889
July 20, 1889
August 24, 1889
August 26, 1889
September 7, 1889
September 12, 1889
September 13, 1889
October 7, 1889
November 16, 1889
December 11, 1889
December 20, 1889
February 24, 1890

March 1, 1890
March 16, 1890
March 18, 1890
April 7, 1890
April 25, 1890
April 30, 1890
May 15, 1890
June 6, 1890
September 20, 1890
November 18, 1890
November 18, 1890
November 20, 1890
November 26, 1890
February 1, 1891
February 5, 1891
February 20, 1891

LETTER TO ARMAND SAVOURÉ

February 11, 1890

Hassan Ali's villa, then and now. Contemporary photo by Jean-Hughes Berrou.

ACKNOWLEDGMENTS

This volume could not have been assembled without the help of many hands more adept than my own.

Photographs and documents are reproduced by kind permission of their gatherers and collectors listed herewith. First among these is Pierre Leroy, who generously provided the cover image of Rimbaud from his growing collection of Rimbaud artifacts. He, along with his collaborators—writer Jean-Jacques Lefrère and photographer Jean-Hughes Berrou—are responsible for two beautiful books of new and archival photographs documenting Rimbaud's African and Arabian peregrinations: *Rimbaud à Aden* and *Rimbaud à Harar.* Gratitude to each for their generosity in supplying me with the images for this book.

Redundant thanks go to Jean-Jacques Lefrère, the great biographer responsible for the definitive book on Rimbaud's life, *Arthur Rimbaud* (Fayard, 2001). It is my hope that an American editor will publish this necessary work in English for the benefit of non-French readers. M. Lefrère clarified many matters relating to chronology and content of the letters, and showed a stranger the warmth customarily reserved for friends.

Thanks to Jean-René Etienne of the Book Office of the French Cultural Services of the French Embassy in New York for arranging a trip to France that resolved many uncertainties. In France, Steve Murphy, the redoubtable Rimbaud scholar, has been invaluable. His authoritative editions of Rimbaud's work offer a vivid picture of Rimbaud's messy output. His fascimile edition of Rimbaud's manuscripts (Volume IV of his never-ending project) was essential to my preparation of this book. I thank him for his patience and generosity with permissions.

In America, Michael Attias read an early draft of the manuscript and resolved a great many uncertainties. John Jeremiah Sullivan at *Harper's* edited and improved the introduction in its first form. Charles Bock was once again essential in making the introduction more comprehensible at every stage of writing and rewriting. The generous assistance of all three reminds me how fortunate I am to have friends far smarter than myself upon whom I can depend.

Working again with everyone at Modern Library has proven the best reason to do a book. They turn a chaotic manuscript into something I can be proud of. They are also lots of fun. Thanks to Evelyn, Kate, Shelley, Gaby, Vincent, Will, and David.

Gratitude to Elizabeth Sheinkman of the Markson Agency, a bottomless source of smarts and support.

And to the Suzanne and William Mason rhetorical trust: I love you guys.

—Wyatt Mason
August 2003

SELECTED BIBLIOGRAPHY

FRENCH EDITIONS OF RIMBAUD'S WORKS
Œuvres complètes. De Renéville and Mouquet, eds. Gallimard, Pléiade, 1954.
Œuvres complètes. Antoine Adam, ed. Gallimard, Pléiade, 1972.
Œuvre/vie. Alain Borer, ed. Arléa, 1991.
Œuvres complètes. Pierre Brunel, ed. Livre de Poche, 1999.
Œuvres complètes, I: Poésies. Steve Murphy, ed. Honoré Champion, 1999.
Œuvres complètes, IV: Fac-similies. Steve Murphy, ed. Honoré Champion, 2002.

ENGLISH TRANSLATIONS OF RIMBAUD'S WORKS
Collected Poems. Oliver Bernard, tr. Penguin, 1962.
Complete Works, Selected Letters. Wallace Fowlie, tr. Chicago, 1966.
Complete Works. Paul Schmidt, tr. Harper & Row, 1976.
Rimbaud: The Works. Dennis J. Carlile, tr. Xlibris, 2000.
Collected Poems. Martin Sorrell, tr. Oxford University Press, 2001.
Rimbaud Complete. Wyatt Mason, tr. Modern Library, 2002.

ON RIMBAUD'S POETRY AND LIFE
A Concordance to the Œuvres complètes of Arthur Rimbaud. William Carter and Robert Vines, eds. Ohio University Press, 1978.
Berrichon, Paterne. *Arthur Rimbaud, Poète.* Mercure de France, 1912.
Cohn, Robert Greer. *The Poetry of Rimbaud.* University of South Carolina Press, 1999.
Delahaye, Ernest. *Delahaye témoin de Rimbaud.* Baconnière, 1974.
Izambard, Georges. *Rimbaud tel que je l'ai connu.* Le passeur, 1991.
Jeancolas, Claude. *Les lettres manuscrites de Rimbaud.* Textuel, 1997.
Lefrère, Jean-Jacques. *Arthur Rimbaud.* Fayard, 2001.

Lefrère, Jean-Jacques, et al. *Rimbaud à Aden.* Fayard, 2001.

————. *Rimbaud à Harar.* Fayard, 2002.

Robb, Graham. *Rimbaud.* Norton, 2000.

Starkie, Enid. *Rimbaud.* Norton, 1947.

Steinmetz, Jean-Luc. *Une Question de presence.* Tallandier, 1999.

ON SUBJECTS RELATING TO TRANSLATION

Baudelaire, Charles. *Les Fleurs du Mal.* Richard Howard, tr. Godine, 1980.

Borges, Jorge Luis. *This Craft of Verse.* Harvard, 2000.

Craft and Context of Translation. William Arrowsmith and Roger Shattuck, eds. University of Texas Press, 1961.

Davenport, Guy. *Seven Greeks.* New Directions, 1995.

Gass, William. *Reading Rilke.* Ecco, 2000.

Random House Book of Twentieth-Century French Poetry. Paul Auster, ed. Random House, 1981.

Rilke, Rainer Maria. *Selected Poetry.* Stephen Mitchell, tr. Vintage, 1983.

ABOUT THE TRANSLATOR

WYATT MASON has translated the works of various contemporary French writers, and has been a finalist for the French-American Foundation Translation Prize. His translation of Arthur Rimbaud's poetical works, *Rimbaud Complete*, appeared in 2002 from the Modern Library. His writing has appeared in *Harper's*, *The Nation*, and the *Los Angeles Times*. He was named a fellow of the New York Public Library's Dorothy and Lewis B. Cullman Center for Scholars and Writers for 2003–2004. His current projects include a new translation of Dante's *La Vita Nuova*, for the Modern Library. He is also at work on a translation of the essays of Michel de Montaigne.

A NOTE ON THE TYPE

The principal text of this Modern Library edition
was set in a digitized version of Janson, a typeface that
dates from about 1690 and was cut by Nicholas Kis,
a Hungarian working in Amsterdam. The original matrices have
survived and are held by the Stempel foundry in Germany.
Hermann Zapf redesigned some of the weights and sizes for
Stempel, basing his revisions on the original design.